# Engaging in Mathematics in the Classroom

What comes first, class management or student engagement? How can the 'real world' be used to engage learners? What is the role of technology in engaging students? And is 'understanding' or 'exam success' more engaging?

In the modern world, success in school mathematics can determine life chances. It is therefore vital to engage children and young people in learning mathematics. *Engaging in Mathematics in the Classroom* brings together the debates concerning mathematical engagement and draws on first-hand experience and key research to promote successful classroom practice. It considers what engagement looks like at different ages and the implications of this for the classroom.

Accessibly written with examples of successful classroom practice, activities and projects, the book covers:

- planning and managing engagement in learning;
- mathematical understandings and meanings;
- early primary and the number system;
- primary/secondary transition and geometrical thinking;
- secondary school: adolescence and algebraic activity;
- post-16 and infinity;
- learning across the lifespan.

Written by a leading authority in the field, this timely text will be essential reading for all trainee and practicing teachers of mathematics.

**Alf Coles** is Senior Lecturer in Education (Mathematics) at the University of Bristol, UK.

# Engaging in Mathematics in the Classroom

Symbols and experiences

**Alf Coles**

LONDON AND NEW YORK

First published 2016
by Routledge
2 Park Square, Milton Park, Abingdon, Oxon OX14 4RN

and by Routledge
711 Third Avenue, New York, NY 10017

*Routledge is an imprint of the Taylor & Francis Group, an informa business*

© 2016 Alf Coles

The right of Alf Coles to be identified as author of this work has been asserted by him in accordance with sections 77 and 78 of the Copyright, Designs and Patents Act 1988.

All rights reserved. No part of this book may be reprinted or reproduced or utilised in any form or by any electronic, mechanical, or other means, now known or hereafter invented, including photocopying and recording, or in any information storage or retrieval system, without permission in writing from the publishers.

*Trademark notice*: Product or corporate names may be trademarks or registered trademarks, and are used only for identification and explanation without intent to infringe.

*British Library Cataloguing in Publication Data*
A catalogue record for this book is available from the British Library

*Library of Congress Cataloging in Publication Data*
Coles, Alf.
Engaging in mathematics in the classroom : symbols and experiences / Alf Coles.
pages cm
"Teaching and learning mathematics from the beginning of school until aged 18"—Galley, pref.
1. Mathematics—Study and teaching. 2. Mathematics teachers—Training of. I. Title.
QA135.6.C642 2016
510.71'2—dc23
2015008180

ISBN: 978-0-415-73368-7 (hbk)
ISBN: 978-0-415-73369-4 (pbk)
ISBN: 978-1-315-69132-9 (ebk)

Typeset in Bembo
by Swales & Willis Ltd, Exeter, Devon, UK
Printed and bound in Great Britain by Ashford Colour Press Ltd, Gosport, Hampshire

A science teacher in a school where I used to work once stuck a note over the staff-room door that read: 'For those of you who are about to teach, we salute you'. This always made me smile and feel good about my career choice. This book is dedicated to those of you about to teach!

# Contents

*List of figures* viii
*List of tables* x
*Preface* xi
*Acknowledgements* xiii

**PART I**
**Issues** 1

1  Engaging in mathematics 3
2  Planning for engagement in learning 14
3  Mathematical understandings and meanings 29
4  Symbolic fluency 43
5  Managing engagement 60

**PART II**
**Curriculum focus** 73

6  Early primary and the number system 75
7  Primary/secondary transition and geometrical thinking 86
8  Secondary school: adolescence and algebraic activity 103
9  Post-16 and infinity 118

**PART III**
**Reflections** 133

10  Engaging in engaging learners 135
11  Learning across the lifespan 146

*Appendix 1* 151
*Appendix 2* 161
*Index* 163

# Figures

| | | |
|---|---|---|
| 2.1 | Schematic showing the effect on extreme temperatures when (a) the mean temperature increases, (b) the variance increases, and (c) when both the mean and variance increase for a normal distribution of temperature | 26 |
| 3.1 | Starting positions for the 'Frogs' game | 29 |
| 3.2 | Whiteboard with results for 'Frogs' game | 30 |
| 3.3 | Descent into meaning and symbol transformations | 36 |
| 4.1 | Representation of a staircase of Cuisenaire rods. The real rods are all coloured differently | 47 |
| 4.2 | Different representations of '2' and '½' | 49 |
| 4.3 | The 'Numicon' number line | 50 |
| 4.4 | Exploring $y = mx + c$ with Geogebra | 54 |
| 4.5 | Working on the concept of gradient | 55 |
| 4.6 | A dynamic geometry sketch to demonstrate the sum of angles in triangles | 56 |
| 4.7 | A triangle mystery | 57 |
| 6.1 | Gattegno's number chart | 76 |
| 6.2 | Three 'journeys' | 77 |
| 6.3 | A connection made! | 77 |
| 6.4 | A student extends to division by 10,000 | 78 |
| 6.5 | A journey into decimals | 78 |
| 6.6 | A journey from one column to a different column | 79 |
| 6.7 | A journey from 3000 to 0.04 | 79 |
| 6.8 | Henry in November 2011 | 81 |
| 6.9 | Henry in May 2012 | 81 |
| 6.10 | Henry in January 2012 | 82 |
| 6.11 | Henry in March 2012 | 83 |
| 6.12 | Henry in April 2012 | 83 |
| 7.1 | Two lines | 87 |
| 7.2 | Tessellated triangles 1 | 89 |
| 7.3 | Tessellated triangles 2 | 89 |
| 7.4 | Tessellated triangles 3 | 90 |
| 7.5 | A student's work on Pick's Theorem | 95 |
| 7.6 | S2's triangle | 96 |
| 7.7 | The chord subtended by angle ß | 98 |

# Tables

| | | |
|---|---|---|
| 2.1 | Approaches to sustainability in teaching mathematics | 24 |
| 2.2 | Historical global population estimates | 24 |
| 3.1 | The transition between process and object | 34 |
| 3.2 | Two student responses | 38 |
| 9.1 | Recurrence calculation for $x = (6x - 7)/x$ | 120 |

| | | |
|---|---|---|
| 7.8 | Creating a graph of the 'sine' line | 100 |
| 7.9 | An image of trigonometry | 100 |
| 7.10 | The tangent ratio | 101 |
| 7.11 | An image of the tangent function | 101 |
| 8.1 | A growing pattern of squares | 105 |
| 8.2 | A matchstick pattern with 6 squares | 105 |
| 8.3 | Graph of a rational function | 114 |
| 8.4 | Graph of a rational function with quadratic numerator | 115 |
| 9.1 | An image of recursion | 119 |
| 9.2 | A simple recursive programme in Scratch | 119 |
| 9.3 | Routes across a square | 121 |
| 9.4 | A numerical approach to finding the gradient of $y = x^2$ when $x = 1$ | 122 |
| 9.5 | Finding the area under a curve | 124 |
| 9.6 | The area under the graph $y = x^2$ | 126 |
| 9.7 | The 'area' under the function $f(x)$ | 127 |
| 9.8 | Visualising the chain rule for linear functions | 129 |
| 9.9 | An alternative chain rule representation | 129 |
| 9.10 | A representation of the product of two functions | 130 |

# Preface

At a time of increasing global comparison and concern in relation to raising mathematical attainment in schools there is a pressing question as to how, as teachers, we can engage students in the same project. This book is about teaching and learning mathematics. A central idea is that all learning requires, to some extent, the creation of symbols for experiences (consciously or unconsciously) and that this can become an engaging activity, in itself.

There are roots of the word 'engagement' that link to marriage (originally, any moral obligation or pledge), to battle (engaging the enemy) as well as appointments (I have several engagements today). All three of these senses of the word perhaps have resonance to the situation of a student sitting in a mathematics classroom today. As teachers there may be a feeling that it is the students' moral obligation to do what is asked of them; from the student's perspective a lesson perhaps can seem like a fight; and, teacher and student are certainly meant to be in the same place at an appointed time. A more typical meaning of the word in the context of schooling, though, would be to capture some judgement about the quality of attention a student gives to the task of a lesson, 'are the students engaged today?' Dick Tahta was fond of the aphorism (adapted from Simone Weil) that the greatest gift we can give someone is the quality of our attention. Perhaps, speaking as a teacher, there is a question too about the quality of my engagement with students in lessons.

This book looks at teaching and learning mathematics from the beginning of school until aged 18. Topics are addressed in two ways. Chapters in Part I focus on an issue related to engaging students, such as planning or gaining symbolic fluency. In Part II, chapters have a different feel as the focus is on a specific age range at school and a particular curriculum area (e.g., early primary schooling and number), with the offer of a range of classroom activities. In Part III, the focus shifts again to considering issues about working with teachers (not students) to make mathematics an engaging study, and to consider themes across the book chapters.

In the preface to David Pimm's (1995) book *Symbols and meanings in school mathematics*, he writes:

> A very familiar tension in teaching mathematics at whatever level is between wanting symbols to be 'iconic', that is readily transparent with respect to their meaning or reference while yet, for fluency and automation, more compact, opaque symbols are frequently more efficient. There is a frequent trade-off: the more transparent a symbolism, the less compact, and hence the less easily manipulated. This is a theme that I shall come back to time and again. (p. xiv)

I also allude to the theme of the tension between wanting to give symbols specific (and 'meaningful'?) objects of reference compared with developing awareness of how symbols relate to each other within a structure. The national curriculum in the UK (first being taught in 2014-15) emphasises three aspects of mathematics (at all ages of schooling) which are: problem solving, reasoning and fluency. The aim of efficient symbol use relates to fluency and it can seem as though there is a dilemma between developing slick, fast symbolic skills and having the depth of awareness needed to solve problems and reason with these symbols. I hope to show some ways in which both sides of this dilemma can be developed simultaneously.

Learning to teach mathematics is also a process that requires symbolising – but the symbols in this case are not related so much to mathematics as to issues that arise in the classroom and which require a different response (for the learning teacher).

I work in a building named after Helen Wodehouse. She was the first woman to hold a chair at the University of Bristol and was Head of the Education department between 1919 and 1931. She was a philosopher of education (see Wodehouse, 1924). As part of the centenary celebrations of the (now) Graduate School of Education, at the University of Bristol, I was motivated to look into her archive to find out a little of the woman whose name was given to our building. I find some of her writing arresting and include several quotations from her work. Wodehouse wrote: '[s]o far educational history, like religious, is not a journey but a continual re-inspiration' (1924: 218), which I interpret being as true from generation to generation as well as from day to day. In education we do not stand on the shoulders of giants, rather each of us, each teacher, must surely re-create the insights from the past in our own practice. But perhaps (to borrow a phrase used in the early years of the Association of Teachers of Mathematics) we can teach with the strength of us all.

## References

Pimm, D. (1995). *Symbols and meanings in school mathematics*. London: Routledge.
Wodehouse, H. (1924). *A survey of the history of education*. London: Edward Arnold & Co.

# Acknowledgements

The ideas in this book have arisen out of conversations. Many of them with members of the Association of Teachers of Mathematics, through which organisation I met Laurinda Brown, Dick Tahta, Dave Hewitt, John Mason and many others – and as a result discovered what a conversation about mathematics in a classroom could feel like. I have not nearly been able to capture in this text the extent to which what I write about has come from others.

I would like to acknowledge a huge debt to David Pimm for his insightful comments on a draft of this manuscript. The text is immeasurably improved as a result.

And thank you to my wonderful family for putting up with all those days when I was glued to my laptop and not playing with them.

# Part I
# Issues

# 1 Engaging in mathematics

In the first two years of my teaching career in the UK, I experienced classes that would rarely listen to what I had to say. I felt I managed to 'turn off' students from mathematics who may have begun the year relatively keen and enthusiastic. Students seemed engaged primarily in an exploration of my boundaries rather than anything mathematical. The failings were of my own making. In my third year of teaching, I moved school and began a research collaboration with Laurinda Brown that was pivotal to my finding a way of being in the classroom that allowed something more interesting to take place. The ideas in this book have been developed almost entirely through that collaboration (see Brown and Coles 2008).

When I began teaching I had little sense of how to set up a way of working with a class so that the focus was on the mathematics. Reading accounts of other people's successful classrooms did me no good, as I was not given access to information on what they did to set up the context in the first place such that students would listen to each other (or the teacher). In writing this book I have partly had in mind that 'me' who began teaching in the UK in 1994. I hope, over the course of the book, to offer some images, experiences and labels (symbols) to help think about what is involved in getting students engaging in school mathematics.

Freud referred to educating as one of the 'impossible' professions (along with healing and governing) 'in which one can be sure beforehand of achieving unsatisfactory results' (Freud 1976: XXII, 248). This reminds me of a story.

> I taught a student Further Mathematics A-level some years ago. We were just starting the subject in my school and so I was allowed to run the course with one student, meeting for just a couple of hours each week. Due to the limited contact time, the student taught himself one module entirely. This was the module in which he received his highest marks.

Reflecting on the experience I can of course comfort myself with the notion that I must have equipped the student with the skills to teach himself. It is still striking, however, that he did best without my direct help. Maybe we should not be surprised. There is a view of biology that suggests the actions of living beings should be seen as a result of their own internal structure – the world around can trigger a response but never determine what that response will be (Maturana and Varela 1992). If I kick a stone, its path is determined by the energy, direction and manner of my strike. If I kick a dog, what happens next will mainly be a result of the dog's character and metabolism, not the energy transferred from my boot (Bateson 2000: 229). Living beings are triggered into action by others, but *how* a living being responds is a result of its structure and history (Maturana and Poerksen 2004). Taking this view of biology to its logical end, suggests that '*instruction*, in the strict sense of the word, is radically impossible' (Stewart 2010: 9). A teacher cannot determine change in her students. As teachers, we cannot *make* students act, all we can do is trigger and provide feedback on actions. How a student responds, and therefore what they learn, is a function of their own self. We cannot instruct/structure a student's mind directly.

The impossibility of instruction resonates with a paradox about teaching and learning which has been recognised since antiquity. Plato (*Meno 80d*) had a view of learning as a recognition of the new, and asked how this is ever possible, since to recognise something I need to know already what I am looking for. More recently, in a presentation, Anna Sfard (2013) referred in her own language to essentially the same paradox: 'To participate in a discourse on an object you need to have already constructed this object but the only way to construct an object is to participate in the discourse about it' (quotation taken from the conference presentation slides).

There is something in these paradoxical statements that points to why teaching is so hard and why students sometimes do not engage in learning mathematics. When things go well, a student participates in the game, takes part in the discourse of mathematics and, in doing so, begins constructing mathematical objects that allow further participation – a virtuous cycle. When things are not going well, a student sees the discourse of mathematics as alien, does not participate and so does not construct the objects that others do, who are participating, and the discourse begins to seem further and further away as a possibility – a vicious cycle. What makes the difference is *engagement*.

Valerie Walkerdine (1990) also sees engagement in mathematics as about learning a new discourse. In a powerful critique of the contemporary practice in classrooms, she demonstrated how participating in the discourse of 'reason' is always harder for the 'Other' in a society: the women, the poor, the minority groups. Logic is seemingly always on the side of the oppressor. Walkerdine tracked the way that girls with high IQs aged four can come to be regarded as 'stupid' by the age of ten. Walkerdine (1990: 55) argued that it is

> necessary to understand how high-performing girls came to be designated as 'only hard-working' when poorly-achieving boys could be understood as 'bright' even though they presented little evidence of high attainment. Poorly-achieving girls in the study, quite simply, were never designated bright.

One of the roles of the teacher, then, is to find a way of hooking students into giving their attention to, and taking part in, the discourse of mathematics or, to borrow a Buddhist phrase, of tripping them into engaging. And the longer students have felt excluded from this discourse, the harder it may be to engage them. Walkerdine's research implies it behoves us all, as teachers, to be particularly mindful of the groups and individuals in our classrooms who are excluded.

It is sometimes possible to catch yourself in a moment of exclusion, to remember what it must feel like to experience the events of a lesson as occurring at some distance from yourself. Another story comes to mind.

> I went into our garden to pick some runner beans from a bean plant in our vegetable patch. Bean plants are tall with large leaves and the runner beans are of the same colour, growing from the stem of the plant. At first I could not make out any runner beans. After some while of looking and wondering if there were any beans on the plant at all, I saw a runner bean, perhaps by chance, and picked it. Then quite quickly I noticed another runner bean, then another. Having started to see the beans, I realised they were everywhere on the plant!

As soon as I start seeing 'beans', I cannot *not* see them; it is then hard to engage with someone who was in the place I was just a moment before (and perhaps easy to interpret them as lacking 'intelligence' or 'ability'). In essence, then, learning changes how we view the world, usually without us even realising.

Marton and Booth (1997) describe how, in the course of life, we normalise our world. As we learn something new and therefore experience a small part of the world in a different way (e.g., looking at a bean plant), that new way of seeing becomes normal and we are rarely sensitive to the shift that has taken place. Freudenthal (1978: 185) describes working with some children and asking them which number was least likely to occur when you roll a dice. The children agreed that '6' was hardest to get (perhaps because you need to roll a '6' to start in some games and it can seem as though you can never roll it). Freudenthal goes on to get students creating nets of dice and writing on the numbers. With no discussion and seemingly no discontinuity for the children, at the end of engaging in making their own dice, no child thinks '6' will be harder to get than the other numbers. We do not always notice how we change.

One of the difficulties for the teacher, therefore, is to be sufficiently open to how students may be seeing situations differently from us (and particularly those students who are 'different' from us). How can we think about what activities to give students when they may be seeing the world in ways that we are no longer able to access and when we know that we cannot directly influence how they see the world? And linked to this question, what will engage students in wanting to change their way of seeing, in wanting to learn, in the first place?

Engagment requires vulnerability. Both teacher and student need to allow themselves to become vulnerable to the other, if there is to be a space where engagement is possible and where experiences can lead to the creation of new ways of thinking and new symbols.

## An image of a classroom

To help think about some of the questions raised so far and to set up the themes of the rest of this book, I want to present an image of a classroom where students are involved in creative and independent work in mathematics. The problem with doing this is that inevitably, as a reader, you can only interpret the events as they appear on paper in terms of your own classroom experiences. Nevertheless, I begin by setting up the context by giving two transcripts from lessons. As you read the transcripts you will inevitably be confronted by reactions that may be judgemental (positive or negative). A recurring theme in this book is the usefulness of being able to put aside evaluations and focus on the detail of experience, to allow the possibility of seeing something in a different light from an initial reaction.

6  *Issues*

After the transcripts and a discussion of issues raised by them, I draw out issues linked to engaging students in school mathematics.

*Context*

The date is 2007 and the classroom is in a state comprehensive secondary school in the UK, on the edge of a city. The school serves a mainly white catchment area, including some wards with high levels of deprivation. One of the major issues faced by the school, as interpreted by many staff, was low educational aspiration among some students and some parents. I was the teacher in the classroom, head of the mathematics department at the time, and this was the start of my eleventh year of teaching at the school. The class was a year 7, meaning the students were aged 11 or 12. They had started secondary school at the start of September, so the transcripts are from some of their first mathematics lessons in their new school.

The problem they are working on is called '1089'. The next section is taken verbatim from the documentation of the mathematics department that would have been used by all year 7 teachers at the time, to guide their planning (i.e., the department 'scheme of work').

---

**The beginning of year 7 – '1089'**

We begin by articulating the purpose of year 7 for the students as being about *becoming a mathematician* and *thinking mathematically,* i.e.: thinking for yourself and so not asking the teacher if things are right, noticing what you are doing, e.g., patterns but then asking why patterns work, writing down everything you notice, being organised, doing things in your head.

We want to establish a purpose for the year that is removed from the content level of what we do in class and is an easily stated label that can gather complexity and meaning for each individual as the year progresses. We believe the purpose of 'becoming a mathematician' supports students in becoming aware of what they do when working in a mathematics lesson, by allowing them (and us) to question and reflect on whether something they (and we) do is mathematical or not.

*Lesson extract*

I issued the following instructions, at the same time going through an example on the board:

|  | *Example* |
|---|---|
| Pick any three-digit number with first digit bigger than third | 7 5 2 |
| Reverse the number and subtract | − 2 5 7 |
|  | 4 9 5 |
| Reverse the answer and add | + 5 9 4 |
|  | 1,0 8 9 |

Several comments were made by students that they also got 1089 and the challenge I gave to the class was: 'Can you find a number that does not end up as 1089?'

---

There are several reasons behind the choice of this activity as the first one with our year 7 groups. It is an activity we are familiar with, but more important for our purposes is the fact that it is *self-generative*. By that we mean that, having set up the task, we do not need to direct students as to what numbers to try out, they can generate their own examples to try. Also, some students typically become convinced very soon that all answers will end up at 1089, so if a student gets a different answer from that they can check their working with someone who thinks it is impossible, so the task becomes *self-checking* among the students. Both of these elements leave our attention free to notice aspects of mathematical thinking that we can highlight to the group and also gives the students an immediate experience of having to 'think for themselves', which we had said was part of 'becoming a mathematician'.

One of the tasks we set ourselves for the year is to comment as much as possible on activity that we consider to be mathematical. Below are two examples from a first lesson.

*Lesson extract*

> This group noticed something about their answers – it proved not to be 100% correct but it's an example of what it means to think as a mathematician.
>
> This group had an idea which they wrote down and tested and found it didn't work so they changed their idea. That's a great example of what it is to think mathematically.

Commenting on activity in this way is part of our attempt to set up a classroom culture in which students' ideas and questions are valued and in which there is an acceptance that it is okay to make mistakes, from which everyone can learn. The self-checking nature of the first activity supports the development of this culture in which we, as teachers, act as a role model.

We move on to looking at the same problem using four digits – where there are several different answers. We set up two 'common boards' for students to write up their answers.

| 9999 | 10,890 | 10,989 |
|------|--------|--------|
| 9271 | 1520   | 1000   |
| 7164 | 9741   | 4551   |
|      | 8304   |        |

On the first board, students write the numbers they started with underneath the total it came to. They write their initials next to their number. If another student checks their number and agrees, they come and write a tick next to it. When a number has two ticks it is rubbed off (by the original student) and written on the second board of checked results. The challenge with four digits is to predict what total your number will come to. These 'common boards' develop the self-checking nature of the activity. The checked results board allows every student access to working on the higher-level questions of looking for patterns in which column different numbers end up in.

8  *Issues*

## Lesson transcripts

The focus of the department on thinking mathematically can perhaps be seen in the write-up of the task above. As a group of teachers we made a decision to use the language of *conjecture, counter-example, proof* and *theorem* with students, in order to describe and guide their work.

In what follows there are two transcripts, taken from video recordings of the lessons. After the transcripts I offer some thoughts about each one.

The transcription has been tidied up slightly to avoid the 'um's and 'er's which are so much part of common speech but don't add to the message being conveyed here. To try to ease reading, I have adopted the following notation: (.) for a pause of less than 1 second; (3) for a pause of 3 seconds; [ ] talk indecipherable on the recording; [text] my best guess at transcription; [*text*] transcriber comments; ACs is me, Alf Coles; students are referred to by a single letter or sometimes S1, S2, etc.

The first transcript begins at the start of work on the 1089 problem in the class's second lesson on the task. The numbers in the left column indicate, in minutes and seconds, how long has passed since the start of the lesson. Lessons last one hour.

### *11th September*

| 11.22 | ACs | Let's remind ourselves what we're doing here (.) Like I say there was some absolutely fantastic work in your books (.) um and I wanted really to just hear from a few people what they discovered (.) so we can set up some more work on this project (.) You'll have got the idea by now that we work on projects in maths over a period of time and it's important we keep track of conjectures or questions that you come across (.) So would anyone like to offer a conjecture or question they came up with (.) in their homework? (2) L |
| --- | --- | --- |
| 12.15 | L | If there's a nine in the number already it isn't going to work. |
| 12.20 | ACs | Okay so we're all on different digit numbers now so (.) When you're talking make it clear how many digits you're thinking about (.) So was this three digits? (3) [*writing on the board*] (.) Say it again. |
| 13.02 | L | If there is a nine in the number in the middle it isn't going to work. |
| 13.08 | ACs | So what will it come to? (2) What are you saying it will come to? (3) What will the final answer be? (10) So are you saying it will come to one thousand and eighty-nine? |
| 13.27 | L | [yes] |
| 13.30 | ACs | Yup (.) So can I write it like that cos some people saying it does and doesn't work there's a bit of confusion [ ] So if there's a nine in the middle (.) in the number in the middle the final answer is one thousand and eighty-nine (.) |
| [*some dialogue skipped*] | | |
| 14.52 | H | I think she is wrong. I've done some sums and they didn't have nines in it. |

| 12.56 | ACs | b is b (.) b must equally b mustn't it (.) S7? |
| 12.59 | S1 | I think I meant d (.) Yeah I meant d. |
| 13.03 | S7 | I agree with S1 but I think there's also other ways of getting one hundred and nine thousand nine hundred and eighty-nine (.) um cos I've done sixty-two thousand one hundred and twenty-four [*for the number 62,124, b = d = 2*] |
| 13.25 | ACs | And what did that come to ? |
| 13.30 | S7 | That came to one hundred and nine thousand nine hundred and eighty-nine (3). |
| 13.40 | P | Yeah but that is S1's conjecture because the two and the two is the same because b is two and d is two. |
| 13.50 | S7 | But did she? (.) She said c equals b she changed |
| 13.53 | S1 | No, I said that d equals b. |
| 13.55 | S7 | Oh right. |
| 13.56 | ACs | Great little interaction there thank you very much (.) So we sorted out (.) so if it had been b equals c that would have been a useful example of another one that might have come to that but P is now saying that one fits with S1's conjecture (.) S9 are you happy about why that fits with S1's conjecture? Are you happy with that? (.) P said that fits with S1's conjecture (.) Are you happy about that or not sure why? |

The start of the lesson is similar to that of the 11th September, although it was more succinct, perhaps because the class knew by then what to expect. It would not be the case that every lesson on the project begins this way. For example, as a teacher I might make a choice at the start of one lesson to focus everybody on a particular idea.

On 11th September, I was the one who asked a student how many digits she was talking about in relation to a conjecture. On 24th September, at 12.25, it was a student who asked of another student how many digits they were discussing. At 13.03, a student made a distinction between agreeing with a conjecture and giving an example, not captured by the conjecture, that suggested there were other types of number that end up with the same answer. There is some awareness here of logical implication – the conjecture states all numbers of a certain kind end up at 109,989, but this still allows that other numbers could also end up the same.

This transcript, like the first one, shows that students interpret things differently. As with the issue of the number of digits, rather than me as teacher having to lead the students, in the second transcript the students resolved the different interpretations for themselves (13.30 to 13.55).

At 13.56, I again made some comments about the preceding dialogue, and I asked S9 if he was happy about what it means for an example to fit a conjecture. The interaction with S9 continued for several minutes, with other students contributing as well, since it became apparent that S9 was not clear why 62,124 'fits' with S1's (modified) conjecture (i.e., since b = d).

## Consciously developing a classroom environment

Looking at the two transcripts, there is perhaps some sense of how quickly a classroom environment can become established, in this case one in which students are involved in:

- making predictions;
- testing their own and other people's predictions;
- asking questions of each other;
- commenting on whether they agree or disagree with each other's ideas;
- using the language of conjecture;
- offering counter-examples to conjectures;
- sustaining involvement in one task over more than three weeks (including the time before the first transcript and after the second one).

As a reader, you will likely notice other elements of the classroom. The language of conjecture is particular to the school context of these lessons, but some of the other features of the transcripts listed above I take to be necessary for engagement in mathematics. For example, to be engaged in the study of mathematics as a student, I must be involved in the project of making sense of my (mathematical) experiences.

As the teacher, after eleven years in this school, I had conviction in what I had to offer, mathematically, and furthermore believed that it would be worthwhile for a sufficient number of students to justify taking up so much of their time. I was quite deliberate about aspects of the kind of mathematics classroom I wanted to establish. When I began teaching, not only did I lack the skills to create a particular classroom environment, I did not know precisely enough what I valued in the teaching and learning of mathematics. In some sense, that situation is unavoidable. When we begin teaching, we often will have few images of a classroom other than those in which we were taught ourselves. Part of teacher training can be the unpacking of how we were taught in order to retain what is useful for our purposes and to question what is not. I know that when I began teaching, I had aspirations to the kind of classroom I wanted, but this was not linked to any practical strategies (for example, of having a problem which allows students to ask and work on their own questions). The tasks I gave my classes were new to me and I was often not particularly aware of the range of interesting mathematics that could come out of them. And this is, again, one of the impossibilities of learning to teach – at the start of the journey into teaching, how can you know the implications of your actions and decisions in terms of overall classroom environment? After eleven years I was closer, perhaps, to the following image:

> Teaching, [Wodehouse] told us, is not so much handing on the torch of knowledge as fumbling with a box of matches, trying to strike one so that your pupils can find the electric light switch for themselves (Humphreys 1964: 2).

After eleven years, I was so familiar with the 1089 problem that my attention could be on supporting students in developing their ideas into conjectures and in supporting them to work with and listen to each other; my fumbling could be deliberate.

Zwicky's (1998: 41) beautiful poem 'Cashion Bridge' begins:

> It would be as well at the outset to admit
> how even to have said this much
> is to have failed.

I have presented images from my own classroom in an attempt to point to phenomena of engagement and learning, and yet I am aware how impossible it is to communicate these things without sharing a classroom experience. And this was the problem I had when beginning to teach: with no sense of what a classroom could look like in which students spoke mathematics to each other, there was little I could interpret from writing about such classrooms – to have said anything is to have failed.

## References

Bateson, G. (2000). *Steps to an ecology of mind*. Chicago: University of Chicago Press.
Brown, L. (2004). It's about learning: from purposes to basic-level categories to metacommenting. In A. Noyes (ed.) *Proceedings of the British Society for Research into Learning Mathematics*, 24(3): 1–6.
Brown, L. and Coles, A. (2008). *Hearing silence: steps to teaching mathematics*. Cambridge: Black Apollo Press.
Freud, S. (1976). *The complete psychological works of Sigmund Freud*, translated from the German under the general editorship of James Strachey. London: The Hogarth Press and the Institute of Psychoanalysis.
Freudenthal, H. (1978). *Weeding and sowing: preface to a science of mathematical education*. Dordrecht: D. Reidel Publishing Company.
Humphreys, D. (1964). *Helen Wodehouse*. Unpublished pamphlet held in University of Bristol, Graduate School of Education, Library Store.
Marton, F. and Booth, S. (1997). *Learning and awareness*. Mahwah, NJ: Lawrence Erlbaum Associates Ltd.
Maturana, H. and Poerksen, B. (2004). *From being to doing: the origins of the biology of cognition*. Heidelberg, Germany: Carl Auer.
Maturana, H. and Varela, F. (1992). *The tree of knowledge: the biological roots of human understanding*, 2nd edn. Boston: Shambhala.
Sfard, A. (2013). Discursive research in mathematics education: conceptual and methodological issues. In A. Lindmeier and A. Heinze (eds), *Proceedings of the 37th annual conference of the International Group for the Psychology of Mathematics Education* (Vol. 1, pp. 157–61). Kiel, Germany: PME 37.
Stewart, J. (2010). Foundational issues in enaction as a paradigm for cognitive science: from the origin of life to consciousness and writing. In J. Stewart, O. Gapenne and E. D. Paolo (eds), *Toward a new paradigm for cognitive science*, pp. 1–32. Cambridge, MA: The MIT Press.
Walkerdine, V. (1990). Difference, cognition and mathematics education. *For the Learning of Mathematics*, 10(3): 51–6.
Zwicky, J. (1998). *Songs for relinquishing the earth*. Ontario: Brick Books.

# 2 Planning for engagement in learning

If, as a teacher, I am going to get students in my classroom engaged, I want them to be engaged in learning mathematics (as opposed to, for example, engaging in an exploration of my boundaries). How do I recognise learning? What does it feel like when a group is engaged in learning? How can I know what is possible? This chapter will explore some of these issues and then focus on the question of how to plan in a way that may lead to engagement in learning.

Returning to the two transcripts from Chapter 1, there is one clear example of change from 11th to 24th September, that has already been alluded to.

**11th September**

| 12.20 | ACs | Okay so we're all on different digit numbers now so (.) When you're talking make it clear how many digits you're thinking about (.) So was this three digits? (3) [*writing on the board*] (.) Say it again. |

**24th September**

| 12.25 | S3 | What digit is it? |
| 12.28 | S1 | Um (.) Five. |
| 12.36 | ACs | Thank you for the question (.) That feels really important that we don't (.) um we can't make sense of it unless we know how many digits (.) um [*writes on board*] |

On 11th September, I pointed out to the class that we needed to know how many digits there are in the starting number to make sense of a student's conjecture. On 24th September, it was another student (S3) who questioned S1 about how many digits were in the sums.

It might be tempting to see the difference in these transcripts as a case of the teacher causing a change (learning) in a student. However, the reflections on the difficulty of teaching in the first chapter suggest an alternative view. On 11th September, I made the comment at 12.20 to everyone in the class. I would also have made several other comments about how mathematicians work. What we observe is that one student picks up on one comment and offers it back a fortnight later. Looked at in this way, it is perhaps clearer to see that what is significant here is the student, S3, not the comment from the teacher. Out of all the comments and all the students, something in the history of S3 meant that she heard this particular distinction about digits and subsequently observed the lack of a distinction between the number of digits on 24th September.

One of the reasons for choosing the task '1089' as the first activity in year 7 (ages 11–12) is that it gives many opportunities for students to notice patterns and make predictions that increase in complexity as the number of digits increases (also there is the possibility, useful for some students, of looking at the simpler situation of two digits). As teacher, I quite deliberately wanted to engage students in the precision of thinking that is required to make conjectures (which they do) such as: 'With a five-digit number $abcde$, if $b = d$ then the answer will be 109,989'. There is the important idea that a conjecture needs to work for all examples that 'fit' its conditions and again, this would be an explicit focus at various points in the project.

John Mason coined the epigram: 'teaching takes place in time, learning taking place over time' (Mason 1998). I do not expect, as a teacher, that saying to students 'conjectures need to work for all examples' will mean that they then 'know' this. In order for students to develop new ways of operating in a mathematics classroom there must be a sustained engagement in a new discourse. The notion of a conjecture and what it means to make one, test one, disprove one are ideas that will take time to become embedded in a classroom environment and different individuals will be less or more quick to pick up on the new language. At the school where the 1089 lessons took place, I knew that for the year 7 students every major project (there were seven of them across the year) would give opportunities for conjecturing and proving.

In any task, as well as learning some mathematics, students are learning about *what learning mathematics is like* in this classroom; the choice to use any task cannot be dissociated from a choice about *ways* of working. Watson and Mason (2007: 210) emphasise

> the importance of developing ways of working, a classroom rubric in which the learners are drawn into patterns of thinking, in which some transforming action takes place.

Embedded within the choice of tasks such as 1089 was an image of a way of working, one in which students would be engaged with a common focus, sharing results and ideas and developing conjectures to guide further activity. There are of course many possible images of mathematical ways of working – what seems significant is that, as a teacher, I have *some* image of what I want to create and I choose tasks that will allow students to engage in those kinds of ways of working. This idea of having some 'story' that, as a teacher, we tell ourself about what we are doing was observed by Laurinda Brown (2014) in her work interviewing teachers about their first lessons with a class. This again raises the difficulties of beginning teaching – at the start of teaching we cannot know what ways of working we will value, or, as in my case, we do not know how to promote a specific way of working. For me, the making of conjectures becomes a 'transforming action' in the classroom in the sense of allowing students to feel some control over the subject. Students themselves can learn to become arbiters of mathematical truth.

Some hints at how, in my own teaching, I tried to promote patterns of thinking can be seen in the transcripts from Chapter 1. On 11th September, I commented about one aspect of conjecturing.

| 16.29 | ACs | So could H and L talk to each other about this one? (5) So L (.) H was offering that one [*indicating 740 on the board*] as what we call a counter-example to your conjecture (1) Do you want talk to H about what you saw in that example? |

One of the things I know I was trying to do was find opportunities to reflect back to the class aspects of what they did that had a mathematical label. In particular, I was sensitive to anything which might approach a conjecture or counter-example. At 16.29, I can be seen providing the label 'counter-example' for what H suggested. At the risk of repeating myself, I am not expecting that even one student necessarily will pick up on this label right away. But I know I will notice counter-examples and flag them up to students. Over time, I expect the word will come to be used by the class and begin to guide their activity.

On 24th September, I commented about examples fitting conjectures, a theme closely linked to that of counter-example.

| 13.56 | ACs | Great little interaction there thank you very much (.) So we sorted out (.) so if it had been b equals c that would have been a useful example of another one that might have come to that but P is now saying that one fits with S1's conjecture (.) S9 are you happy about why that fits with S1's conjecture? Are you happy with that? (.) P said that fits with S1's conjecture (.) Are you happy about that or not sure why? |

Later in this chapter, I will return to what happened (in the interaction with S9) after this comment, but there is a sense perhaps of a consistent teacher focus across these two transcripts on specific aspects of mathematical thinking. What I observed is that over time more and more students picked up on what it meant to make and test conjectures and became actively engaged in looking for patterns and connections in *any* piece of mathematics they were given.

## Inner and outer tasks

There is an issue, identified in the literature, around what students do in response to tasks, compared to the intentions and plans of the designer or teacher. Mason *et al.* (2005: 131) see the problem as one of how a mathematician's awarenesses can be translated into instructions or procedures that lead to those same awarenesses for students. The problem is that it is all too easy to get students performing the same actions as a mathematician but without the same awarenesses. Tahta (1980) raises a similar issue when he distinguishes 'outer' and 'inner' aspects of tasks. The outer task is what is made explicit to students by the teacher; the inner task is the relationship or awareness the teacher hopes students will gain. The problem for teachers (and again this speaks to the difficulty of teaching) is that the more precisely the desired behaviours in students are specified, the less these behaviours are likely to emanate from students' own awareness. Watson and Mason (2007: 209) put it this way, alluding again to transformation:

> Engaging learners in activity is important, but in order to learn from that activity they need to experience some kind of shift or transformation in what they are sensitised to notice and attend to mathematically.

And, to repeat, the more precisely we specify the behaviour that would indicate a transformation or shift, the less likely it is that students will experience a transformation or shift. When I metacommented to the year 7 class about counter-examples (11th September, 16.29), what I was not doing was telling students how to find a counter-example. Instead, I gave students a description of what H had done and a suggestion that this kind of activity is significant. An implicit (inner) task for all students is that part of their role is to look for counter-examples and try to modify conjectures if necessary.

## Mathematical thinking

So, what kinds of awareness, shifts and transformations are important in doing mathematics? If I want to plan for my students to be doing mathematics, what will this look like? My view of mathematics has been influenced by Caleb Gattegno. Before getting to Gattegno's view of mathematics, it is important to say a little about a key word I have been using, which I take from his writing: awareness. Gattegno (1987: 25) thought of awareness as a technical term: 'to illuminate our fields of action'. He turned 'awareness' into a countable noun – we can enumerate awarenes*ses*. I can uncover my own awarenesses by observing myself operating in any field of action. For example, think for a moment about how you would go about doing this calculation: $17 \times 23$. If you would use a paper and pencil method, you must have an awareness about the appropriateness of a particular algorithm in relation to the problem (as well as awarenesses linked to the use of the algorithm itself). If you translated the problem into $(20 - 3) \times (20 + 3)$ and hence into $20^2 - 3^2$, then you must have an awareness of 'the difference of two squares' and how this idea can be used to simplify some calculations.

Gattegno (1965) saw mathematics as the awareness of relationships. For Gattegno, all mathematics was algebraic, since awareness of relationships implies a consideration of inner connections that he associated with algebra. '[A]ll is algebra in mathematics, because to say "algebra" is to say the awareness of the mind at work on whatever content' (Gattegno 1965: 22). This is a complex quotation and one that is worth dwelling on for a while. In order to make sense of an algebraic expression as simple as $x + y$, I must be able to step back from the particular addition of two numbers and consider the process of adding two numbers as an object in its own right. The expression is a static representation of a dynamic process (and perhaps this is part of the reason for the difficulties students have with algebra). I must move from considering the content of the addition of two numbers, to an awareness of that content (that addition). It is such a movement that Gattegno considers to be algebraic.

Gattegno (1971) distinguished 'powers of the mind' that he believed all humans possess, which would mean that all humans are able to think mathematically. These powers (also referred to in Brown and Coles 2011: 866) are:

> 1) *extraction*, finding 'what is common among so large a range of variations'; 2) making *transformations*, based on the early use of language '*This* is *my* pen' to '*That* is *your* pen'; 3) handling *abstractions*, evidenced by learning the meanings attached to words; and 4) *stressing and ignoring*, without which 'we cannot see anything' (paraphrased from Gattegno 1971: 9–11).

Therefore, the kinds of transformation and shift I can expect *all* learners in my classes to be able to make are: noticing what is the same or different from a collection (extraction/

stressing and ignoring); considering and naming both sides of a relationship (transformation/abstraction). To take a non-mathematical example, young children have no difficulty in handling linguistic relationships such as: 'she is my sister' and 'I am her brother'. In the 1089 task, all students can engage in looking at lists of numbers that are linked to different 'finishing' numbers and noticing what is the 'same/different' (a phrase of Laurinda Brown's). In recognising that just because a conjecture states some kinds of number will end up at a particular finishing point, that this does not preclude other kinds of number also ending up at the same point, students show they can consider both sides of a relationship.

Gattegno privileged the visible and the tangible in the learning of mathematics. He worked with imagery and felt that mathematics 'is shot through with infinity' (Gattegno 1984: 20). The connection here is that once we become aware of a relationship it is possible to imagine that relationship as an action that is iterated, potentially an infinite number of times. The 1089 task I see as shot through with infinity in several ways. Students can choose any three-digit number to work with and although there is not an infinite choice here, there is something powerful about the *any*. And then, most obviously perhaps, there is an unlimited number of digits that students can potentially consider (four-digit, five-digit, etc., numbers).

With this view of mathematics in mind, before moving on to issues around the planning of whole-class tasks, I want to think about how, as teachers, we might notice mathematical shifts and transformations in our students.

### An awareness 'at hand'

If, as a teacher, my focus is on students' awareness rather than their behaviour then there may be times that I focus attention on one individual, if I am confident that there is an 'awareness at hand' (to use a phrase of Gattegno's). And, rather than offer more and more precise descriptions of the behaviour that is desired, there can be an uncomfortable *non-reduction* in the level of challenge. An example of what I mean follows from the end of the Chapter 1 transcript of the 24th September lesson. The context was that there was a conjecture, made by S1, that *if* a five-digit number '*abcde*' had $b = d$, then the answer should come out as 109,989, and students were discussing the number 62,124 (which therefore should end up at 109,989, according to S1's conjecture).

The transcript from Chapter 1 ended with my comment:

| 13.56 | ACs | Great little interaction there thank you very much (.) So we sorted out (.) so if it had been b equals c that would have been a useful example of another one that might have come to that but P is now saying that one fits with S1's conjecture (.) S9 are you happy about why that fits with S1's conjecture? Are you happy with that? (.) P said that fits with S1's conjecture (.) Are you happy about that or not sure why? |// 

I cannot recall why I chose to ask S9 at this moment, but I know he was one of the less confident students in the class (mathematically speaking) and that he had arrived from primary school with low attainment compared to most of the others in the class. He responded to the question by saying that he was not sure.

| 14.25 | S9 | [not sure why] |
|---|---|---|
| 14.27 | ACs | Could somebody help? (.) Could somebody explain why does that fit with S1's conjecture? (.) S10? |
| 14.39 | S10 | Because on $b$ it's the same as $d$ because they're both [two] and on her conjecture it says if $b$ equals $d$ it should come to that thing (.) That number. |
| 14.51 | ACs | (2) Does that make sense? [*looking at S9*] (2) Can you explain that in your own words? (7) What was S10 saying? (.) What does the conjecture say? (2) Go on, M. |
| 15.00 | M | It's saying that $b$ is the same number as $d$ (.) which means that on there $b$ is (.) on the answer it's the same. |

At 14.51, I waited two seconds for S9 to respond, then repeated my question and waited seven seconds, repeated again and paused for a further two seconds. A seven-second pause is a long time in a whole-class discussion. Perhaps sensing the discomfort of the pause, another student, M, indicated that he wanted to respond, which he did at 15.00. I then returned to focus on S9 and there were more long pauses.

| 15.10 | ACs | (2) Is that making sense S9? [*S9 nods*] (2) Yeah? (.) Can you try and say that in your own words then? (7) I'm sorry to put you on the spot S9 (.) but it just feels quite important (.) I mean be honest with me (.) If it doesn't make sense then say (.) but if you're saying it makes sense it would just be helpful for lots of people/ |
|---|---|---|

At the start of my turn, S9 nodded to indicate that it was 'making sense'. There is another seven-second pause. I commented on what I imagine was my own discomfort 'I'm sorry to put you on the spot'. As M did earlier, another student (D) intervened (at 15.36) to say it does not make sense to him.

| 15.36 | D | [doesn't make sense to me] |
|---|---|---|
| 15.40 | ACs | Right it doesn't make sense to D (.) Thanks, D (.) Good (.) So can you try and say what you understand by this? (.) or by P saying it fits S1's conjecture? (11) Can you give us another number that according to S1's conjecture might come to one hundred and nine thousand nine hundred and ninety-eight? (3) D go on then. |
| 16.01 | D | Alright then (.) um (.) seven um three five three four. |

At 15.40, I changed my focus to work with D and he was able, straight away, to provide a number that could be used to test the conjecture (for 7.35.34, $b = d = 3$, so the conjecture predicts it will end up at 109,989). I then returned again to S9.

| 16.08 | ACs | S9 do you think (.) S9 (.) does that one fit S1's conjecture? (3) |
|---|---|---|
| 16.12 | S13 | [how many digits is it] |
| 16.20 | ACs | Five digits (2) Does that fit S1's conjecture S9? [*S9 nods*] Why? (6) |

*(continued)*

*(continued)*

| 16.39 | S9  | [b equals d] |
|-------|-----|---|
| 16.45 | ACs | Because b equals d (.) That's what she's saying (.) if b equals d it should come to that (.) Great (.) C could you give us another number we could use to test? (.) I'll put a question mark there because D was making a prediction which is brilliant (.) So once you've got a conjecture you need to be making predictions (.) S9, see if you can give me one in a minute as well (.) C can you give me another prediction from S1's conjecture? |
| 17.07 | C   | Eight four seven four six. |
| 17.15 | ACs | Great (.) S9 could you give me another one? |
| 17.20 | S9  | Two [three nine three seven] |

The two student interventions (by M and D) from earlier in some sense made things easier for S9, and rather than having to explain the conjecture he now needed to say if he thinks an example will fit the conjecture. However, at 16.39, S9 put forward something that, to me at the time, I took as indicative of a new awareness. I then returned to S9 at 17.15 and asked him to provide a number of his own, to confirm (perhaps to himself as much as to me) that he was now able to generate numbers that could be used to test the conjecture. In the context of the 1089 task, there is a rule that the first digit must be larger than the last (to avoid getting negative numbers after the subtraction), so his response at 17.20 needed a little work – but, for me, this was a minor detail compared to the capacity he demonstrated to distinguish numbers where $b = d$.

Looking back at the transcript, I would see this distinction made by S9 as the 'inner task'; the 'outer task' was variously, 'S9 are you happy about why that fits with S1's conjecture?'; 'Can you try and say that in your own words?'; 'Does that one fit S1's conjecture?' What I imagine the less experienced 'me' in the classroom might have done would have been to point out the '$b$' and '$d$' in some examples and 'show' S9 how they are the same. What this lessening of the complexity of the task would do, however, is rob S9 of the experience of interpreting some text and coming up with his own example. Arguably the interventions of other students do lessen the complexity for S9, but the 'inner task' remains unspecified. I had conviction that there was no way S9 would be incapable of distinguishing numbers where $b = d$, given that extraction and stressing/ignoring are powers of the mind. He perhaps needed my help and the help of others in the class to focus his own attention. Gattegno coined the phrase 'forcing awareness', to describe one of the roles of the teacher, which could be another description of what I was doing here. Perhaps I sensed that there was an awareness 'at hand' for S9 and that he could discover something about himself (that he was capable of making connections, for example) if 'forced'. I have always found this phrase of Gattegno's uncomfortable, with overtones of doing damage to students. We cannot know how S9 experienced the discomfort of being put 'on the spot', but if his answers came from a genuinely new awareness, then I would hope that the overall experience would be one of the excitement of making sense of the new.

## Planning for engagement

The analysis of the interaction with S9 was about noticing shifts and transformations and trying to align student experience of a task with teacher intentions. The example with S9 was, in essence, a one-to-one interaction; the question remains how to plan activities for a whole class that may lead to engagement in mathematical thinking.

From my experiences of working with prospective teachers, one of the major challenges of the journey to becoming an effective teacher of mathematics is finding a way of reducing planning time. How, as teachers, do we choose what tasks to give our students? The internet offers a seemingly unending supply of lesson ideas, activities and resources. Prospective teachers report on the 'trap' of spending hours trying to find the 'perfect' resource for their particular purposes. Having some principles to guide planning is one way to reduce planning time.

An underlying theme so far has been the connection between learning and the making of a new distinction. In Chapter 1, the example of my looking at the bean plant was one of a moment of learning in which I became able to distinguish beans from the background plant. In the example of S9, by the end of the transcript there is some evidence that he was able to distinguish five-digit numbers whose second and fourth digits are the same from all other five-digit numbers.

There is a research tradition within cognitive science called 'enactivism' that views the making of distinctions as the most basic mental function (and not just for humans). Thompson and Stapleton (2009) give the example of an amoeba in a sugar gradient which will always move towards the higher concentration. In order to do this, the amoeba must be making a distinction. In the interaction between amoeba and sugar solution, there is the creation of 'value' for the amoeba. This view of mental functioning is a contemporary take on Gattegno's powers of the mind and the extraction or stressing/ignoring that is required to make a distinction or notice a similarity or difference.

To translate these insights into the classroom, one answer to the problem of how to engage learners in the doing of mathematics is to design tasks where students are exposed to the possibilities of making the same distinctions that teachers (and mathematicians) make. In the 1089 task, students quite naturally become curious about whether all numbers will end at 1089 and hence begin making distinctions about predictions that work for all or only some examples.

Arising directly from a belief in the importance of making distinctions, the design principles that operated in the school where I was head of department included the list below (first articulated in Coles and Brown, 2013). This list is not presented as a finished product and was not made explicit within the department. However, over the course of the last fifteen years, within the community around the school, various of these principles were spoken about and worked on as a group. During my time at the school, two mathematics teachers moved to become heads of mathematics in different schools, and established their own curricula based on similar principles for activities. The principles are:

1 Start with a closed activity (which may involve teaching a new skill).
2 Consider at least two contrasting examples (where possible, images) and collect responses on a 'common board'.
3 Ask students to comment on what is the same or different about contrasting examples and/or to pose questions.
4 Have a challenge prepared in case no questions are forthcoming.
5 Introduce language and notation arising from student distinctions.
6 Provide opportunities for students to spot patterns, make conjectures and work on proving them (hence involving generalising and algebra).
7 Provide opportunities for the teacher to teach further new skills and for students to practise skills in different contexts.

Principles 2, 3, 5, and 7 come from the view of knowing and learning which is linked to the making of distinctions. By working with at least two examples, we support students in sharing distinctions and, through this sharing, making new distinctions, which is tantamount to learning. Language and notation are introduced to label distinctions students make, to support new ways of seeing. Taking the opportunity to introduce the label 'counter-example' (see the transcript in Chapter 1) would be one example of introducing a label to name a distinction made by students. It was a student who offered the example that contradicted the conjecture. Providing a label makes it more likely that this action can be kept in mind and repeated by other students. Labelling students' distinctions is likely to be far more effective (in terms of supporting more and more students to use that label) than introducing labels for distinctions students have not yet made.

By 'examples' (Principle 2), I mean to capture a wide range of possibilities, including images, animations and procedures. Principle 6 comes from the view of mathematics as being essentially about the activities of conjecturing, no matter what content is being covered. Principles 1, 4 and 7 derive from Gattegno. The closed activity will, where possible, involve something visible or tangible and be something that all students can do. The challenge and opportunity to teach skills in different contexts are linked to the power humans have of extraction. When we do something in different contexts, it is more likely we can extract the skill and retain it for use another time.

So, thinking about the activity '1089' that was described in Chapter 1, it is possible to see each of these principles in operation:

- The activity start is closed (Principle 1) – students have to choose one number and perform a pre-defined process.
- Through the whole class doing the process on their own number, the teacher can collect a wide range of responses (Principle 2) most of which will have the answer 1089, but typically some students will have made a mistake with the process and got a different answer.
- Having collected the range of answers from the class and worked through the anomalies, the teacher asks what questions anyone has (Principle 3), knowing at the same time that the challenge 'Can you find me a starting number that does not end up at 1089?' is an engaging one (Principle 4).
- As indicated in the transcripts, the 1089 activity is an excellent vehicle for introducing the language of conjecture, counter-example and proof (Principles 5 and 6).
- Alongside the work on noticing pattern, students get a lot of practice at addition and subtraction (Principle 7). A further purpose of this task – assisting the teachers – was to provide space to sort out problems with any student who came to the school lacking confidence in these processes.

The 1089 activity in itself does not completely fulfil the requirements of Principle 7 since, to take just one issue, students will only have had practice at adding and subtracting numbers which have an equal number of digits. Hence, the activity can mask problems students might have 'aligning digits' (if they are using one of the standard algorithms). Therefore part of the curriculum at the school involved other activities (that could come from textbooks) where students were required to use the same skills as those in the longer tasks, such as 1089, but in a different context.

The principles above are, of course, quite particular to the school where I worked. Although the principles were largely implicit, there was a sense that, as a group of teachers, we knew what we wanted from a task – to allow the kind of conjecturing and proving evident in the transcripts. What is important, as ever, is not the particular principles used but the idea of having some principles to guide planning.

To take just one alternative (and in the spirit of offering contrasting examples), in the rest of this chapter I consider the principle of planning for engagement by making use of the 'real world' and mathematical modelling.

## Using the real world

Mathematics can be seen as an abstract subject with little relevance to students' lives outside school. One response to this view of the subject has been to introduce more 'real-world' examples when teaching, for example, using percentages to look at mobile phone tariffs or mortgages. There is an assumption that students will be engaged by the 'real' or perhaps that students will value the subject when they see it has 'real-world' applications. However, it is not universally accepted that 'real' means 'good' in the context of teaching and learning mathematics. Anne Watson, in a 2008 plenary lecture, argues powerfully about the limits of the 'real', particularly when working with adolescents. It is worth quoting from this lecture at some length.

> Realistic tasks can provide contexts for enquiry and often enquiry methods of teaching and learning are recommended for adolescent learning. Historically, mathematics has been inspired by observable phenomena, and mathematicians develop new ideas by exploring and enquiring into phenomena in mathematics and elsewhere. It is also possible to conjecture relationships from experience with examples, and thus get to know about general behaviour. But mathematics is not *only* an empirical subject at school level; indeed it is not *essentially* empirical. Its strength and power are in its abstractions, its reasoning, and its hypotheses about objects which only exist in the mathematical imagination. Enquiry alone cannot fully justify results and relationships, nor can decisions be validated by enquiry alone. Many secondary school concepts are beyond observable manifestations, and beyond everyday intuition. Indeed, those which cause most difficulty for learners and teachers are those which require rejection of intuitive sense and reconstruction of new ways of acting mathematically (Watson 2008: 23).

Watson is suggesting that at the heart of mathematics is the learning of ways of acting that are not (centrally) about noticing aspects of the empirical world and making predictions based on past experience. Mathematics, essentially, is about the development of reasoning about objects that do not appear in the world but have come about through the use of human mathematical imagination. While being mindful of these concerns, I consider possibilities for using mathematical modelling to provoke engagement.

## Mathematical modelling

Is it possible to start with genuine problems in the world and support students in turning them into mathematical models that can be manipulated, analysed and then interpreted back into the situation from which they arose? The idea of introducing mathematical modelling into the curriculum to motivate the learning of mathematics is not new.

Conrad Wolfram has developed an entire curriculum based on modelling that is being implemented across all schools in Estonia.[1]

*Teaching secondary mathematics as if the planet matters* (Coles et al. 2013) contains many ideas for introducing elements of mathematical modelling into the classroom.[2] Before considering some of the possibilities from this book, it is worth noting a useful framework that can be used to think about different modes of integration of wider issues into the mathematics classroom. In Table 2.1, Barwell (2013a) summarises a framework from Renert (2011) to help focus on ways in which sustainability can be incorporated into the teaching and learning of mathematics. Although the focus of this chapter is not only on sustainability, the framework provides a useful way to think about how a mathematics classroom can be connected to broader issues.

Drawing on Coles et al. (2013), I will give examples of activities within each of these approaches to sustainability. It is important to note that the boundaries between these approaches are not clearly marked, and Barwell (2013a) suggests they are better conceived as lying on a continuum.

## Accommodation approach

In an accommodation approach, as a teacher, my focus remains firmly on the mathematics that students will learn. I use real-world examples whenever I can but the focus in each lesson perhaps quickly shifts away from the context and into a consideration of the underlying mathematics. This underlying mathematics has been determined by me in advance and is not open to question.

For example, if I want to work on linear sequences, I might present a class with the data in Table 2.2 and ask them to predict what happened next.

*Table 2.1* Approaches to sustainability in teaching mathematics

| | | |
|---|---|---|
| Transformation | Teaching and learning mathematics to analyse and critique the perspectives that shape how the world is understood and engage in action to change the world | Outside world as origin of sustainability problems, for which mathematics may be one tool (or part of the problem) |
| Reformation | Teaching and learning mathematics to relate mathematics to the world and to refine how things are done | Outside world as origin of mathematics problems |
| Accommodation | Teaching and learning mathematical facts and procedures | Outside world used as a way of presenting mathematics |

Source: Barwell (2013a: 8)

*Table 2.2* Historical global population estimates

| Year | Population estimate | Population (billions) |
|---|---|---|
| 1750 | 640,000,000 | 0.64 |
| 1800 | 970,000,000 | 0.97 |
| 1850 | 1,300,000,000 | 1.30 |
| 1900 | 1,630,000,000 | 1.63 |

Source: Coles (2013:111)

Students might notice that the population appears to increase by 0.33 billion every 50 years. This would be enough information to be able to predict the population in 1950, 2000, 2050 and/or to generate an algebraic rule. At this point, the connection to the real world is in the balance. As a teacher, do I want to engage students in thinking about how realistic this model is and about what actually happened between 1900 and the present day? The pressures of the school curriculum may suggest that such discussions are a luxury and therefore the focus of this hypothetical lesson would shift to, say, techniques for finding the rule of any linear sequence.

Students may be suspicious of the regular increase in population between 1750 and 1900 and, indeed, the numbers in Table 2.2 have been chosen (within the bounds of historical population numbers) to make the increase appear linear. The activity could easily be moved into a reformation setting by considering the bounds of population and, for example, which vested interests might want to take different values.

*Reformation approach*

In a reformation approach there is more of a sense that the starting point for planning is not some particular piece of mathematics that I want to teach, but rather a problem in the real world. Barwell (2013b) considers how, as teachers, we might want to tackle issues of climate change. It is possible to access historical temperature records for anywhere in the UK[3] and many other areas of the world. A starting point for activity could simply be the question: is our climate changing? Or, as Barwell (2013b) suggests, the more provocative: if the climate is warming, why is there still so much cold weather around? Analysing weather records can be done simply through finding the means of various datasets. A more sophisticated analysis involves finding the variance also. Considering possible changes to mean and variance, there are three scenarios (on the assumption that something is changing and that neither measure is decreasing):

- mean increasing, variance constant;
- mean increasing, variance increasing;
- mean constant, variance increasing.

It is possible to test, experimentally, with weather data from a local area which, if any, of these scenarios has taken place. The different scenarios can be visualised in Figure 2.1 (reproduced in Barwell 2013b). It is likely that local historical weather data will show that mean and variance have both increased. Why there is still a similar amount of cold weather as there always has been can now be interpreted from the graph.

*Transformation approach*

An activity based on considering climate change would shade into a transformation activity, to the extent that the mathematical tasks are used 'to analyse and critique the perspectives that shape how the world is understood and engage in action to change the world' (see Table 2.1). So, for example, if a consideration of weather data was followed up (or preceded) by an analysis of media reporting on climate change, the activity would begin to have some features of transformation. If students were encouraged to analyse and engage in the political debate around climate change, again, the activity would begin to have characteristics of a transformation approach. The policies of the school and local

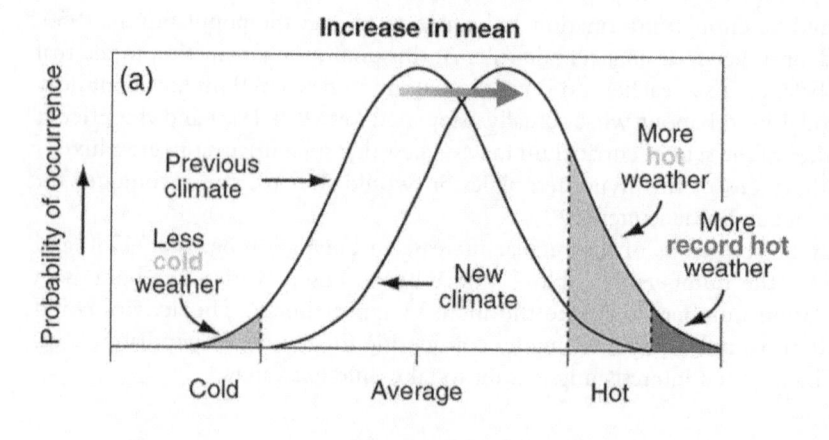

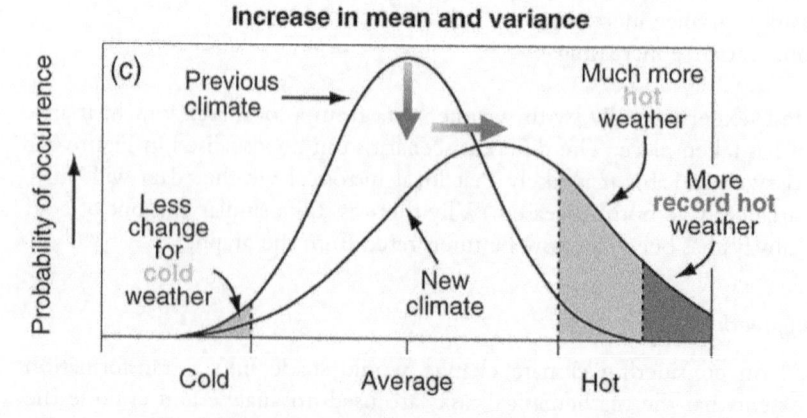

*Figure 2.1* Schematic showing the effect on extreme temperatures when (a) the mean temperature increases, (b) the variance increases, and (c) when both the mean and variance increase for a normal distribution of temperature

Source: IPCC 2001: 155, quoted in Barwell 2013b: 42

district might be investigated and critiqued in the light of what these administrative bodies are doing to combat the effects of climate change. Campaigns of change might be launched, backed up by mathematical analysis.

This image of schooling may seem a long way from the realities of a typical classroom, with the demands of standardised testing and performance-related pay for the teacher. However, it is perhaps useful to consider extreme cases in order to think about possibilities that may be around, spaces for differences that exist, but are not always recognised. Perhaps once a year, a class might be able to engage in a problem originating in the outside world, the analysis of which has the possibility of leading to action for change. The problem, of course, with one-off activities that are different from the norm is that classroom environments can become set and a class may not value an activity too far outside what they have come to expect.

Helen Wodehouse (1924: 215) reminds us that we act out of habits we not even be aware of, even when doing things for the first time:

> When the inexperienced teacher . . . is confronted with the problem of a child to be educated, he [sic] brings to it not the hypothetical fresh and empty mind, but a mind with a history, a mind filled and formed by his own up-bringing and by tradition and memories and hearsay. He clings to remembered scraps as to supporting planks in the ocean.

How can we not, in a sense, do anything other than teach as we were taught, to begin with? One of our tasks as teachers, therefore, is to try to bring to awareness of those habits we fall into which perhaps do not serve our purposes. Some patterns of acting can seem unchangeable, and yet perhaps may be no more than our clinging to Wodehouse's 'remembered scraps as to supporting planks in the ocean'.

## Notes

1 See www.computerbasedmath.org, for further details.
2 See also nrich.maths.org/10054.
3 From the Met Office; see www.metoffice.gov.uk/

## References

Barwell, R. (2013a). The role of mathematics in shaping our world. In *Teaching secondary mathematics as if the planet matters,* pp. 3–15. London: Routledge.

Barwell, R. (2013b). Climate change. In *Teaching secondary mathematics as if the planet matters,* pp. 31–49. London: Routledge.

Brown, L. (2014). Stories of learning as a mathematics teacher educator through narrative interviewing. In *Perspectives on storytelling: framing global and personal identities.* Oxford: Inter-Disciplinary Press.

Brown, L. and Coles, A. (2011). Developing expertise: how enactivism re-frames mathematics teacher development. *ZDM, 43*(6–7): 861–73.

Coles, A. and Brown, L. (2013). Making distinctions in task design and student activity. In C. Margolinas (ed.), *Task design in mathematics education: proceedings of ICMI Study 22,* pp. 183–92. Oxford: ICMI.

Coles, A., Barwell, R., Cotton, T., Brown, L. and Winter, J. (2013). *Teaching secondary mathematics as if the planet matters.* London: Routledge.

Gattegno, C. (1965). Mathematics and imagery. *Mathematics Teaching, 33*(4): 22–24.
Gattegno, C. (1971). *What we owe children: the subordination of teaching to learning.* London: RKP.
Gattegno, C. (1984). Infinity. *Mathematics Teaching, 107*: 18–22.
Gattegno, C. (1987). *The science of education. Part 1: theoretical considerations.* New York: Educational Solutions Worldwide Inc.
Intergovernmental Panel on Climate Change (IPCC) (2008). *Climate change 2007 synthesis report.* Geneva: IPCC.
Mason, J., Graham, A. and Johnston-Wilder, S. (2005). *Developing thinking in algebra.* London: Paul Chapman Publishing.
Renert, M. (2011). Mathematics for life: sustainable mathematics education. *For the Learning of Mathematics, 31*(1): 20–6.
Tahta, D. (1980). About geometry. *For the Learning of Mathematics, 1*(1): 2–9.
Thompson, E. and Stapleton, M. (2009). Making sense of sense-making: reflections on enactive and extended mind theories. *Topoi, 28*(1): 23–30.
Watson, A. (2008) Adolescent learning and secondary mathematics. *Proceedings of the 2008 Annual Meeting of the Canadian Mathematics Education Study Group*, pp. 21–32. Available online at www://cmesg.ca/ (accessed 17 September 2010).
Watson, A. and Mason, J. (2007). Taken-as-shared: a review of common assumptions about mathematical tasks in teacher education. *Journal of Mathematics Teacher Education, 10*(4): 205–15.
Wodehouse, H. (1924). *A survey of the history of education.* London: Edward Arnold & Co.

# 3 Mathematical understandings and meanings

It seems a prerequisite of engagement in mathematics that tasks are meaningful to students. The plan to base mathematics on the real world (discussed in Chapter 2) is one way of trying to make mathematics meaningful. In contrast, I begin with another classroom transcript that, for me, gives an image of a group of students making meaning of mathematics in a context that is game-like rather than real-world. The activity they are engaged in is called 'Frogs'. A description of the task is below, followed by the transcript.

> **'Frogs' activity**
>
> The starting challenge for this task is best done actively. Set out seven chairs in a line at the front of the classroom, facing the room. Invite three girls to come and sit on one side and three boys to sit on the other, with the spare chair in the middle, as shown in Figure 3.1. Students can slide into an empty chair or jump over one student into an empty chair. The task is for the boys and girls to swap where they are sitting.
>
> Students will probably need several goes to do this. Rather than explain how they can move – demonstrate. At some point, introduce the challenge of swapping seats in the minimum number of moves (this challenge might come from students). You may want to get different students trying it at the front.
>
> When you are happy that the class has figured out how the game works and have been hooked by the idea of trying to find out the minimum number of moves, students can be invited to continue working at their tables, for example using counters.
>
> If they become convinced they have the minimum number (15), they can be invited to try to record how they do it. They are likely to suggest, themselves, trying it for more people on each side. Can they predict the total number of moves for everyone in the class? or the school?

*'Frogs' transcript*

In the transcript below, italicised text is a commentary. It was written up, from memory, a couple of days after the lesson, which took place in 1998 with a class of year 7 (age 11–12)

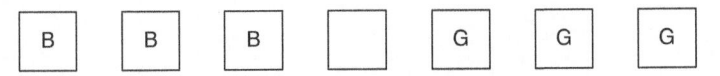

| B | B | B |  | G | G | G |

*Figure 3.1* Starting positions for the 'Frogs' game

30  Issues

```
No. each side    No. moves
     1    →    3 +5
     2    →    8 +7
     3    →   15 +9
     4    →   24 +11
     5    →   35 +13
     6    →   48
```

*Figure 3.2* Whiteboard with results for 'Frogs' game

students. Punctuation has been included in this transcript as it is not a verbatim account. There were 12 students in the class, who were all in one group because they were thought to need extra support in mathematics. Names have all been changed. By the end of the transcript, the board looked like Figure 3.2:

This was the students' second lesson working on 'Frogs'.

| 1 | | *One of the first students to arrive is Paige, who was away for the first lesson on this activity. I arrange some chairs at the back of the classroom. Tom arrives, who had also been away last lesson.* |
|---|---|---|
| 2 | | *Their homework from the last lesson was to write up 'How to play Frogs' and to explain how to do it in 15 moves with three people on each side (we had established this as the minimum number of moves when doing it practically at the start of the first lesson). Suzie and Jean came in saying they wanted to show me their homework, and so did Jake, who had written out a system for solving the three-a-side problem and wanted to try it out with six people to see if it worked.* |
| 3 | ACs | Okay, everyone, because Paige and Tom have missed what we have done so far on 'Frogs', I'd like to begin by doing it again on chairs at the back, so that they can see what this is about. Jake has shown me his homework and he has written out a system that he'd like to try out to see if works in 15 moves, so can you three and three go onto the chairs at the back . . . Yes, Paige and Tom you have to be on chairs, otherwise you won't learn how it works. |
| 4 | Jake | E (to himself) . . . that's you . . . to D (again, said to himself, then looking up and pointing) there . . . then C . . . Paige . . . to D . . . there (pointing). |
| | | *As he continued, the class picked up his system of classifying the chairs and so for the last few moves he simply said "C to E . . . D to C" and the students knew what to do. It came out as fifteen moves.* |
| 5 | Jake | I can do it for four on each side as well, it comes out as twenty-four moves |
| 6 | ACs | Great, we'll try that in a minute, but I just want to see if the people sitting here can do it in fifteen moves without being directed. |

|   |     | *The group do it twice in fifteen moves, two or three students point to who they think should move where and one student, Karen, waves her arms, saying "No!, back!" when she disagrees with a move. In terms of going for the minimum number of moves, her sense of 'false' moves is correct each time, and is followed by the others. Jake then had to go to a music lesson at this point.* |
|---|-----|---|
| 7 | ACs | Okay, let's see if we can do it, without being directed, for four on each side. |
|   |     | *Twenty-four moves is what it takes. They try it again, again twenty-four. There is a table of results on the board from last lesson, with the minimum moves for 1, 2, 3-a-side. I now write in the result for 4-a-side.* |
| 8 | S   | Can we try it for five? |
| 9 | ACs | Yes! Can anyone predict how many moves it will take? |
| 10 | Ss | "Thirty"; "Thirty-one"; "Thirty-five" |
| 11 | ACs | Okay, we'll see . . . |
|   |     | *We swap in thirty-five. I write that on the board as a second attempt also ends in thirty-five moves.* |
| 12 | S  | Can we try six? |
| 13 | ACs | Okay, but can anyone say how many moves it will take? |
| 14 | S  | It's going up in twelves. |
|   |     | *The student who said this had recently been writing out multiples of 12, one story I have of where this comment came from is that he recognised 24 as being in the 12-times table and perhaps thought 35 was as well.* |
|   |     | *There are several guesses.* |
| 15 | ACs | What is it going up in? |
|   |     | *I go to the board:* |
| 16 | ACs | The difference here is . . . |
| 17 | S  | Five (*I write in 5*). |
| 18 | ACs | Here it is . . . |
| 19 | S  | Seven (*I write in 7, then point to the next gap and look at the class saying nothing.*) |
| 20 | Ss | "Eleven"; "No"; "Ten"; "No"; "Nine" (*I write in 9.*) |
| 21 | S  | It'll be eleven next |
| 22 | ACs | Good, so can anyone say what the difference will be here? |
| 23 | S  | Thirteen |
| 24 | ACs | So what should we get for six |

*(continued)*

*(continued)*

| 25 | Ss | "Thirteen"; "No, forty-two"; *(several other guesses before someone says "Forty-eight!", which I write in)* |
|----|----|----|
|    |    | *I have to join in to make up numbers for six-a-side. We try it twice and both times come out as forty-eight moves. There are now three or four people, Karen being one, who wave arms at any 'false' moves and who prompt 'correct' ones.* |
| 26 | ACs | Okay, that was brilliant! You need to now carry on with your write-up of this problem. Make sure you can do it yourself with three on each side, you can use counters, and see if you can, like Jake did, come up with some way of showing the moves you need to make so you won't forget how to do it. |

What are some of the elements that lead to the task being meaningful? I wrote about my own decision-making in this lesson at the time of writing up the transcript and I draw on some of that writing below.

I see this transcript as an example of 'meaning-making' partly because of the way students take the initiative, in terms of making suggestions of what to do next (turns 5, 8 and 12). In response to my question (turn 13) about how many moves six on each side will take, a student did not give an answer, but made a more general suggestion of the overall number pattern (a suggestion that was not, in fact, correct). I followed up the more general idea of a rule and supported the class, partly through writing on the board (see Figure 3.2), to spot the more complex pattern behind the numbers. In my planning I had wanted to at some stage focus students on the number pattern in the minimum moves to get them predicting. I had not had a sense that we would focus on rules in this lesson and that had not been my explicit intention.

As with the 1089 write-up from Chapter 1, I am struck by the power of students coming into the room with something they have done that they want to share. In this particular school it could be hard to get all students to engage in homework. I felt I was most successful when homework was linked to the classwork and was obviously going to be used. So, the lesson begins with Jake using his homework to try to direct other students. The physicality of the lesson start is surely significant as well. There is a particular 'move' when doing 'Frogs' that can often go wrong and will lead to students not swapping the groups in the minimum number of moves. It can be easier to get a sense of this move physically than when working with counters or marks on paper.

Time is not spent at the start of the class setting up the task. When Paige arrived, saying she had been away and asking what we had been doing, I had a strong sense that it would be impossible to explain to her what the task was about and I started putting out chairs at the back of the class. I was clear in my mind that Paige and Tom had to be involved physically if they were to gain any access to the challenge and so I did not give them a choice about this. I think that in my first or second year of teaching I may have let them simply watch if they had expressed a desire not be on the chairs.

I decided at the moment of turn 2 to let Jake have a go at directing others from his written account. I was aware, from having invited my mixed ability year 7 from the previous year to do exactly this task, that it can be difficult to do. No one in the class the previous year had a way of writing which moves to make that enabled them to direct a group of people on chairs. However, I had had a glimpse at Jake's recording system and it seemed to me that it might be possible. This sense of going with what a student brings to class is something I did not recognise when I began teaching. I would have planned a beginning and, for the 'me' then, students coming up and telling me about their homework would have been a distraction.

A change in my teaching around the time of this lesson, one that seems important in relation to meaning-making, was that of allowing more time and space in my classroom to allow as many students as possible to become involved in what is going on. Whereas previously I may have been concerned about what was happening at around turn 6 for Karen (and other seemingly confident students) and so gone straight on to trying four-a-side, my sense of delaying here was that it allowed others to develop their awarenesses of what moves to make and to avoid, and so contributed to an increasingly shared focus of attention.

I registered surprise, when writing up this lesson, that I did not ask for reasons behind the answers in turns 10/11, something that feels like a natural question for me. I was not aware at the time of this as a decision point and in fact I think it may well have broken the flow of events if we had got too deeply into that question. Hewitt (1992) calls attention to important issues around the extent to which we focus on number patterns or the structure that underlies them.

The writing-up of this activity (referred to in line 26) was a background task that was around from the lesson before and in planning I had identified that at some stage we would return to it. I had not anticipated spending so long as a whole group, but it felt as though all the students, not just Paige and Tom, now had something to work on and write up as well as a sense of where the problem goes, in that they knew what totals they had to aim for when doing the problem individually.

Clearly, the 'Frogs' problem in itself is not significant for students to know about in terms of their mathematical development. However, through making meaning of this context they develop a sense of how problems have particular structures, how number patterns can arise from problems and (later in the project) how rules can be expressed algebraically and used for prediction and consideration of proof. Through making meaning of the problem, students gain access to understanding aspects of number pattern and algebra. This analysis of meaning-making raises the question of students' longer-term development. Is it plausible to believe that students will learn more general ideas from such particular activities? What kinds of experience help students make meaning and understand more formal aspects of mathematics (such as, for example, rules of how to transform algebraic expressions)? In the next sub-sections, I draw on a range of recent and past research to help think about these questions, starting with the issue of what has been said about human conceptual development.

## Concepts and conceptual development

There has been considerable work carried out within mathematics education on how concepts are learnt. Table 3.1 is a summary of fifty years' work about the way humans come to be able to operate with mathematical concepts.

There is a suggestion, taking in the views of all these authors, that the movement in learning is from top to bottom. A commonality across these perspectives is the sense of starting with a process and ending with some kind of object that either contains the

Table 3.1 The transition between process and object

|  | Piaget (50s) | Dienes (60s) | Davis (80s) | Greeno (80s) | Dubinsky (80s) | Sfard (80s) | Gray & Tall (90s) |
|---|---|---|---|---|---|---|---|
| Process | action(s), operation(s)... | predicate | visually moderated sequence... Each step prompts the next | procedure... | action... Each step triggers the next | interiorised process... process performed | procedure... specific algorithm |
| ... | ... | ... | integrated sequence... seen as a whole, and can be broken into sub-sequences | input to another procedure... | interiorised process... with conscious control | condensed process... self-contained | process... conceived as a whole, irrespective of algorithm |
| Object | thematised object of thought. | subject, a noun. | a thing, an entity, a noun. | conceptual entity. | encapsulated object. | reified object. | procept. symbol evoking process or concept |

Source: adapted from Tall et al. (1999: 4)

process as a 'thing' or allows a flexible evocation of object or process. There is an implication, therefore, that teaching should start with a process and the question of how we come to understand mathematics shifts to what kinds of processes we can offer students that will make the transition to 'object' smooth and meaningful.

A common assumption in the UK seems to be that it is helpful for students to have experience working with concrete materials in order for the move to handling more abstract objects to retain meaning. So, for example, in primary school students will be invited to do one-to-one mappings between different collections of objects and, from this process, it is hoped they will begin to conceptualise something about the 'fiveness' (for example) of different collections. At secondary school, students might be presented with a balancing scale to work on transforming algebraic equations. Again the hope is that the awarenesses gained through the process of manipulating the scales will translate into awareness of how to manipulate algebraic expressions (in any context).

## Manipulatives, models and objects

Several researchers have raised potential problems with the use of manipulatives and concrete models for mathematical concepts. In essence, the criticism raised is that to make sense of the concrete model, you need to have already gained some sense of the mathematical concept in the first place. Materials or other resources may seem like a powerful way to introduce a new concept to students. The danger is that in giving students the materials to work with, they may gain fluency with using the materials but not develop the mathematical concept – the point is similar to Watson's (2008) critique of the use of the real world, quoted in the last chapter. Key to mathematical concepts is their appropriateness to vastly different contexts and great care is needed in the use of concrete models for these not to become limiting. For example, if fractions are introduced as slices of cake or pizza, how are students meant to think about multiplication (let alone division) of fractions? If algebraic equations are introduced as balancing scales, what does this do for students' thinking about graphing functions?

These critiques lead to a more general worry about the implications of viewing the learning of mathematics as the gaining of 'objects'. Some of the considerations in Chapter 1 about how even seemingly fixed aspects of what we have learnt may need to be 're-thought' or worked out again suggest that equating knowledge to 'objects' is a misleading approach.

Yet the sense of learning mathematics as the gaining of 'objects' is rarely questioned and perhaps fits with how it subjectively feels when learning. But, to quote from Dick Tahta (1989), seeing concepts as objects

> inevitably leads to metaphors of ownership and control: obtaining the meaning, having the understanding, getting the concept. And, consequently, of course, there will be the mathematical descaminados, the shirtless who have not understood, who never get the concept . . . I always have some concept of what we may both be considering. I will certainly never have yours.

And once we conceptualise there being mathematical 'haves' and 'have nots', it is a short step to placing them in different 'ability groups'. In the UK, it would not be uncommon for four-year-old children to be taught different mathematics, dependent on a judgement

36  Issues

of their prior attainment. There is evidence that there is often little significant movement between 'ability' sets and that life chances are largely determined by mathematical achievement at aged 16, which in turn is largely determined by your 'set'. And, in the UK, the strongest predictor of being labelled one of the descaminados for your entire school career is social class. It is, therefore, in part a question of social justice to investigate alternatives to a view of conceptual development as the obtaining of mental objects, and the task of learning as the understanding of these objects.

## Meanings and fluency

One distinction that has been written about (Pimm 1995), in relation to making meaning of mathematics, is the idea of a vertical 'descent into meaning' and a horizontal symbolic transformation. Thinking about the students' written work on the 'Frogs' problem, the analysis might be something like that shown in Figure 3.3.

When the table of values is first being completed, there is perhaps a strong link between the number symbols and the physical actions that have just been performed. The '24' may still carry the echo of the movements across the chairs. As the table of values is then worked on and the focus turns to the number patterns within it, the link to the chairs and the context from which the table arose is suppressed. We work with the number symbols themselves, for example to make a prediction for six on each side. Depending on the situation, we may then re-interpret these transformations back into a 'meaningful' statement, as in the 'Frogs' transcript, where the class try out the problem with six people on each side to check that the prediction fits what happens. Also, the question of 'why' the number pattern is as it is (which is the important mathematical awareness that Hewitt (1992) draws attention to) requires a return to the context and the structure of the problem situation.

One of the orthodoxies of what might be seen as 'good' teaching of mathematics is to spend time on the vertical movements before working on the horizontal, and the

| No. each side | No. moves |
| --- | --- |
| 1 | 3 |
| 2 | 8 |
| 3 | 15 |
| 4 | 24 |
| 5 | 35 |
| 6 | 48 |

Symbol transformations

| No. each side | No. moves |
| --- | --- |
| 1 | $3_{+5}$ |
| 2 | $8_{+7}$ |
| 3 | $15_{+9}$ |
| 4 | $24_{+11}$ |
| 5 | $35_{+13}$ |
| 6 | 48 |

Descent into meaning

Movements on chairs

Predictions about movements on chairs

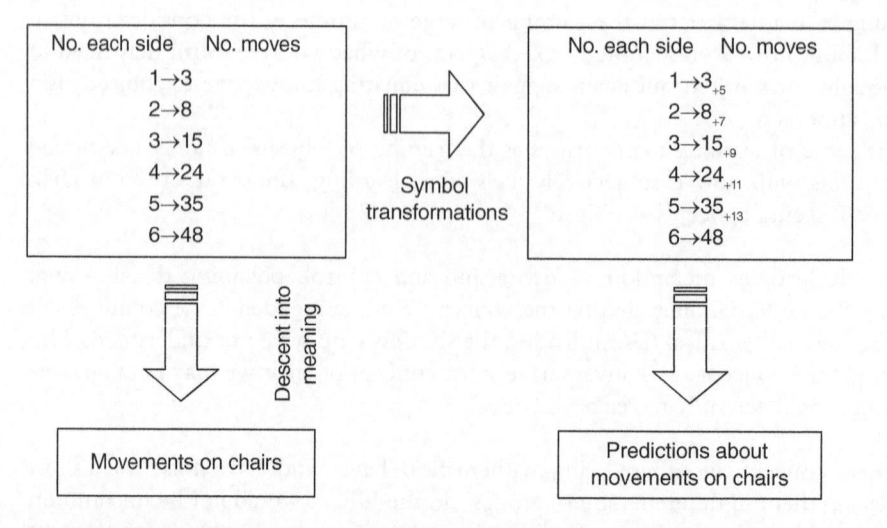

*Figure 3.3* Descent into meaning and symbol transformations

gaining of symbolic fluency. According to this image, the alternative to an explicit focus on developing student understanding might seem to be: rote learning, or 'traditional teaching'. There can be worries about getting students manipulating symbols before these symbols are 'meaningful' to them.

Walkerdine (1990) reports on a student discussing in an interview the fraction ⅘, which was significant to him because there were five people in his family and only four lived at home – his mother lived somewhere else. Several students had similarly poignant associations with symbols. There are associations we may have with symbols that will not be helpful in the doing of mathematics and that have to be suppressed. Part of the skill of the mathematician is knowing which association(s) to bring to the fore in any particular context. Part of the skill of the teacher is knowing how to introduce symbolism in a manner that allows students to leave behind the unhelpful connections and develop a mathematician's intuition.

I have come to wonder if the vertical/horizontal contrast between meaning-making and symbolic transformation is ultimately an unhelpful one in terms of thinking about how to balance the two aspects of linking symbols to context and linking symbols to other symbols. The symbols we use in mathematics have a myriad of connections, to other symbols, other objects or wider aspects of our life.

The philosopher Jan Zwicky (2014: §2) writes about the experience of understanding something as 'the dawning of an aspect that is simultaneously a perception and reperception of a whole'. At the moment of insight, we re-see, re-think, re-cognise what we have been attending to. Zwicky (2014: §3) continues, 'all genuine understanding is a form of seeing-as'. Moments of re-seeing, or 'seeing-as' can just as easily occur in the case of considering a symbol's relationship to another symbol, as the case of a symbol's relationship to an object. In the 'Frogs' task, the link between the table of values and the movements on the chairs, I would argue, becomes transparent and unproblematic to students. The moment of insight in the transcript was around the connections *between* the symbols in the table of values; there may have been excitement about translating the predicted values back into the context, but the moment of seeing differently, 'seeing-as', was around being able to see a new pattern within the symbols. Meaning was created in relation to the number pattern predictions. The link back from the table to the number of moves expected with six people on each side was not the moment of learning and indeed the link between values and chair movements hardly needed remarking upon.

What these reflections lead to is that what exists is not so much a horizontal–vertical axis of meaning versus rote symbol manipulation but more a symbol at the centre of a sphere of connections – to other symbols, to contexts (that could include concrete materials) and to other affective aspects of life. Some of these connections will be the result of a moment of insight. Some will have been created without my even noticing. When I make use repeatedly of a symbol in a particular way, the link loses its surprise (if it ever had surprise). So, for example, in the context of performing algebraic manipulations, if I solve equations using the model of a weighing scale, the connection to that scale can become as 'rote' or un-thinking as if I use a rule I have memorised such as 'change of side, change of sign'.

What seems important, to be successful at mathematics, is that I am able at times to consider a symbol's wider connections and at other times suppress those connections and efficiently work through an algorithmic procedure (for example to solve an equation).

## An alternative vision

Gattegno (1974) developed a curriculum that he claimed could teach the entire UK secondary mathematics curriculum (which takes most students the five years between ages 11 and 16), to mastery, in eighteen months. Gattegno's concern was with the efficiency of learning and with what, as teachers, we can do to minimise the time we take from students in, for example, the study of mathematics (something he labelled the 'economy' of teaching). Gattegno's vision for mathematics teaching is one where the teacher places little attention on encouraging 'understanding' but rather on supporting gains in symbolic mastery, letting students generate over time what meaning they will, for what they are doing. In Dick Tahta's (1989: 1) pithy summary: 'the teacher looks after the symbols. The sense looks after itself'.

What Gattegno does offer students are 'plenty of things to try out which give students something to do and something to talk about' (Tahta 1989: 1). Rather than the assumption that students need to 'understand' symbols before they can use them, consideration can be given to setting up contexts, or structures, in which symbols can be introduced with a limited number of dimensions of variation (Marton and Booth 1997; Mason 2011), but yet with the capacity for these dimensions of variation to increase with no rupture to the original conception. On Gattegno's approach, students are supported in developing symbolic fluency – understanding develops over time.

One of Gattegno's insights was the realisation that, for the mathematician, what is *most* significant is a symbol's connection to other symbols. I once attended a conference where a primary teacher trainer reported on some work she had done on which student characteristics might indicate that they would be successful at secondary school (age 11–18). She invited us to think about the problem: if $23 \times 35 = 805$, what else do you know? This question had been given to a group of year 6 (age 10–11) students. The two responses in Table 3.2 were both given by students deemed to be 'ready' for secondary school (I have re-created these from memory, to give the gist of the differences – the responses ran to fifteen or more statements).

The suggestion was that Student 2 is far more likely to be successful in later mathematics. What is striking is the way Student 2 appears to be able to play with the symbols. It is evident that the number symbols being used have rich connections to each other. Gattegno's challenge, then, is that if it is the case that successful mathematicians develop rich and varied connections between number symbols, then why not *begin* by showing students this way of working with symbols?

Recently, there has been an intriguing confirmation of the potential of Gattegno's approach from a neuroscience lab in Canada. Ian Lyons, who has led this work, considered

*Table 3.2* Two student responses

| Student 1 | Student 2 |
|---|---|
| $23 \times 350 = 8050$ | $23 \times 17.5 = 402.5$ |
| $230 \times 35 = 8050$ | $(20 + 3) \times 35 = 805$ |
| $23 \times 3500 = 80{,}500$ | $46 \times 35 = 1610$ |
| $230 \times 3500 = 805{,}000$ | $805 \div 35 = 23$ |
| $230 \times 35{,}000 = 8{,}050{,}000$ | $70 \times 23 = 805 \times 2$ |

what neuroscience can tell us about the development of number sense and he began by distinguishing between two aspects of number, the ordinal and the cardinal.

## A neuroscientific story

Ordinality refers to the capacity to place numbers in sequence, for example, to know that 4 comes before 5 and after 3 in the sequence of natural numbers. Cardinality refers to the capacity to link numbers to collections, e.g., to know that '4' is the correct representation to denote a group of four objects. I find it easier to think about the difference between these two aspects of number as 'attention to sequence' (which is ordinal and is linked to attention to number structure) and 'attention to quantity' (which is cardinal). A significant question dealt with in the twentieth century was: which aspect of number is most primitive? On the assumption that sequence and quantity are the two key dimensions to developing an initial concept of number, there are three possibilities for which is most important and each one had its proponents. It could be that attention to quantity is primary (Russell 1903), it could be that attention to sequence or structure is primary (Gattegno 1974), and it could be that both are equally primary (Piaget 1952). I will briefly summarise each perspective.

### *Quantity as primary*

Russell (1903) based his analysis of number on the concept of cardinality (quantity). For Russell, a number was what was common to sets containing members that could be placed in one-to-one correspondence. Lest there be doubt that questions of mathematical philosophy have relevance, it is only necessary to look at the prevalence of one-to-one mapping tasks in the first years of schooling in the UK, or the fact that, in the early years, work on number is limited to the integers 1–20 (the ones we can grasp) to see the influence of Russell's thinking.

### *Sequence as primary*

An opposing view is that ordinality (attention to sequence) is the more primary. This view was used to inspire at least one mathematics curriculum (Gattegno 1970) and the use of Cuisenaire rods. In Gattegno's curriculum, students' first experiences are to play with the Cuisenaire rods (wooden blocks with 1cm square faces and different lengths – each length associated with a unique colour) and work on relations (bigger than, smaller than). The first number to be introduced is '2', to represent the action of placing two rods of the same size to match the length of a single rod. Numbers are introduced as structured relations, i.e., in relation to each other rather than as linked to specific objects.

### *Quantity and sequence as primary*

A third perspective is that both ordinality and cardinality are equally primitive, and such a view was advocated by Piaget (1952), who believed that the development of our awareness of sequence and quantity was characterised by the same stages, which occurred at the same age, hence his conclusion that they are acquired simultaneously. Experiments in the 1970s appeared to suggest that awareness of sequence occurred in young children at a much earlier age than awareness of quantity (Brainerd 1979).

## *ANS and number awareness*

Recently, the kind of ingenious psychological experiment conducted in the twentieth century has given way to brain research. One of the findings of broad agreement from neuroscience is that humans share an early (in evolutionary terms) 'approximate number system' (ANS), our 'number sense', which we use to judge the relative size of groups of objects (Nieder and Dehaene 2009). The ANS is a non-symbolic source of numerical reasoning. Research is currently being undertaken to try to map out how the ANS links to our symbolic use of number, since there is evidence that ANS skill is correlated with later mathematical achievement (e.g., Gilmore *et al.* 2010).

There is a research lab in Canada that has been experimenting with students' skill at tasks involving both number symbols and number as represented by collections of dots (e.g., see Lyons and Beilock 2011). So, for example, participants might be asked to say which is bigger and shown two single-digit numbers (testing symbolic quantity awareness). Or they might be shown two collections of dots and asked which has more (testing non-symbolic quantity awareness). Then there are tests where 3 single-digit numbers are shown and participants asked if the numbers are in order or not (testing symbolic sequence awareness) or the same task with three collections of dots (non-symbolic sequence awareness).

Lyons and Beilock have therefore considered five aspects of number awareness:

- approximate number system;
- non-symbolic attention to quantity;
- non-symbolic attention to sequence;
- symbolic attention to quantity;
- symbolic attention to sequence.

On discovery of the ANS, the assumption of much work in neuroscience in this area has been that our ANS transitions into non-symbolic awareness of quantity and then into symbolic awareness of quantity in the development of number sense. What Lyons and Beilock (2011) have found, however, considering the five aspects of number above, is that symbolic attention to sequence is the 'odd man out'. In other words, they have found that qualitatively distinct areas of the brain are active during sequencing tasks with number symbols, compared to tasks involving collections of objects and tasks involving number symbols and quantity. Their hypothesis (Lyons and Beilock 2011: 257) is that the key to moving from the ANS to being able to work with symbols directly, is being able to attend to numbers as a sequence.

Lyons and Beilock (2011, 2013) have evidence that in the development of our concept of number, distinct processes are occurring in relation to our awareness of relations between symbols (in an ordinal sense) and our awareness of how to link objects to numerals (with the emphasis on quantity). Furthermore, there is evidence (also from brain imaging) that when working with numbers in more complex mathematical contexts, areas of the brain significant for linking numbers to objects are not activated (Lyons and Beilock 2011). A study of a large sample of Dutch students in grades 1 to 6 found that, from grade 2 onwards, of the five aspects of number awareness above, skill at symbolic sequencing was most highly correlated with overall mathematical attainment and as students got older, the correlation got stronger (Lyons et al. 2014).

The conclusion that, for students aged 7 onwards, what is most significant in the learning of number is awareness of sequencing and structure, i.e., symbol-symbol relations, is a radical one. Current practice in the UK places emphasis in the first years of schooling firmly on linking number symbols to collections of objects. Furthermore, if students start to fall 'behind' in mathematics they tend to be given more and more concrete resources and materials. The implication of the work from this neuroscience lab is that such 'help' may be reinforcing the very way of conceptualising number (one strongly linked to quantity) that students need to move away from if they are to become successful at mathematics.

Thinking back to the transcript of the lesson on 'Frogs' from the start of this chapter, there is an interesting relationship between the objects of the chairs and movements and the numbers students are using. Although the starting point is a concrete situation, what students end up attending to is the underlying structure of the number patterns. The concepts that students are working with are not embodied by the concrete situation (the numbers are not 'there' in the chairs) but arise from playing with the concrete objects. The theme of engaging students in the development of symbol-symbol awareness or symbolic playfulness is taken up in the next chapter.

## References

Brainerd, J. (1979). *The origins of the number concept*. New York: Praeger Publishers.
Gattegno, C. (1970). *Gattegno mathematics textbook 1*. New York: Educational Solution Worldwide Inc.
Gattegno, C. (1974). *The common sense of teaching mathematics*. New York: Educational Solution Worldwide Inc. Available at www.calebgattegno.org/teaching-mathematics.html. (accessed 17 September 2012).
Gilmore C., McCarthy S. and Spelke E. (2010). Non-symbolic arithmetic abilities and mathematics achievement in the first year of formal schooling. *Cognition, 115*: 394–406.
Hewitt, D. (1992). Trainspotters' paradise. *Mathematics Teaching, 140*: 6–8.
Lyons I. and Beilock, S. (2011). Numerical ordering ability mediates the relation between number-sense and arithmetic competence. *Cognition, 121*: 256–61.
Lyons, I. and Beilock, S. (2013). Ordinality and the nature of symbolic numbers. *The Journal of Neuroscience, 33*(43): 17052–61.
Lyons, I. M., Price, G. R., Vaessen, A., Blomert, L. and Ansari, D. (2014). Numerical predictors of arithmetic success in grades 1–6. *Developmental Science, 17*(5): 714–26.
Marton, F. and Booth, S. (1997). *Learning and awareness*. Mahwah, NJ: Lawrence Erlbaum Associates Ltd.
Mason, J. (2011). Explicit and implicit pedagogy: variation theory as a case study. In C. Smith (ed.) *Proceedings of the British Society for Research into Learning Mathematics, 31*(3): 107–113.
Nieder, A. and Dehaene, S. (2009). Representation of number in the brain. *Annual Review of Neuroscience, 32*: 185–208.
Piaget, J. (1952). *The child's conception of number*. New York: Humanities.
Pimm, D. (1995). *Symbols and meanings in school mathematics*. London: Routledge.
Russell, B. (1903). *The principles of mathematics*. Cambridge: Cambridge University Press.

Tahta, D. (1989). *Take care of the symbols*. Unpublished paper in his personal archive.
Walkerdine, V. (1990). Difference, cognition and mathematics education. *For the Learning of Mathematics*, *10*(3): 51–6.
Watson, A. (2008). Adolescent learning and secondary mathematics. *Proceedings of the 2008 Annual Meeting of the Canadian Mathematics Education Study Group*, pp. 21–32. Available online at www://cmesg.ca/ (accessed 17 September 2010).
Zwicky, J. (2014). *Wisdom and metaphor*. Edmonton & Calgary: Brush Education.

# 4 Symbolic fluency

In Chapter 3, there were two sources for the idea that engaging in mathematics and mathematical meaning-making may be powerfully provoked through a focus on developing symbol–symbol awareness, or awareness of the structure of, say, the number system, rather than by an over-riding concern that each symbol we introduce has a 'meaning' in itself. These sources were the pedagogy of Gattegno and the neuroscientific research of Ian Lyons and colleagues.

Almost forty years ago, Dick Tahta (1985: 49) suggested: 'We do not pay enough attention to the actual techniques involved in helping people gain facility in the handling of mathematical symbols'. The starting point for this chapter is the thought that despite the intervening four decades, questions remain: how do we learn to become fluent symbol users? How can we introduce symbols in a way that learners find engaging? And what role might technology play in feeling at home with symbols?

In order to think about techniques for engaging students in gaining facility with handling symbols, I have found it instructive to look back at some archive video footage of two extraordinary teachers. One is Caleb Gattegno himself who has been mentioned many times already in this book and the other is Bob Davis. Davis worked with Gattegno at one time and researched the effective teaching of mathematics in the United States (e.g., see Davis 1990). Davis started a major research programme (the Madison Project) that led to successive funded work, video recording students' long-term mathematical development. The unique video archive from these projects is now available online.[1] In the next two sections, I describe teaching episodes from Gattegno's and Davis's teaching and then analyse them in terms of how symbolism is introduced and used. The final sections of the chapter consider issues around technology and the development of symbol use.

## Classroom example – Bob Davis

Rutgers University, in the USA, is home to a unique video library of mathematics teaching spanning over 50 years. Part of this collection is some historic video footage of Bob Davis working with different groups of students.

In one clip he is teaching children who look to be around age five. The clip begins with him at the front of the class with two children. One of the children, Nora, is holding a bag of stones. The other child, Jeff is standing nearby. In the transcript below, RD indicates that Bob Davis is speaking.

| RD | Okay, Jeff is going to tell us when to start and (.) you say 'go'. |
| Jeff | Go. |
| RD | Okay, you say go (.) and I'm going to put three stones in the bag that Nora is holding (.) three stones in |
| | *[RD drops three stones into the bag, one by one, so we hear them drop]* |
| RD | Are there more stones in the bag now or less than there were when Jeff said go? (1) Charlotte, what do you say? |
| Charlotte | More. |
| RD | And how many more? (.) As if you all didn't all know (.) How many more? Laurie? |
| Laurie | Three |
| RD | Three (.) huh |
| | *[RD writes '3' on the blackboard]* |
| RD | And now I'm going to take some stones out of the bag (.) How many stones do you want me to take out of the bag? (.) Barbara, how many stones do you want to take out? |
| Barbara | Three. |
| RD | Three (.) I'll take three out (.) Okay (.) Barbara says take three out so I'll take three stones out (.) There's one (.) There's two (.) There's three (1) Three stones out (.) and I'd better write that |
| | *[RD adds to the board, so it now reads '3 – 3 =']* |
| RD | Took three stones out (.) Now are there more stones in the bag than there were when Jeff said go or are there less? (.) Brett? |
| Brett | There's the same amount. |
| RD | There's the same amount (.) And I bet that's right and what will I say here? (.) As if you didn't all know (.) Sandy? |
| | *[RD is pointing with his chalk to the space to the right of the equals sign in '3 – 3 =']* |
| Sandy | Zero's what I'll say. |
| Others | Negative zero. |
| | *[RD completes the statement on the board to read: '3 – 3 = 0']* |
| RD | Zero (.) Okay that was that time (.) I need two other assistants (.) Thank you very much |
| | *[The two assistants at the front return to their seats.]* |
| RD | I need somebody to hold the bag (.) Paul, would you come? (.) and I need somebody to say when to go (.) Bruce would you come? |
| | *[Paul and Bruce come to the front.]* |
| RD | You're going to tell us when to start (.) Good. |

| Bruce | Go. |
| --- | --- |
| RD | Go (.) Bruce said go (.) How many stones do you want me to put in the bag? Nancy (.) how many? |
| Nancy | Five. |
| RD | Five (.) I'll see if I've got five (.) Turns out I've got five (.) I've got five (.) There's five stones there and I'm going to put all five of these in the bag. |
|  | *[RD has laid five stones on his palm and puts them one by one into the bag, again each stone makes an audible noise as it hits the other stones in the bag.]* |
| RD | And I better write that before I forget. |
|  | *[RD writes '5' on the blackboard.]* |
| RD | Are there more stones in the bag than when Bruce said go or are there less? Jeff? |
| Jeff | More. |
| RD | And how many more? |
| Jeff | Five |
| RD | Five (.) Five more, huh? (.) Okay (.) How many do you want me to take out? Nora, how many do you want me to take out? |
| Nora | Five |
| RD | Er (.) I don't want to do that (.) Some other number. |
| Nora | Six. |
| RD | Six (.) Take six out. |
| Student | Did you have stones in the bag to start with? |
| RD | I better have had hadn't I? (.) I wouldn't be able to do this if I didn't. |
|  | *[RD reaches into the bag and removes some stones that he then counts out onto his palm.]* |
| RD | Let's see (.) One two three four five six (.) That was more good luck than good management (.) I got exactly six (.) Okay I'll write it. |
|  | *[Write on board: '5 – 6 =']* |
| RD | Have I got more stones in the bag than when Bruce said go or have I got less? Jeff what do you think? |
| Jeff | Less. |
| RD | And anyone know how many less? Nora, how many less? |
| Nora | One less. |
| RD | Okay and how do I write this one to show that it's one less? Ceri? |

*(continued)*

46    Issues

*(continued)*

|    | [RD writes: '5 – 6 = 1'] |
|----|--------------------------|
| Ceri | Negative one. |
| RD | Negative one (.) And that's just what I'll do. |
|    | [RD writes: '5 – 6 = –1'] |

In this clip, we see Davis setting up a game-like situation with the class. What I want to point to is the relationship between the actual stones and their representation with symbols. When Davis writes '5' on the board, he is indicating that five stones have been added to the bag, the presence of the symbol therefore represents a change in the number of stones in the bag. The symbols do *not* represent the concrete objects in an absolute sense. Instead, the symbols represent *relationships* between the objects, or *actions* on those objects.

I have shown the video containing this clip to several groups of people and for teachers with primary school experience there is generally an air of amazement at the seeming ease with which these young children are able to handle expressions involving negative numbers. If number symbols are linked to physical objects then, of course, negative numbers do become problematic. Some evidence for the analysis above (that in this extract the number symbols represent a relation between objects rather than the objects themselves) is precisely that negative numbers arise so fluently.

By associating symbols with relationships, the symbols (from the outset) are abstracted from objects. In the beginning of work with the symbols, the concrete can still be called upon and the initial dimensions of variation in the task can be kept limited. Yet it is not hard to imagine that attention soon could turn to dealing with the symbols in their own right, evoking, if necessary, the actions they represent. The way the material situation is symbolised provides an initial entry into considering relations between the symbols. Inverse operations can be dealt with because when symbols themselves are relations, unlike physical objects, there is no problem in considering the symbol being 'done' and 'undone'. A 'change' in number of stones can just as easily be a change higher (resulting in a positive number) as a change lower (resulting in a negative number).

## Classroom example – Caleb Gattegno

The second example comes from the teaching of Caleb Gattegno and another historic video clip.[2] At 6.50 minutes through this clip, Gattegno starts getting students naming Cuisenaire rods. Up to this point in the lesson, the rods had been named by their colour and Gattegno had done some activities getting students to recognise different colours by their feel. Students had all made 'staircases' of rods, which were on the tables in front of them (Figure 4.1) at the point in which the transcript below begins.

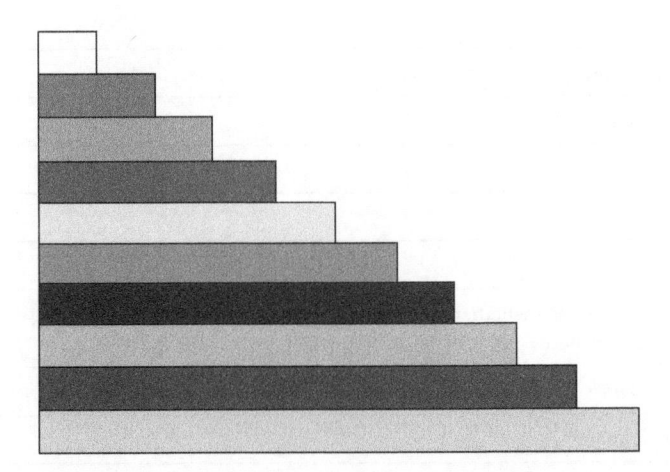

*Figure 4.1* Representation of a staircase of Cuisenaire rods. Please note that the real rods are all coloured differently

| 1 | CG | Now let's find the new names . . . if we call the white one one (.) If the white one is one (.) what's the name of the red? |
|---|---|---|
| 2 | chorus | Two. |
| 3 | CG | And the light green? |
| 4 | chorus | Three. |
| 5 | CG | And the purple? |
| 6 | chorus | Four. |
| 7 | CG | And the yellow? |
| 8 | chorus | Five. |
| 9 | CG | The dark green? |
| 10 | chorus | Six. |
| 11 | CG | The black? |
| 12 | chorus | Seven. |
| 13 | CG | The brown? |
| 14 | chorus | Eight. |
| 15 | CG | The orange? |
| 16 | chorus | Nine. |
| 17 | chorus | Ten. |

*(continued)*

*(continued)*

| 18 | CG | The orange? |
|---|---|---|
| 19 | student | Oh, ten. |
| 20 | chorus | Ten. |
| 21 | CG | And the blue? |
| 22 | chorus | Nine. |
| 23 | CG | Now let me see whether you can find which (.) how many white ones will go into this? |
| 24 | | [CG kneels down and holds up a black rod, some students put up their hands.] |
| 25 | CG | Say it. |
| 26 | chorus | Seven. |
| 27 | CG | Into this? |
| 28 | | [CG holds up a light green rod] |
| 29 | chorus | Three. |
| 30 | CG | Into this? |
| 31 | chorus | Two. |
| 32 | CG | Into this? |
| 33 | chorus | Eight. |
| 34 | CG | Into this? |
| 35 | chorus | Nine. |
| 36 | CG | Into this? |
| 37 | chorus | Five. |
| 38 | CG | Into this? |
| 39 | chorus | Six. |
| 40 | CG | Into this? |
| 41 | chorus | Seven. |
| 42 | CG | Into this ? |
| 43 | chorus | Nine. |
| 44 | CG | Into this? |
| 45 | chorus | Ten. |
| 46 | CG | Into *this*? |

| 47 |  | [CG holds up an orange and blue rod held end to end and now stands up. There is a pause of five seconds before one student, followed by others, says 'nineteen'.] |
| 48 | CG | What is it? |
| 49 | chorus | Nineteen. |
| 50 | CG | Into this? |
| 51 |  | [CG rotates the way he is holding the rods, which had been horizontally, to be vertical, there is a two-second pause] |
| 52 | Student | Nine . . . |
| 53 | chorus | Nineteen. |
| 54 | CG | Into this? |
| 55 |  | [CG alters again the direction in which he is holding the rods] |
| 56 | chorus | Ninteen. |
| 57 | CG | And into this? [alters again] |
| 58 | chorus | Nineteen. |

There is a lovely moment of humour at turn 15, as Gattegno holds up rods that are 5, 6, 7, 8 cm long and then holds up the orange 10 cm rod and all the class call out '9', carrying on the sequence rather than paying attention to the rod Gattegno holds up.

What is significant here is that number names are introduced in relation to a unit (the length of the white rod). The yellow rod does not represent '5' (in an absolute sense), it represents the relation: '5 of the white rod'. This is a subtle distinction and yet it is a vital one. For a start, what the relational naming means is that the same number can have multiple representations with the rods. The number '2' can be created by placing two white rods against the red rod, or two yellows against the orange or several other ways (e.g., see Figure 4.2).

In the lesson on the video, Gattegno goes on to make use of the relational naming of the rods to introduce the first-grade children to the inverse view of the relations just described. Each of the images in Figure 4.2, as well as being ways to represent the number '2' are, of course, also ways to represent the number '½'. If 2 red rods make 1 pink, then 1 red rod is ½ of the pink. By the end of the lesson, Gattegno has these children (aged 6, perhaps) successfully working out the following questions:

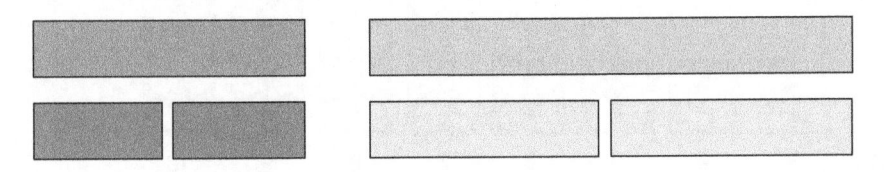

*Figure 4.2* Different representations of '2' and '½'

$$\frac{1}{2} \times (36-18) =$$

$$\frac{1}{3} \times (18+9) =$$

$$\frac{1}{4} \times (9+27) =$$

$$\frac{1}{2} \times (9+\frac{1}{3}\times 27) - \frac{1}{4} \times 36 =$$

As with the Bob Davis video, it is striking what young children are capable of doing mathematically, when symbols are introduced in a manner that makes them easy to handle.

## Absolute and relational symbolism

There is a subtle but vital distinction visible in the work of Gattegno and Davis in relation to what is being symbolised. The difference can perhaps be appreciated by considering the difference between introducing number names in a context such as the Gattegno video clip as the relation between the lengths of rods, and an introduction in the context of a resource such as 'Numicon' (see Figure 4.3).

The manipulable objects shown in Figure 4.3 offer an *absolute* symbolism of number: number '3' *is* the 'L' shape piece and it can be made, for example by putting the '2' and '1' piece together. The symbol '3' is used to represent just that particular object – hence the label 'absolute symbolism'. In contrast, Figure 4.2 is an alternative representation of the number '2'. Here the symbol '2' points to a relationship between the rods, not a concrete object, this is therefore a *relational* symbolism. Two differences are pertinent. The first is that, using the Cuisenaire rods, alternative representations of '2' are possible (for example, 2 white rods make a red rod; 2 reds make a pink rod). Secondly, it is apparent that the representation of '2' in Figure 4.2 can just as easily be seen as a representation of '½'. The representation, via Cuisenaire rods, gives a relational view of number and, as seen in both video clips discussed above, when such a *relational* representation is used, there is little difficulty in considering the inverse.

The suggestion, then, arising from considering the teaching of Davis and Gattegno is that presenting students with a relational (rather than absolute) symbolism of mathematics may prove a powerful mechanism to help students to gain facility with those symbols. With a relational symbolism of mathematical concepts, students can have powerful, simultaneous access to inverse processes (negative numbers with the Davis lesson; fractions with the

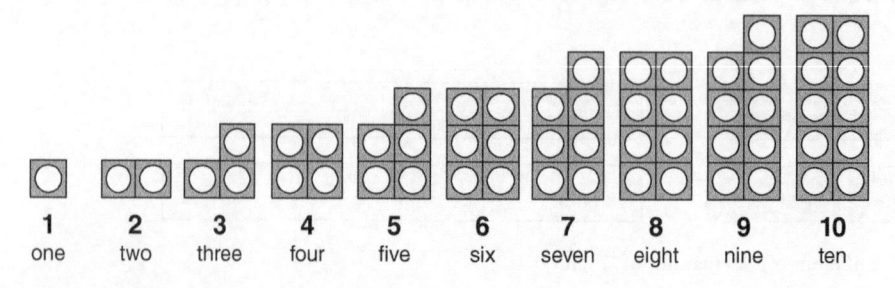

*Figure 4.3* The 'Numicon' number line

Gattegno lesson), which are typically seen as hard and left until later in the curriculum. There may also be advantage in terms of allowing students access to the ambiguity of mathematical symbolism. In Figure 4.2, the number 2 can be seen as the process of placing 2 rods against a bigger one, or as the object that results. Indeed it is important for their mathematical development that they *are* able to interpret '2' in these different ways. Gray and Tall (1994) argue that being able to use a mathematical concept as a process or an object is what successful mathematicians do (and what unsuccessful mathematicians do not do). One of the powers of a relational representation is perhaps that it symbolises a process (e.g., an action or a change) and at the same time can be seen as the result of that process (see Coles (2014) for further examples of the ambiguity of relational representations).

The idea of introducing symbolism in a relational rather than abstract manner has implications for other parts of the curriculum. For example, one might introduce area not as an 'absolute' ("this shape has area 4") but by emphasising the unit ("this shape is 4 of that shape"). In turn, this suggests a possible reordering of the more usual topic sequence in mathematics. If a relational symbolism of the concept of 'area' draws attention to the role of the unit, then working on enlargement could be a *precursor* to working on area (and similarly for volume).

Relational symbolism of fractions would initially lead to an emphasis on their role as operators (rather than more absolute representations as, say, sectors of a circle). Work on angles would emphasise movement and comparison, work on symmetry and rotation might focus on geometrical transformations as operations. A relational view of functions might emphasise transformations of functions. Would it be possible to deal with transformations of functions before, or as a route in to, working on the functions themselves? A transformation approach to circle geometry is possible. In general, teaching becomes economical when a relational symbolism of mathematical concepts draws attention to larger mathematical structures. Symbols become meaningful in their connections to each other, as they are not linked directly to particular objects. And what we can observe from the teaching of Gattegno and Davis is that students can become highly engaged in activity with symbols. There is something engaging, perhaps, in the power that comes with gaining control over the manipulation of new symbols.

One commonality between Gattegno and Davis is that they were both academic mathematicians at one point in their lives. Their understanding of mathematics was clearly deep and relational. Seeing Bob Davis work with young children on the distinction between an identity and an equation (in a different video) is to see someone with a view of the long–term development of mathematical thinking. Mathematics is presented as a coherent structure. There is an observable faith in students' sense–making. Challenges are not made easier when they appear inaccessible to students.

In terms of the design principles discussed in Chapter 2, the snapshots from both the Gattegno and the Davis lessons take place during relatively 'closed' phases, where there is one task for students (Principle 1). As discussed above, the context of the activities means that the labelling and symbols capture distinctions that students observe and/or re-create (Principle 5). For Davis, the negative symbol is introduced to distinguish between ending up with 'more' or 'less' than when they started. For Gattegno, fractions are introduced to label actions that students carry out on the rods (placing copies of one kind of rod against another).

One insight from Dick Tahta and Laurinda Brown and their work within teacher education is that role models of teaching are not there to be cloned. We can study in detail what, for example, Bob Davis was doing in his teaching and the video clips give an image of what is possible with children, but if the aim is to support students in operating mathematically in a fluent manner, our parallel aim, as teachers, must be to theorise our own practice, in order to gain our own fluency in the act of teaching. Gattegno and Davis put forward an image of how economical mathematics teaching can become. Tahta and Brown remind us that their challenge is not one of copying, but instead finding within ourselves what we need to work on in order to meet the needs of our students and colleagues – a theme I return to in Chapter 10.

In the tasks in the rest of the book, the implications of offering relational symbolism of mathematics will recur. In all of the tasks in the second half of this book, one aim is that symbols will be introduced in the context of relationships between objects or actions on objects, or introduced in a way that emphasises how the symbols relate to each other.

In the final section of this chapter, the role of technology is explored as a potential means to introduce symbols in a relational manner.

## The promise of technology

There is a danger in any writing on technology that it becomes outdated almost before it is finished. However, technology is not something we can ignore, especially since seemingly each new technological innovation is cited as a panacea for student engagement. It can be instructive to look back over the last thirty or more years of technological innovation in schools, to see how change has occurred.

In a survey article looking at the integration of new technologies into the mathematics classroom, Ruthven (2014: 59) remarks how

> it was widely assumed that, as interaction between student and computer moved to the heart of schooling, the (human) teacher would become more peripheral (Ruthven 1993). However, as new generations of digital technology came and went with surprisingly little impact on school mathematics, attention turned towards the ways in which educational institutions and individual teachers shape patterns of uptake and use.

Ruthven takes the example of the interactive whiteboard (the technology that perhaps has had the fastest and most widespread take up in mathematics classrooms in the UK in recent years) in order to interrogate how technology use develops. Ruthven (2014: 61) concludes:

> By and large, teachers have appropriated the interactive whiteboard to facilitate – and accentuate certain characteristics of – an established instructional pedagogy.

In other words, it was perhaps misguided to look to technology to alter and change classroom practice. The lesson from the past would suggest, instead, that technologies are taken up to the extent that they fit within teachers' existing pedagogies. An implication of this suggestion is that any new technology will only be effective if it supports already-existing ways of working in a classroom. Of course, once taken up, a new technology will entail differences in ways of working – the tools we use ultimately change us as well as changing what we do in the world.

Perhaps rather than ask what technology I want to use in my classroom, an initial question might be: what ways of working do I want to establish? and then to ask: what technologies might support these ways of working? If, as a teacher, the technology does not fit with my overall aims for a classroom, it is perhaps unlikely that its use will be sustained. In keeping, therefore, with the aims of this chapter, the focus here will be on the potential for technology to support students engaging in gaining symbolic fluency.

There is clearly potential for technology to expose students to the dynamics behind mathematical concepts. Rather than draw a static triangle on the board to represent 'any triangle', in a program such as Geogebra or Geometer's Sketchpad, vertices can be dragged and the potential variation can be observed. I have come to wonder, however, if there is a danger that the symbols introduced dynamically via technology can assume a new absoluteness, an idea discussed below.

Rather than focus on particular tools, the next section is organised around a range of purposes for which different technologies are commonly used within mathematics. These are: graphing; making geometry dynamic and representing statistics. My assumption here is that, regardless of what platform or software we might want to use in a classroom, these are purposes we will want our technology to perform.

## Graphing

I have seen, and taught, many lessons introducing the concepts of gradient and $y$-intercept of linear functions (functions of the form $y = mx + c$) through the use of a graphing package. Students might be given a software package in which '$m$' and '$c$' can be varied, perhaps with slider bars so that changes in the graph $y = mx + c$ can be observed on screen.

In my experience, there is something quite underwhelming for students in playing with this kind of application. The letter '$m$' can simply become a way to manipulate the steepness of the line and perhaps no symbolising is needed in order to gain control over the line's direction. Without some other aim or purpose for the manipulations, it is not clear what distinction there is to make for students. They quickly learn how to control the line and there is little surprising in this. The issue perhaps links back to the discussion earlier in this chapter, about the problems of using concrete models for mathematical concepts. It is almost as though playing with sliders to manipulate the graph of $y = mx + c$ only becomes an engaging activity if you already have some concept of graphing and functions. If you know about gradients, it can be engaging to see how the line gets steeper and steeper the more you raise the value of $m$ (Figure 4.4). If you do not know about gradient, I wonder if there is a danger that $m$ comes to symbolise, in an absolute manner, the steepness of the line?

I have often felt, with graphing programs in particular, that there needs to be some way of slowing the technology almost – of forcing students to pay attention to the variations. How can we get students to make the distinctions that mathematicians make? The key question, arising from the discussion of absolute and relational symbolism, is to ask whether technology can allow *actions* to be symbolised? Can the technology or software offer a dynamic that allows a distinction/relation/action to be made by students that can be named, rather than trying to illustrate the concept in a more direct (absolute) manner?

In contrast to lessons getting students to explore graphing packages, I recently observed a lesson focusing students on the idea of gradient. The teacher had set up a sketch that looked a little like Figure 4.5(a).

With this simple sketch and image the teacher engaged the class in discussion about what the 'gradient' would become if the points or lines were moved to different places.

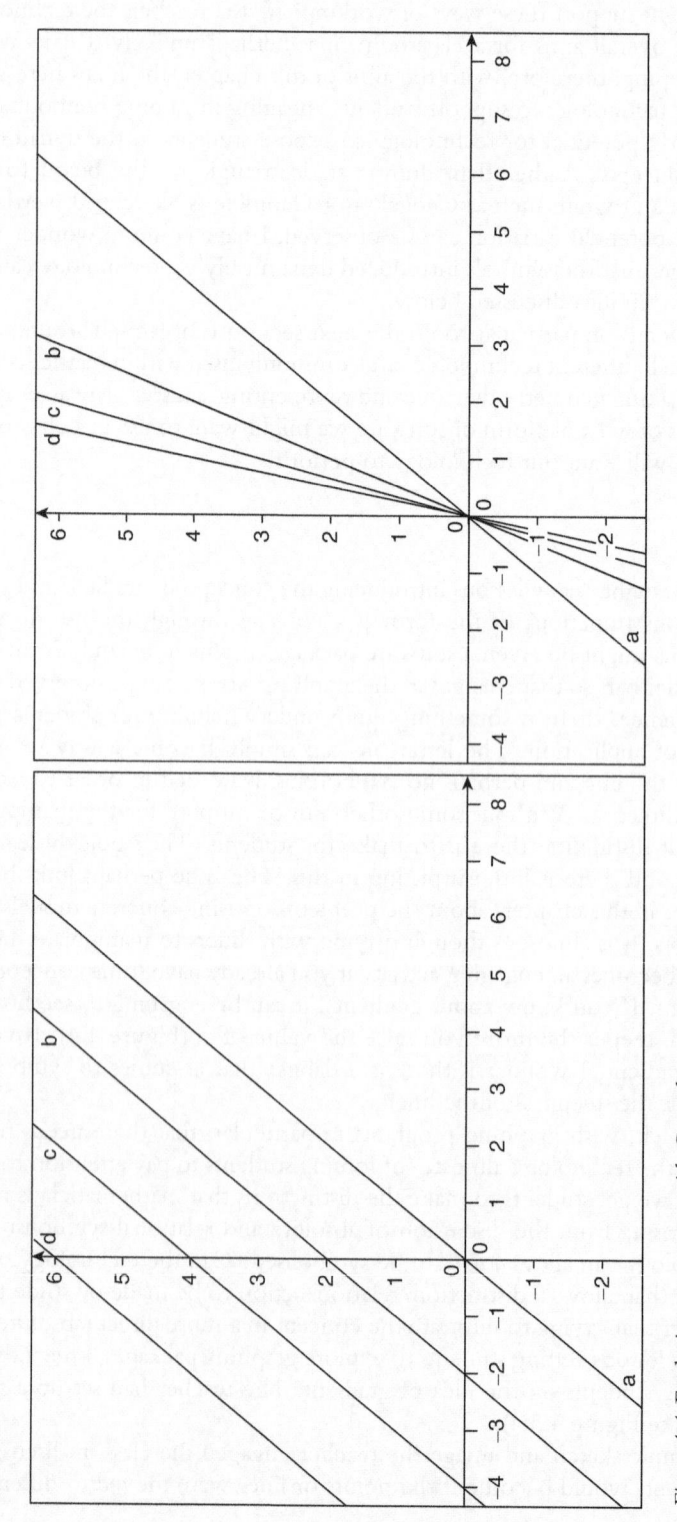

Figure 4.4 Exploring $y = mx + c$ with Geogebra

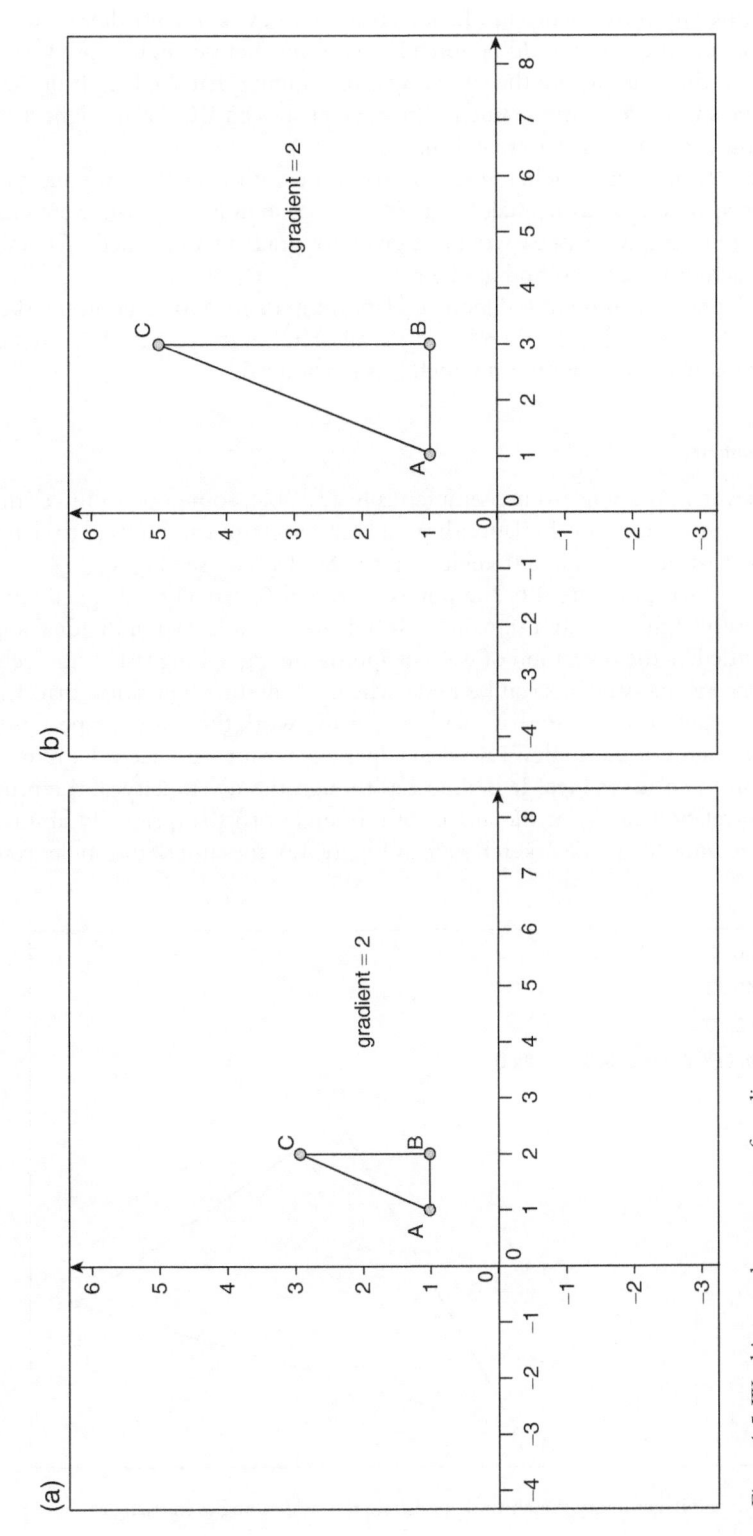

*Figure 4.5* Working on the concept of gradient

56  *Issues*

Before making any movement (and hence creating a new gradient) there would always be discussion and the class would be forced to commit themselves to a prediction of the new value. At the stage where the students were thinking that the length of the vertical line BC gave the value of the gradient, the teacher moved BC to the right, to create a base of 2 units, as shown in Figure 4.5(b).

With this device, the teacher was able to address directly the misconception that students can assume the 'horizontal' length is always one unit. The class were engaged in the task of predicting what value would be given for gradient and ended up being able to explain to each other how to find gradient.

The label 'gradient' is used to denote a relationship that can be seen in the sketches in Figure 4.5. The label is therefore a relational symbol in this treatment, abstracted from the very beginning from the context in which it is introduced.

## Dynamic geometry

There are several programs (some commercially available, some open source) that allow an exploration of geometrical relationships. These programs can be used to demonstrate 'empirically' that the angles in a triangle sum to 180 degrees (see Figure 4.6).

In a sketch such as Figure 4.6, the points A, B and C can all be dragged around and it can be observed that the sum remains at 180 degrees, while each individual angle does change. A little like the discussion of ways of approaching graphing tasks with technology, my experience is that students can be underwhelmed by the observation that the sum of the angles remains constant. Perhaps without further work there is no expectation either way about the sum of the angles. I need to experience some variance if I am to notice or pay attention to an invariance. It is almost as though the dynamicity of the programme can rob the relation between the angles of a triangle of its surprise. By animating the relation itself with the use of a sketch such as Figure 4.6, the sum of the angles can assume

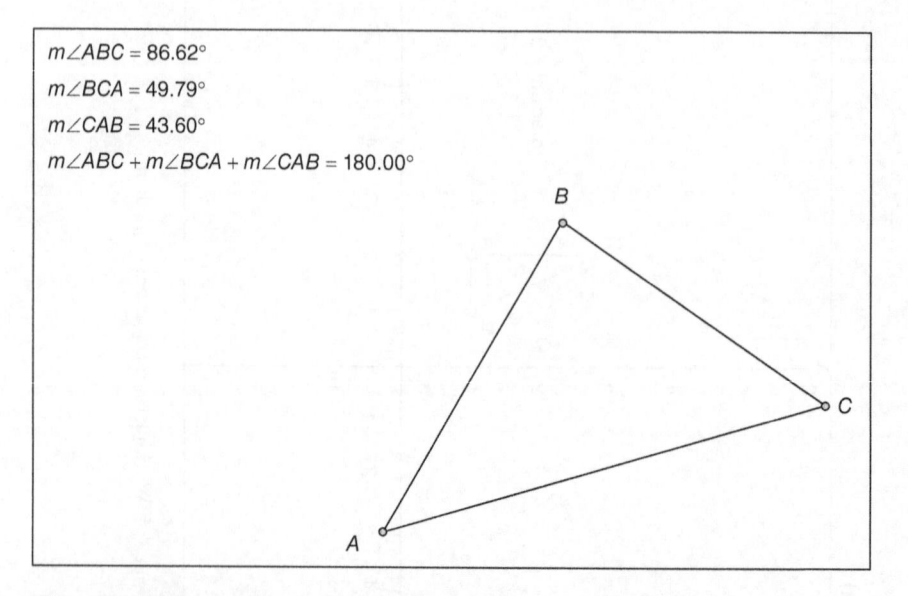

$m\angle ABC = 86.62°$
$m\angle BCA = 49.79°$
$m\angle CAB = 43.60°$
$m\angle ABC + m\angle BCA + m\angle CAB = 180.00°$

*Figure 4.6* A dynamic geometry sketch to demonstrate the sum of angles in triangles

an absoluteness. As with the example of graphs, perhaps the sketch is only engaging if you already have some sense of the concept already. If you 'know' the angles in a triangle, there might be a pleasure in seeing this remembered fact 'demonstrated' no matter how eccentric you make the triangle.

An alternative use of dynamic geometry to support students to work on their awareness of relationships is to set up sketches in which they have to explore constructions that have been hidden.

In Figure 4.7, I have set up a construction of three points linked to a triangle that can be moved freely. As the triangle is altered, the points move in relationship. Questions naturally arise. When are the points all inside the triangle? When are they in a line? This leads to an exploration of how the points are created and the challenge for students to re-create the sketch. Working with this file, students gain a sense of how some standard constructions behave and inevitably become involved in the naming of properties they have noticed, leading to geometrical awarenesses. Nathalie Sinclair has created a series of 'mystery' files that operate in a similar manner, to provoke exploration and awareness.[3]

## *Statistical representations*

The study of statistics is, to some extent, about ways of presenting and re-presenting. Computing power means that it is now increasingly possible to work with whole datasets, leaving behind questions of and issues with sampling. With the wealth of raw statistics now available on the web, it is hard to imagine why you would work with made-up data for even the most routine of exercises. There are obvious connections between the use of computers to work with statistics and the discussion of mathematical modelling in Chapter 2.

There are now several web-based applications that allow the representation of a staggering amount of data in a single diagram. Perhaps the most well–known is Gapminder,[4] where historical data about each country in the world can be visualised on a 2D scatter graph, making use of the two axes, the size of circle (for each country) and the colour of each circle. In other words four variables can be investigated over time (which adds a fifth variable) on a single 2D graph. The Gapminder website allows for choice of variables from a single database. Google Public Data Explorer[5] allows similar functionality within a choice of databases.

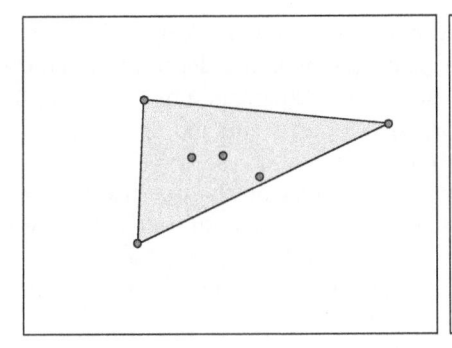

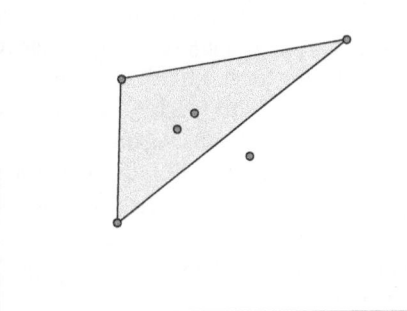

*Figure 4.7* A triangle mystery

It is not straightforward to plan engaging activities that make use of this functionality. Running the animations in front of a class may well provoke interest, but how do you move from this to working on awareness of statistical relationships, or developing statistical thinking? What is the potential of this software for developing symbol use in relation to statistics? Students could perhaps be challenged to find strong negative and positive correlations and also examples of no correlation. They would then need to search the databases and try to find variables that have a connection and perhaps try to explain any correlations they observe.

## The future for technology

I am conscious that in the brief discussion of technology above I have not addressed the potential for social media or for making use of the personal digital devices that students in the UK increasingly bring to school. It has been suggested to me that nowadays students already have to 'power down' as they walk through the school gates. Change is inevitable and it can be helpful to take a long view:

> When we are disposed to say of any custom, 'This has been from the beginning and can never be changed,' it may be well to look back to the beginning and to see how recent it is; how small and new and young are the inventions of the new half-conscious maker of history. An effort is needed, because this ability to be conscious of our newness is itself so new (Wodehouse 1924: 1–2).

Particularly at secondary school, students carry around with them computing power in their phones that is in excess of the hardware that landed an Apollo mission on the moon. In the UK, most schools currently ban the use of phones in the classroom, but it seems to me that at some point the power of the technology students bring to school will make this an impossible position to maintain.

For example, a recent development called 'Virtual Math Team'[6] allows a teacher to set challenges in which students can collaboratively engage. Students can post comments about solutions and each others' ideas in an online space that can be monitored, assessed and aided by the teacher. Research into the quality of discussions in which students engage in this online space have been encouraging. The software is free to use and perhaps taps into the skill students have in an environment with which they are already familiar from social media.

Another relatively recent development is the concept of 'flipped learning' where students make use of videos and other internet resources at home in order to make sense of a new idea and then come to class to discuss and practise. There are now many apps that allow students to record work (using audio or video if they want) and upload it to a class list for the teacher to assess (again using audio if wanted).

Through all these new possibilities, there is the tension that on the one hand what needs to come first is a vision for the kind of classroom you want and only after that is it worth considering what technology might support you. And, at the same time, technology may offer potential that we had not even considered was possible. The tools we use do change the way we work.

## Notes

1 At: www.videomosaic.org/
2 Available at www.youtube.com/watch?v=JrMty8v2DqI
3 See www.oame.on.ca/Sketchmad/stories/david.html
4 Available at www.gapminder.org
5 Available at www.google.co.uk/publicdata/directory
6 See www.vmt.mathforum.org/VMTLobby/

## References

Coles, A. (2014). Transitional devices and symbolic fluency. *For the Learning of Mathematics, 34*(2): 24–30.
Davis, R. (1990). *Learning mathematics: the cognitive science approach to learning mathematics*, 3rd edn. Norwood, NJ: Ablex Publishing Corporation.
Gray, E. and Tall, D. (1994). Duality, ambiguity and flexibility: a proceptual view of simple arithmetic. *Journal for Research in Mathematics Education, 26*(2): 115–41.
Ruthven, K. (1993). Technology and the rationalisation of teaching. In C. Keitel and K. Ruthven, (eds), *Learning from computers: mathematics education and technology*, pp.187–202. Berlin: Springer.
Ruthven, K. (2014). Integrating new technologies into school mathematics. In P. Andrews and T. Rowland, (eds), *Masterclass in mathematics education: international perspectives on teaching and learning*, pp. 58–74. London: Bloomsbury.
Tahta, D. (1985). On notation. *Mathematics Teaching, 112*: 49–51.
Wodehouse, H. (1924). *A survey of the history of education*. London: Edward Arnold & Co.

# 5 Managing engagement

One of the ideas raised in Chapter 1 was that engagement requires vulnerability to change, both on the part of the students and the teacher. In this chapter, I reflect on my own journey of developing skill with managing the engagement of learners and consider some of the issues around listening and hearing in the classroom. I conclude by briefly touching on insights from psychoanalysis in terms of working in groups.

Without making ourselves vulnerable to the new it is possible to so constrain the world that we do not allow the unexpected to occur. As humans, we are good at experiencing the world in a way that fits our preconceptions: we are good at ignoring evidence that contradicts our assumptions as it requires deliberate effort to do otherwise. In thinking about the life journey of a teacher who does not open himself to change, Wodehouse (1924: 215–6) comments:

> At first the need of keeping things going somehow may be too confusing and overwhelming to allow of new thought. . . . Afterwards . . . he (sic) is preoccupied with the pressing matters of each day . . . Finally he reaches the assurance of the elderly man, that what he has always known must be the best

I find this quotation a sobering reminder of the effort needed to continually question the way I do things. When I began teaching, perhaps ultimately to my good fortune, my students made it very clear to me that the way I was working with them needed to change!

## Folklore

One of the pieces of folklore in learning to teach is the maxim: 'Don't smile until Christmas' (in the UK, the academic year starts in September). The sense of the advice, presumably, is that as a teacher you need to start off 'hard' with a class to establish boundaries and only once these have been entrenched firmly can you begin to show more of your personality, or humanity even. There is a sense within this folklore that once you have 'lost' a class, once boundaries have been breached, that it is a hard job to 'get them back'.

The flip side is a competing maxim: 'You become what you do'. This is not so much a maxim within the folklore of teaching as one about human nature. The implication of this maxim is that if you begin work with a class by presenting an austere face and trying to clamp down on the smallest misdemeanour, then you establish the pattern for your relationship with the class and possibly the pattern for your relationship with any class – and these patterns are hard to shift.

There is a level of classroom management that is essential before any student is likely to become engaged in mathematics; on the other hand, a classroom where students are scared of their teacher is also unlikely to be conducive to engagement. How is it possible to find a balance?

I have come to wonder if one source of tension within a school comes from the different timescales on which teachers and students view events. When I began teaching, I had a classroom next to a first-storey corridor between the science and mathematics departments that was called 'the bridge'. Students were not allowed to use the bridge and so, for example, if they had a science lesson followed by a maths lesson they were meant to leave the science block, walk outside and around the maths block, up the stairs and end up perhaps just a few metres from where they started. Unsurprisingly, many students would try to sneak across the bridge to save themselves time. As the teacher in the room next to the bridge, I was expected to police this and send students back and around. When I began teaching, I found it hard to enforce this rule with any conviction and really would have rather let students use the bridge. It seemed an arbitrary and unnecessary rule to me, and to many students. I then experienced, one time, what happened when 120 students in maths wanted to get to their next lesson in science, and it just so happened that 120 students in science wanted to get to *their* next lesson in maths. The bridge was only a couple of metres wide, with glazed sides – this was not a safe place for 240 people to try to cross! After this experience, I found I was much better at enforcing the rule. Instead of seeing one student crossing the bridge as a single and isolated incident, I saw the student as the start of a chain of events that I knew could end with danger and chaos if this became an expectation among students. Of course, the students themselves would continue to experience their own attempts to cross the bridge as isolated incidents and hence the enforcing of this rule as petty and unnecessary, but I had a story for myself, that I would often share, about why this was important. With conviction, I was motivated not to turn a blind eye.

On the one-year teacher training course, the Post Graduate Certificate of Education (PGCE), at the University of Bristol on which I work, we are explicit that student teachers have to find their own way through the issue of how to take the authority position in a classroom. For many, this is an uncomfortable shift and one that can touch on deep personal issues. About the only thing we can say – which will be true for everyone – is that you need to learn the students' names and learn them fast. After a few years of teaching, I would always make my first lesson with a year 7 class a name game, so that by the end of that hour I would know every student's name. A lot of managing a classroom seems to involve the routines you establish over time so that students enter your space knowing what to expect and knowing that they are learning.

## My own journey

At the start of my own teaching career, I did not find classroom management straightforward. In my first year of teaching in the UK, I suspect that many students only got engaged by an exploration of where my boundaries were, rather than by anything mathematical. It took me some time to gain the conviction that I had something to offer the students in front of me and that it was worthwhile for me to pay the price to establish boundaries on their behaviour so that exploration could turn to the mathematics. I found that four mechanisms helped me. These are offered only as a reflection on what helped me and to suggest that having *some* mechanisms can be useful (i.e. I do not suggest that these particular mechanisms will be useful for everyone: they were peculiar to the context of 'me' at that time and those classrooms I was working in).

### 'I only speak about mathematics in this room'

As human beings, we generally answer questions that are asked of us. However, as a teacher, having just got a class quiet in order to launch a lesson, if someone asks to borrow a pen, this is not a helpful moment to break my attention to the whole group in order to respond. I had to learn to educate my students not to ask questions at these kinds of moments and also to deal with such questions, if they did arise, with as little fuss and time as possible.

I feel privileged that Dick Tahta spent a couple of days in my classroom, a few years after I began teaching in the school where I eventually became head of department. I remember he sat at the back of my year 10 class with a student who was often disengaged by the study of mathematics. Dick reported afterwards that this student had initially not made any move to start the work I had given to the class. When Dick questioned him as to why he had not begun, the student replied, 'I don't like maths', to which Dick responded, 'What's that got to do with anything?' At this moment, the student laughed and then allowed himself to engage with Dick on the task I had set. I repeat this story as an example of the power of *not* engaging in dialogue about why students might not like mathematics, or feel they are not good at it. All these discussions 'about' working on mathematics are distractions – I only speak about mathematics in this room.

### Establish boundaries as early as possible

I was told on my own PGCE year that as you get more experienced at teaching, you do not necessarily handle conflicts and difficult behaviours situations in class any better, but you do get better at making sure those incidents do not arise in the first place. And here again is the vital connection between engagement and learning and the setting up of ways of working on mathematics. If students become engaged in a process of mathematical thinking they will not be seeking other distractions. There is something, however, about establishing boundaries from the start of a relationship. If I let one student do something but punish the next student who does the same thing, I act unfairly. From my perspective, the warning I give the first student may seem like it is given to the whole class, but this is unlikely to be the students' perspective – what they are likely to see is one student 'getting away with it' and another one not. My actions may, to the students, appear arbitrary – what is the criterion for responding differently to the same misdemeanour? And when boundaries and expectations are not clear, this can be unsettling for students. So, in my own teaching, I began to look out for opportunities to establish boundaries in the first lesson with a group. But a mistake I made when beginning teaching was to start off in my first lesson trying to set out boundaries about a whole range of behaviour (underlining dates, having top buttons done up, always bringing calculator, rulers and pencils) that there was no chance of my possibly noticing every infraction – and half the time I did not really care anyway. The message I was giving my class was that they could ignore what I said, as many of them duly did within a few lessons. In other words, if you are going to set up a boundary, and set it up early, it has to be about something you care about, care about enough to notice every time it occurs, and care about enough to do something about, every time you notice it.

## Planning to conviction

The phrase 'planning to conviction' was one used by Laurinda Brown. In the early years of our research collaboration, we would spend time planning lessons. Over time, I became aware of the moment when I could imagine myself walking into the classroom and knowing what I would say first, or perhaps knowing what would be my overarching purpose and having a sense of some interesting mathematics that students might be able to access. Gattegno's sense of mathematics being 'shot through with infinity' is important to me – if I can get to where the infinity is, in any topic, then I know I can get students working in this area and they will not run out of things to do! To take one example, 'expanding brackets' may be an item on a scheme of work that requires teaching. Although my first instinct now would always be to look for the larger mathematical structure within which any specific concept finds meaning, there still could be times when a specific focus is needed on a specific skill. At first it appears hard to see where any sense of infinity might lurk within 'expanding brackets'. But at its simplest, if I get students expanding a sequence of brackets, there may be patterns that they spot and predictions they can make that engage them in trying out further examples.

$(x + 1) (x + 1)$

$(x + 2) (x + 2)$

$(x + 3) (x + 3)$

$(x + 4) (x + 4)$,

etc. . . .

There could be any number of different sequences that students could try out and then try to predict.

I looked for activities that could become self-checking (for example, in the 1089 activity of Chapter 1, students can check answers as a class) and self-generating (again, with 1089, as with the sequence of brackets above, I do not need to direct students as to what to look at next).

David Fielker (1963) wrote about ways of altering textbook exercises into ones where there is something more engaging for students, through the use of pattern. The example of working on expanding brackets of a sequence of questions would be one inspired by Fielker.

## Having a meta-focus

Part of planning to conviction, for me, came from making sure that each lesson had a purpose that was in a different place to the doing of the task. So, if I was going to ask students to do something, the reason could not be just in order to do it. Thinking again about the 1089 task, when students first start working with three-digit numbers, the challenge is not, for example, to do ten calculations and see what they notice, but rather to 'Find me one that does not work'. Students can be engaged in the challenge and end up doing many calculations quickly, with their focus on the 'meta' purpose. The more focused example of work on expanding brackets can be set up, not with the task of doing the calculations, but rather to 'see what patterns you notice' or to 'see if you can start predicting these without needing to work them out'.

## Listening

My PhD research (written up in Coles 2013) looked into how patterns of communication are established with a class from early in the school year. I took video recordings of several teachers' classrooms over the course of two years in the department where I worked. One teacher (Teacher A) was explicit about students engaging in a process of conjecturing and proving. In the first video recording I have of her teaching a year 7 class (aged 11, in their second lesson of mathematics at the school) the word 'conjecture' is used 42 times in a twenty-minute discussion, 36 times by Teacher A and 6 times by students. Perhaps surprisingly, over the course of the year, the occurrence of this word in discussion steadily decreased, until by the end of the academic year the word was hardly used. However, it was clear that conjecturing was increasingly what students *did* in lessons. This finding mirrors an observation of Laurinda Brown's when she was working in my own classroom over time, that the occurrence of 'metacomments' is especially high at the start of the year when a particular classroom culture is being established. As routines and ways of talking become the norm, there is seemingly less and less need for metacomments.

A recent piece of research in the USA looked at the 'speeches' made by a well-respected and successful teacher in a large, non-selective urban school (Johnson et al. 2013). This teacher used what the researchers call 'speeches', or 'instances in which Mr. Lee would interrupt his mathematics instruction and speak with the students about more general issues concerning their behaviour or motivation' (p. 1). These speeches were used 'to convey to his students a sense of purpose for engaging with mathematics' (p. 1). In the language of this chapter, it is evident that Mr. Lee would regularly metacomment to his class and that these metacomments seemed to be quite central to the success he had in the classroom. Whereas Mr. Lee's metacomments focus mainly on behaviour and motivation, Teacher A's (and my own) would be mainly about mathematical thinking. What seems important is not the particular focus of any metacommenting, but having some focus or purpose that is consistent and is commented on. In my own PhD, I became interested in how a teacher must be listening to students, in order to be able to make metacomments.

At the heart of the management of a classroom is the manner in which listening takes place (students listening to each other, students listening to the teacher and the teacher listening to the students). As a teacher, I need to listen in quite a particular manner if I am going to be able to comment about students' conjectures, or any other meta-focus. I must hear student contributions not just for the content of what is said, but also for the *category* of the comment. For example, the teacher in my PhD study had clearly attuned herself to notice when a student contribution was a mathematical conjecture or not. So the listening takes place on at least two levels: both to the content of what is said, and to the *kind* of content. In a previous study, I suggested the label 'heightened listening' for this kind of twin-track listening, which was meant to suggest that often some conscious effort is required to pay attention both to what is said, and to what a kind of a thing is being said.

The idea of listening to twin tracks in what is said links to the discussion of teachers viewing student actions on an extended timescale. As a student tries to cross the 'bridge' by my classroom (substitute here any equivalent action), I am aware of the action (the content) and the kind of an action it is – and it is because of the *kind* of action it is, rather than the specific action on this occasion itself, that I impose a boundary. During adolescence, students may try to engage teachers with an invitation to negativity, trying to provoke a negative response in order to confirm that they are not liked, or not successful, or not like other people. Again, perhaps it is helpful to recognise the 'kind of comment' being made in order to not become pulled into that negativity.

## Silence

One aspect of listening can be a deliberate silence on the part of the teacher. One of the first teaching strategies I consciously used (as a 'purpose' for my own planning) was the idea of starting lessons in silence. This label emerged from an early conversation with Laurinda Brown (see Brown and Coles 2008). In my experience, there can be a magic to the deliberate silence of the teacher. There is a powerful but unstated message to students that it is their role to make sense of the situation. One of the first lessons where I used the strategy was using the task arithmogons. The task, as written up in the scheme of work is as follows. Laurinda and I wrote about this lesson soon afterwards (Brown and Coles 1996).

---

**Year 8: Algebra – Arithmogons**

*A lesson start (taken from a write-up in Alf's 2nd year of teaching)*

The students filed in as usual, in a noisyish way, and slowly got their stuff out of their bags. I took the register over murmurings of conversations, choosing to ignore them. I then went to the board, with most eyes on me. I tapped with my pen and waited for everyone's attention.

We were going to do some work on arithmogons, I drew one in silence, put a number in two circles, paused and filled the box in between, paused . . . put a number in the third circle . . . filled in the other two boxes.

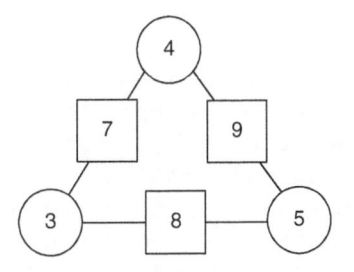

A few hands had gone up, there was silence. Another example, still silence, a couple of students bursting to tell the answers in the boxes, but still silence (this was surprising) . . . I was making eye contact with many of the class and looking a lot at a

*(continued)*

---

*(continued)*

girl who I felt might be the last to pick up what was going on, there was concentration, but still no understanding on her face. A third example . . . I turned to look at the class and *everyone's* eyes were burning into the board, I hadn't experienced this before. Still silence . . . I now took two answers from the class for what should go in the boxes, everyone's hand seemed to be up except the girl; she was straining and seemed to have just twigged; she half-whispered an answer, not quite committing herself, but it was correct. One more example . . . two boys had lost concentration, staring brought them back. The girl's hand was now up with the rest – the boys seemed to be following, after all, so I nodded at her and a correct answer came.

I then drew an arithmogon with only the boxes filled in and invited the class to try to find what the numbers in the circles could have been . . . no one needed a further explanation, which, for me, is rare!

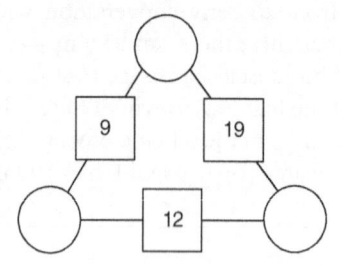

Questions:

- Can you find a method or strategy for solving *any* arithmogon?
- Are there any arithmogons that have no solution? (*You might want to write on the board any the class come up with which they can't solve.*)
- Is there ever more than one solution?
- Can you use algebra to find a solution? (or just to describe how they work eg if a, b and c are in the circles, what is in the boxes?)
- What happens with square arithmogons? pentagonal arithmogons?

The list of questions at the end of the task write-up could all provide a potential 'meta-focus' for the class and the potential infinity is present in the 'any' that appears in several of them. There are also strong links to the design principles discussed in Chapter 2. The arithmogon start described above could be contrasted with a start in which, as a teacher, I tried to explain how arithmogons worked. I can just see the early 'me' as a teacher, standing at the front of the board trying to explain how circles and squares are connected to puzzled faces that quickly disengage and find other more interesting things to occupy their attention. The silent start focused students' attention and engagement seemed to spread. So, another way of thinking about how to manage the engagement of students is to have a range of strategies for focusing attention. This moves into the realm of psychology and even spirituality. There is Buddhist notion of 'presence' that captures, for me, the experience of suddenly having all of my attention taken up by the task in hand. All worries or thoughts about past and future dissipate as I am able to dwell in the present experience – perhaps an unexpected and beautiful view, or a sporting challenge, or a mathematical problem. When 'present', time is experienced differently and typically I am surprised by how much time has passed.

A psychological description of the experience of 'presence' is that we are engaged, as humans, when we are in 'flow' (Csikszentmihalyi 2002); in other words, when there is an absence of self conscious deliberation and all attention is taken by the task in hand. The issue, as teachers, is how to create these conditions in the classroom. In my first year of teaching in the UK, I suspect that students were rarely in this kind of 'flow'. However, there was one lesson I took where something remarkable took place in terms of student engagement.

> When I began teaching in a school in London, I had responsibility for a tutor group. In one session, I invited the class to write about 'The worst (or a bad) experience I have had'. Part of my purpose was to compare and contrast with the students their responses to responses I had got running the same activity with a class of students when I taught for a year in Eritrea. I gave students fifteen or so minutes to write on their own and then invited someone to begin by reading out what they had written. The first student to speak was a girl who at times could be isolated socially. She had written a long piece that she read out fluently, about the illness of her grandmother. The second student to speak was a girl who was usually confident and popular within the class. She also read her piece, in which she described living with her brother who had Down's syndrome. I did not know about this family situation. The effect on me was of a profound sadness and feeling of sympathy. I cannot re-capture the content of subsequent student contributions. But from then on, students no longer read out what they had written, but spoke about personal and close experiences. The conversation continued until the end of the lesson, during which time most students had contributed. I found myself at a loss to know how to end the class, so moving had I found what had been said.

This story I interpret as an example of what can happen when students trip into 'flow'. Social divisions that sometimes took the attention of students dissipated. My sense was that we somehow 'saw' each other and each others' humanity in this hour. The trigger to the change in the classroom atmosphere was the student speaking about her Down's syndrome brother. These are not events that can be planned as a teacher.

One theorisation of conditions for 'flow', that is perhaps helpful in terms of thinking about mathematics teaching, suggests there is a need for a match between challenge and skill (Csikszentmihalyi 2002: 75) and for learners to gain immediate feedback from their environment. Unless, as a teacher, you are going to take on the responsibility for finding that precise match between challenge and skill for every individual in the group, there is a need to develop a way of working in which students see their role as challenging themselves. And that returns to the question of developing ways of working and, hence, what metacomments (or 'speeches') might support such a development. However, one technique for focusing attention or encouraging students to become present/in flow, and that requires careful listening, is taken up in the next section.

## Visualising

Making use of our powers to visualise is a routine that can be exploited to powerful effect. Every student in a mainstream school possesses the capacity to conjure and manipulate visual images. Tristan Needham, in the introduction to his book on complex analysis, writes (Needham 1998: vii):

> Imagine a society in which the citizens are encouraged, indeed compelled up to a certain age, to read (and sometimes write) musical scores. All quite admirable. However, this society also has a very curious – few remember how it started – and disturbing law: *Music must never be listened to or performed!*
>
> Though its importance is universally acknowledged, for some reason music is not widely appreciated in this society. To be sure, professors still excitedly pore over the great works of Bach, Wagner, and the rest, and they do their utmost to communicate to their students the beautiful meaning of what they find there, but they still become tongue-tied when brashly asked the question, 'What's the point of all this?!'
>
> In this parable, it was patently unfair and irrational to have a law forbidding would-be music students from experiencing and understanding the subject directly through 'sonic-intuition.' But in our society of mathematics we *have* such a law. It is not a written law, and those who flout it may yet prosper, but it says, *Mathematics must not be visualized!*

In his book, Needham demonstrates how visual methods can be employed to give a meaning to mathematical processes which are widely seen as having no visual analogue, such as complex integration. The parable he relates, though, surely has resonance right down to the earliest years of mathematics education.

More recently, Christoff Weber has written about the power of making use of mental imagery and working with images has become central to how he works with groups of secondary school students. Weber (2014: 129) gives, as an example, the following task for students.

> Please close your eyes. . . . Imagine a ladder in a light and empty room. Take the ladder and lean it closely against the wall. Imagine yourself at the left-hand side of the ladder and lean your left shoulder against the wall. You now see only one side rail of the ladder leaning against the wall of the room. A lamp is attached to the middle of the side rail facing you. Darken the room and turn the lamp on. You see it shining as a point of light. The bottom end of the ladder begins to slide slowly along the floor to the right, away from the wall. The top end of the ladder continues to touch the wall and slides down it. When it touches the floor, it stops sliding and comes to rest. What is the shape of the trace of light drawn by the lamp as a result of the ladder sliding? What did you imagine during the exercise?

Weber then describes a process he goes through with a class to develop work on a mind image such as the one above. The process could be applied to any image where there is scope for mathematical thinking. Weber starts with some questions for the class. For example, for this image (Weber 2014: 129):

a) What is the shape of the trace of light 'drawn' by the lamp as the ladder moves? Describe your conjectures and draw a sketch. b) Note down all of the mind-images and mind-actions you imagined during the exercise. c) Which of your mind-images and mind-actions were useful with regard to your conjectures? Which ones hindered you?

The class work in journals and after attempting to answer these questions on their own they swap journals with a partner and have to answer these questions (Weber 2014: 130):

Read what your classmate has written in his or her journal and give feedback: d) Which visualisation do you think is of particular interest? e) Which visualisations are useful for answering question a)? In what way?

Work can continue for several lessons. One teaching strategy Weber described is to take in students' journals and, for the next lesson, choose one or two students' work as the starting point for further discussion. For example, there may be two students who are getting quite different results. The mind image quoted above provokes in many people an immediate reaction that the curve created by the light at the mid-point of the ladder will be convex – as it turns out this is a common misconception.

Through careful choice of mind image, it would be possible to provoke work in any area of the curriculum. To take just one example of a topic that might seem far away from possible work with visualisation, the variance of two distributions, consider what a class (perhaps aged 14–15) might do in response to the following:

Imagine every student in your secondary school standing in order of their height . . . in one long line, starting with the smallest and ending with the tallest . . . imagine we know the mean, or the average, height of the students . . . picture this average as a horizontal line, that is above the heads of some students and below the heads of others . . . for each student, find the *difference* between their height and this height of the average . . . now place the students so that the difference between their height and the average height goes from smallest to biggest, it doesn't matter if the student is taller or shorter than the mean, the focus here is *just* on the distance from the mean, so the first student in the list will be the one closest to the average height . . . are students in a new order now compared to before? . . . now multiply the value of the difference in height from the mean, of each student, by itself (square the differences) . . . and find the average (or mean) of the squared differences . . . Now imagine we did the same for students in a primary school . . . which school will have the biggest mean of the squared differences? Why?

## The psychology of the classroom

A lot is known about the psychology of young children and adolescents and there is also a branch of psychoanalysis dedicated to an exploration of what happens when humans get together in groups. Few of these insights have made their way into general thinking about teaching.

One of the earliest theorisers of group processes was Wilfred Bion, who worked with groups of shell-shocked soldiers during World War I. It was while reflecting on and developing his own work with these groups that he began noticing and then theorising some common processes. Bion (1970) developed the concept of the 'work group'. I interpret a 'work group' as one where participants are 'present', in the Buddhist sense. Groups generally meet for a purpose and when a group acts as a 'work group' there is a common focus and participants of the group are engaged in the task of the group. Starting from the notion of an ideal working group, Bion analysed some common things that 'groups' seem to do in order to *avoid* becoming a work group. One of Bion's surprising findings was that groups can be threatened by acting as a work group. In other words, there may be processes taking place within the group to make it unlikely that anyone becomes 'present' or gives attention to the task of the group. The defence mechanisms he initially noticed were: fight–flight, dependency and pairing.

In 'fight–flight' the group identifies an enemy and rather than focus on the work of the group, energy is put into the survival of the group itself, which is seen as being under threat. In a classroom, there is clearly the opportunity for the teacher to become the enemy figure and for the group process to be dominated by 'fight–flight'; equally perhaps the idea of 'mathematics' can become an enemy from which the group must be protected. When groups move into 'dependency' there is again an identification with a figure, but in this mode, the figurehead is seen as the saviour of the group. Again, it is not hard to see how a teacher could adopt such a 'messianic' role and for students to become dependent on the teacher (perhaps for insights into and access to mathematics). And lastly, Bion noticed that groups can adopt a 'pairing' strategy – two individuals this time are seen to be capable of carrying the responsibility for the whole group, the rest of the group listen and attend to the 'pair' who can take on shades of the parental couple. This mechanism is perhaps harder to see in a school context, but the image this conjures for me is of a classroom environment dominated by the antagonism between the teacher and one student. I can remember in the early years of my teaching finding with some classes that a lot of my attention (and worries) were taken up by concerns with one student (who I experienced as disruptive). Perhaps the rest of the class found a safety in giving their attention to individual conflicts between a teacher and student pair.

Bion's ideas are challenging and do not have an immediate link to action. If there is a use to these ideas, it will perhaps be in supporting an altered attention to classroom events, labelling the 'kind' of event that takes place in a different manner. As a teacher, if I recognise (and can describe) an event I am involved in as 'pairing', this may support me acting differently, or doing something to move out of a communication rut.

## References

Bion, W. (1970). *Attention and interpretation*. London: Rowman & Littlefield Publishers.
Brown, L. and Coles, A. (1996). The story of silence. In L. Puig and A. Gutierrez (eds), *Proceedings of the Twentieth Annual Conference of the International Group for the Psychology of Mathematics Education*, 2: 145–52. Valencia, Spain.
Brown, L. and Coles, A. (2008). *Hearing silence: steps to teaching mathematics*. Cambridge: Black Apollo Press.
Coles, A. (2013). *Being alongside: for the teaching and learning of mathematics*. Rotterdam: Sense Publishers.
Csikszentmihalyi, M. (2002). *Flow: the classic work on how to achieve happiness*. London: Rider (first edition published by Harper & Row, 1992).
Fielker, D. (1963). "Now do the following 50 examples . . .". *Mathematics Teaching* 22: 13–15.

Johnson, W., Nyamekye, F., Chazan, D. and Rosenthal, B. (2013). Teaching with speeches: a black teacher who uses the mathematics classroom to prepare students for life. *Teachers College Record*, *115*(2): 1–26.

Needham, T. (1998). *Visual complex analysis*. Milton Keynes: Open University Press

Weber, C. (2014). Exercise in mathematical imagining: setting out a teaching instrument that evokes imaginings and utilises visualisation in secondary school mathematics. *Informal proceedings of the day conference of the British Society for Research into Learning Mathematics*, *34*(1): 125–31. Available online at: www.bsrlm.org.uk/informalproceedings.html (accessed 23 November 2014).

Wodehouse, H. (1924). *A survey of the history of education*. London: Edward Arnold & Co.

#  Part II
# Curriculum focus

# 6 Early primary and the number system

In Chapter 4, the work of Ian Lyons and colleagues was mentioned in relation to the suggestion that there could profitably be a re-focusing of attention in the early years of schooling on ordinal aspects of number. Ordinality can be a slippery concept that I take to be involved in any attention to sequencing. The suggestion from the neuroscience of Ian Lyons is that facility with sequencing aspects of number is the key predictor of mathematical attainment, from age 7–8 onwards. Furthermore, the older children get, the stronger the correlation, i.e. as children get older, facility with ordinal tasks becomes a better predictor of overall mathematical attainment.

Working on numbers as a part of a structure or sequence foregrounds the relational nature of number (again, drawing on the language of Chapter 4). Numbers do not so much stand alone as referents to particular groupings of objects in the world but rather allow the imposition of a certain structure on the world. In fact, even when using '3', say, to pick out three objects in the world, there is an implicit relation being called upon: there are three 'of this particular kind of item'.

## Creativity and number

This chapter draws on the findings of a research project aimed at tackling under-achievement in primary mathematics through a focus on creativity. The project was a collaboration between myself, at the University of Bristol, and the charity '5×5×5=creativity'. We defined creativity, in the context of mathematics, as follows:

- students asking their own questions;
- students following their own lines of enquiry;
- students noticing patterns;
- students making predictions and conjectures;
- students choosing and sharing methods of representation.

This list, for me, could equally be characteristic of 'thinking mathematically'. In 2012–13, the project took place in five schools. All these schools wanted to develop more creativity in their teaching of mathematics. The project teachers in these schools meet six times a year and I made visits to their classrooms between one and three times a month. On these visits I sometimes took lessons and sometimes observed the teacher. There were always reflection meetings afterwards and discussion of what to do next. In all five schools, students were offered the challenge of 'becoming a mathematician' and

| | | | | | | | | |
|---|---|---|---|---|---|---|---|---|
| 0.001 | 0.002 | 0.003 | 0.004 | 0.005 | 0.006 | 0.007 | 0.008 | 0.009 |
| 0.01 | 0.02 | 0.03 | 0.04 | 0.05 | 0.06 | 0.07 | 0.08 | 0.09 |
| 0.1 | 0.2 | 0.3 | 0.4 | 0.5 | 0.6 | 0.7 | 0.8 | 0.9 |
| 1 | 2 | 3 | 4 | 5 | 6 | 7 | 8 | 9 |
| 10 | 20 | 30 | 40 | 50 | 60 | 70 | 80 | 90 |
| 100 | 200 | 300 | 400 | 500 | 600 | 700 | 800 | 900 |
| 1000 | 2000 | 3000 | 4000 | 5000 | 6000 | 7000 | 8000 | 9000 |

*Figure 6.1* Gattegno's number chart

it was noticeable in lessons that teachers were emphasising 'noticing pattern' and 'asking questions' to students.

Gattegno developed a chart (see Figure 6.1 – with younger students, the decimal rows can be hidden) that has been a powerful tool both in creating a sense of excitement in classrooms and also in supporting students' development of a strong sense of pattern and structure within the number system.

In this chart, symbols are presented in relation to each other. The chart makes available the possibility of visualising and verbalising relationships between our number system and the symbols for that structure.

The national curriculum in the UK focuses early number acquisition on the numbers 1 to 20. In the English language, this is almost the only irregular part of the number system. For example consider, linguistically, the differences between '6' and '60', '7' and '70', '8' and '80'. The number ten times bigger is generally denoted by the suffix '-ty'. Following this pattern '30' should be named 'three-ty', '20' should be 'two-ty' and '10' labelled 'one-ty'. Such a naming system would then make saying two-digit numbers a case of saying the first digit, saying '-ty' and saying the second digit. '72' is 'seven-ty-two', '35' would be 'three-ty-five'.

In the absence of such a naming system (although it has been fun to introduce young students to this way of naming numbers) one strategy to support the awareness of structure and pattern has been to work with larger numbers than suggested in UK curriculum documents. The naming of 'hundred' and 'thousand' numbers follows an entirely regular pattern. Teachers involved in the creativity project have all commented on the seeming joy, for children, in 'going big' – trying to say and work with thousands, tens of thousands, hundreds of thousands, perhaps exercising power over these unfathomable numbers.

## Multiplication journeys on the tens chart[1]

In this section, I discuss a project in one school that lasted over four one-hour sessions. I had been asked to support the students in working on multiplication and division. The school is a rural state primary school, with levels of attainment broadly in line with national averages.

I pinned a large copy of the Gattegno chart (Figure 6.1) at the front of the classroom. I began by tapping (with a long stick) at numbers on the chart and getting the whole class to chant back to me the number name. If I tapped on two numerals (e.g. 20 and 5) the class chanted back the name of those numerals combined ('twenty-five'). Having established how to say numbers on the chart, I then tapped on a number and got the class to chant back that number multiplied by 10. I wanted students to appreciate that multiplication

*Early primary and the number system* 77

by 10 (on this chart) can be done by a visual movement ('go down one row'). I then got the class to chant back the number I tapped divided by 10 ('go up one row').

After working with the students on how to multiply and divide by 10 and 100, a challenge was issued: choose a number on the chart, go on a journey multiplying or dividing by 10, 100 and get back to the starting point. The examples of students' responses to this task (Figure 6.2) are taken from a mixed year 3–4 class (ages 7–8).

This student has completed three journeys and ticked their own work since they have recognised that they got back to where they started. In the project, teachers have emphasised to students the need to write down anything they notice and any questions they have. For example, in Figure 6.3, a student has written: 'I've noticed it is clever because if ÷ by 10 you × 10 then get back'.

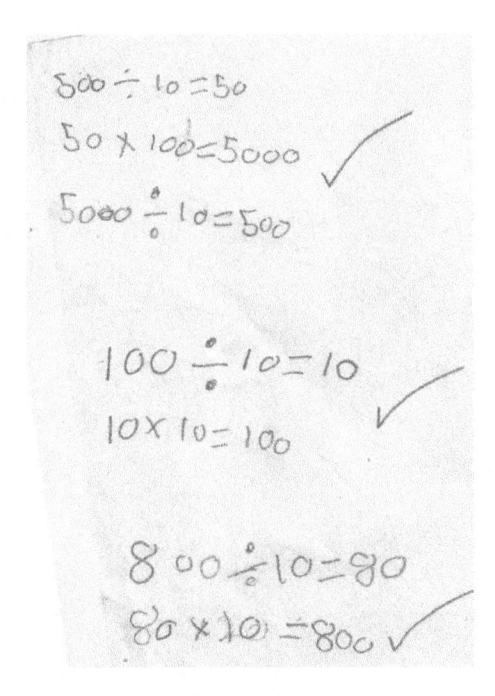

*Figure 6.2* Three 'journeys'

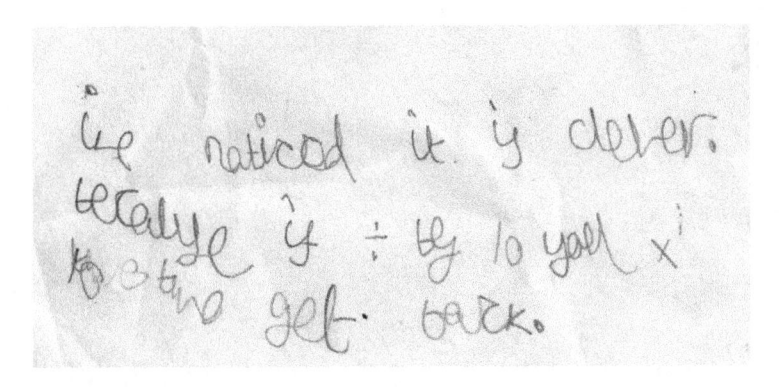

*Figure 6.3* A connection made!

78  Curriculum focus

The student in Figure 6.3 is expressing a key awareness and gives an example of the connection between multiplication and division.

Several students went beyond the operations involving 10 and 100 that had been shown to them. The student in Figure 6.4 was challenging herself to go on a journey and then return in one step.

There is evidence here of the student extending the pattern of how to divide by 10 and 100, to work out what she must do to undo ×10, ×10, ×10, ×10.

In the second session, some students wanted to explore the decimal part of the chart (Figure 6.5).

The structure of the tens chart meant that students found little difficulty in extending what they had done with journeys in whole numbers to journeys into decimals. At the

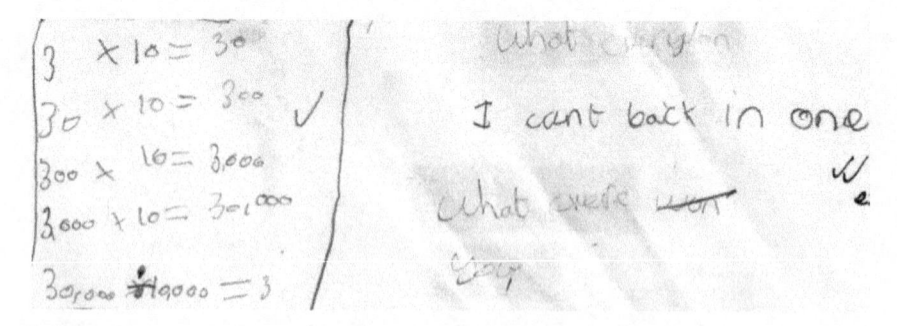

Figure 6.4 A student extends to division by 10,000

Figure 6.5 A journey into decimals

*Early primary and the number system* 79

end of the second lesson, one student asked if they could make a journey from one column to a different column (all journeys to this point had been within a single column of the chart). As teachers and researchers we had not expected this question nor ever used the chart to do this. However, we took on the challenge and in the third lesson, I put forward the idea that to go from, say, 7 to 4 on this chart, since we only use multiplication and division, we would have to divide by 7 to get to 1 and then multiply by 4 to get to 4. With this new possibility, students were then challenged to choose a starting point and a different end point for their journeys (Figure 6.6).

Several students were able to combine moving across columns with moving (as they had been) up and down a column. The student in Figure 6.7, for example, wanted to do a journey from 3000 to 0.04

Although there is a small error in the last line, this student demonstrates a striking control of the symbols she is using. This student was seen by the school as having low levels of prior attainment.

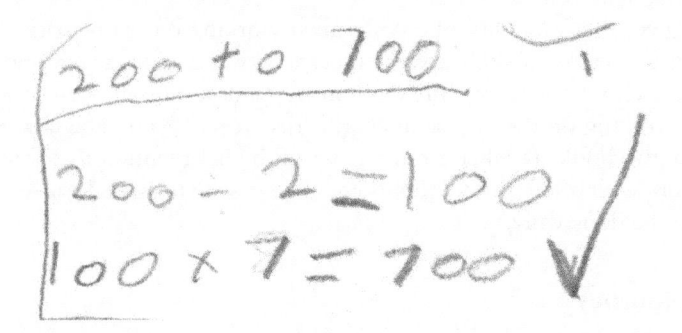

*Figure 6.6* A journey from one column to a different column

*Figure 6.7* A journey from 3000 to 0.04

80  *Curriculum focus*

One of the teachers, in reflecting on this particular project, commented on how she had previously always approached multiplication through a concrete manipulation and grouping of objects. In this treatment, we observed students being able to begin with a visual tool that is already abstract (the tens chart) and build further abstractions from there. At some point they will need to connect their use of multiplication and division with real objects, but in this treatment the fluency comes first. It appears that students are able to work with numbers (e.g. decimals) and operations (e.g. division by 10,000) that would not normally be introduced until considerably later in the curriculum in the UK. The work on journeys supported students in gaining awareness of the inverse relation between multiplication and division; awareness of place value (without this being explicitly mentioned); and, in the work moving between columns, the beginnings of the 'unitary method' for solving problems. I make no claims about what students do or do not understand about multiplication and division. What I observe is that they have become energised by gaining fluency in symbolic manipulations and have developed awarenesses linked to these symbols.

The Gattegno chart gives the possibility of a communal working on mathematics as the children chant responses in unison. As this research on creativity and under-achievement developed, some schools chose to devote fifteen minutes a day, not in their usual mathematics lessons, to working on the Gattegno chart across years 1 to 6. The tasks in Appendix 1 at the end of this book are taken from one set of the intervention materials I produced for these schools, with brief introductory notes. These were imagined as a series of fifteen-minute tasks to be done daily.

### Case study: Henry's journey[2]

The next section of this chapter is a case study that follows the work of one child and charts his development, particularly in terms of being able to work with pattern in mathematics. The student was chosen for this study because his teacher had decided to document his development (not because he was necessarily different or remarkable in terms of the progress he made compared to others in the project). Figure 6.8 shows Henry's (a pseudonym) work in November 2011 and Figure 6.9 his work in May 2012.

It is evident that Henry has moved from some uncertainty about the processes or symbols of addition and subtraction to being able, by the end of the year, to solve a relatively complex examination question. While our focus has been on supporting student creativity, we do want students to succeed in formal assessments as well and there is evidence in this case study that there is no contradiction between these agenda. Through getting excited about 'being a mathematician' and noticing pattern and working with big numbers, Henry has developed his awareness of number to the point where the exam question in Figure 6.9 was unproblematic.

I believe a key factor in Henry's striking development came through his appreciation of the role of pattern in mathematics, coupled with his teacher's growing emphasis on the processes of mathematical thinking (including providing repeated opportunities to spot and use pattern).

By January 2012 (Figure 6.10) Henry can be seen to have extended a pattern in the five times table, up to 14 multiplied by 5. His teacher recorded two comments Henry made: 'It's all five or zero', and in response to a question about how he had done this work: 'I used a hundred square and used the pattern'.

```
6 + 1 = 6  —
5 + 6 = 1  ~~~
9 + 10 = 1  —
10 + 9 = 1  —
6 + 1 = 7  ✓
3 + 2 = 5  ✓
2 + 4 = 6  ✓
8 + 5 = 10 —
10 + 8 = 2  —
```

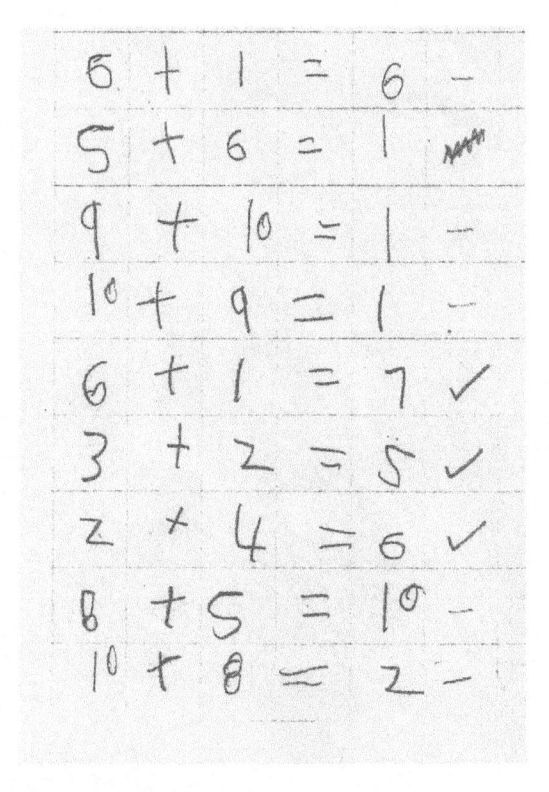

*Figure 6.8* Henry in November 2011

Use [46] and [54] each time to make these correct.

8 + [46] = [54] ✓

[46] + 8 = [54] ✓

[54] − 8 = [46] ✓

[54] − [46] = 8 ✓

*Figure 6.9* Henry in May 2012

82   *Curriculum focus*

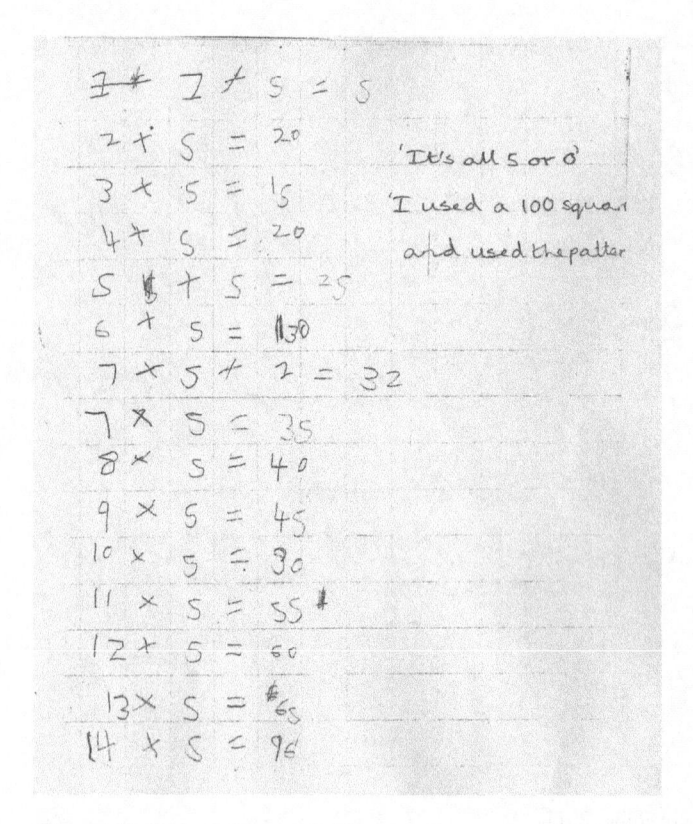

*Figure 6.10* Henry in January 2012

By March 2012 (Figure 6.11) Henry demonstrated that he was able to complete a 'journey' of multiplication and division by 10, apparently working confidently with numbers as big as 90,000.

During April 2012, the emphasis on pattern in Henry's written work continues. In the work in Figure 6.12, rather than needing a teacher to write down his comments (as in January 2012, Figure 6.10), he is able to write for himself about the pattern he noticed: 'Inside goes up in order, outside goes up in twos'.

Henry has been able to work in a systematic manner (increasing the size of his rectangle by 1 unit each time) and, as a result, has been able to notice a pattern in his results. Henry's teacher wrote (in her own learning journal):

> Henry continued this [see Figure 6.12] over 2 days, keen to carry on and use patterns he had spotted.
>
> He used I for inside and O for outside.
>
> We used the word area when talking about it together.
>
> Henry is discovering links between area and perimeter.

In May 2012, Henry was working on the link between multiplication and addition. He wrote some multiplication sentences, $4 \times 2 = 8$ and then wrote out $2 + 2 + 2 + 2 = 8$, using images of beads to help him. His teacher wrote:

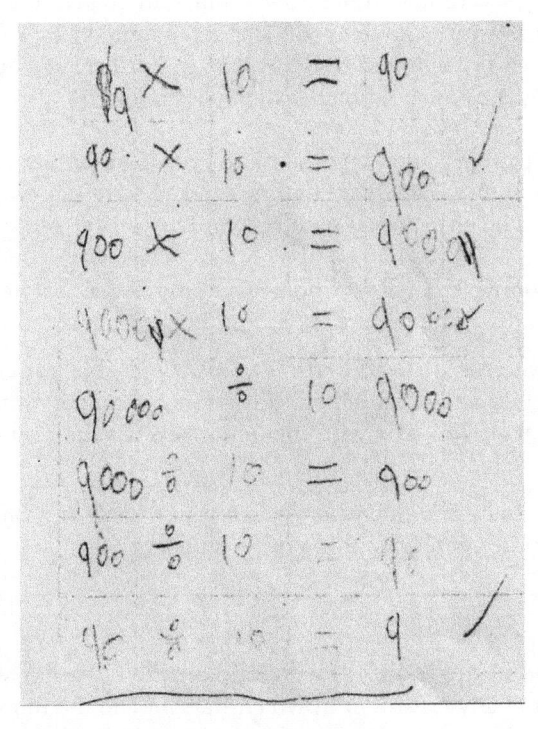

*Figure 6.11* Henry in March 2012

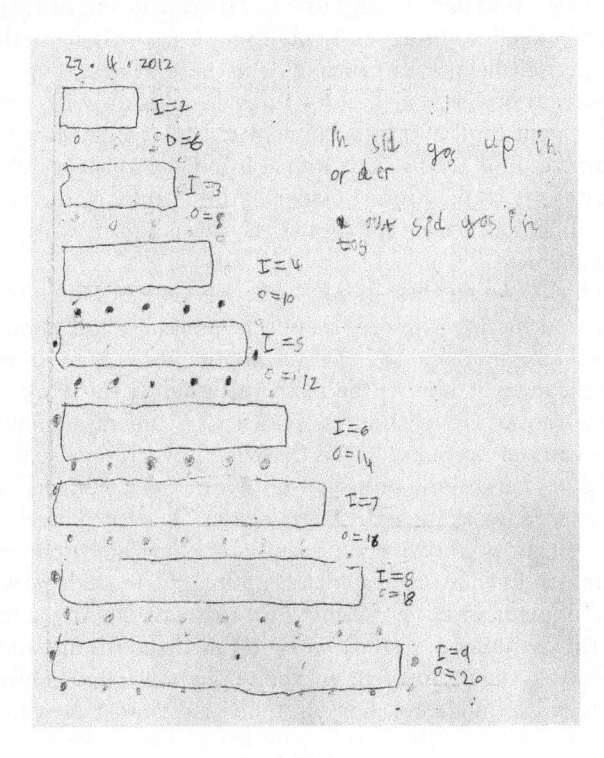

*Figure 6.12* Henry in April 2012

84   *Curriculum focus*

Discovery focus for Henry today was to investigate how + and × are linked. Henry sensibly took the 2s to work with because he felt confident at counting in 2s. After making some mistakes, he noticed the link and could explain it. Further, he could take the pattern into answering questions about higher multiplication facts.

There is a shift here into noticing a pattern (April) and then into noticing a pattern and being able to extend it (May). In the summer of 2012 Henry was asked to reflect on his own mathematical learning journey. The chapter end with his words:

I love doing times tables on my journeys. And I love doing Cuisenaire because it helps me do the right writing. If I want to write the sum, I can just use the right colour.

Numbers are easier if I spot patterns. If it goes 10, 20, 30 it will be a pattern. When Alf came I used big numbers and I was happy. If I use small numbers at the start it will get bigger and bigger. If you start with small numbers it helps you do big numbers.

I like being a mathematician because it's fun when you can just keep on going. Numeracy makes me happy because I just want to do more numbers.

## Discussion

Many of the tasks in this chapter (and in Appendix 1) revolve around the Gattegno tens chart. I would want this on the wall of any classroom in which I taught and the more I work with it the more useful I find it. However, this is not to say either that the chart is all you need for number work, nor that it is straightforward to use. To maintain engagement in a communal chanting the teacher needs to bring sensitivity to the sense-making of the group of students, in order to repeat challenges, or to make them more or less complex. In Chapter 5, there was a description of Gattegno using Cuisenaire rods to work with young children and I am sure that some kind of manipulative materials are significant for students' learning, especially if they can be used in a relational manner. However, what I find so powerful about the tens chart, as mentioned earlier in this chapter, is the way that it gives students access to number structure and allows the possibility of a playful engagement in gaining symbolic fluency.

One of the implications from the neuroscientific studies I described in Part One is that we need to find ways of offering students access to ordinal aspects of number and gaining fluency with number symbols. Linking numbers to objects is important but it need not hold students back from gaining the fluency of successful mathematicians. In the work on journeys on the tens chart, or the case of Henry, there is evidence of students manipulating numbers with confidence without necessarily even knowing how to say some of them. This disturbed some of the teachers on the project, who worried that students did not 'understand' the numbers they were working with. There is certainly a feel of fluency being in advance of something – depth of knowledge perhaps? I see one of Gattegno's challenges as the idea that working on fluency in a way that is meaningful to students is a mechanism to make the learning of mathematics economical for students in terms of the time it takes. What I take from the examples of student work in this chapter is that such fluency can be engaging for students as they gain a sense of their own power and control over a subject that can feel alien and intimidating. Giving students a context in which they can make meaningful and creative mathematical statements sets up the virtuous cycle of engaging in the discourse of mathematics and hence constructing the mathematical objects that allow you to engage further in the discourse of mathematics.

## Notes

1 This section draws on an article first published in the journal *For the Learning of Mathematics* (FLM), 34(2), pp. 24–30 and is reproduced here with kind permission of the FLM Publishing Association.
2 This section draws on data derived in part from an article published in *Research in Mathematics Education*, (forthcoming), copyright British Society for Research into Learning Mathematics, available online: www.tandfonline.com/ (forthcoming). See also Coles (2014).

## Reference

Coles, A. (2014). Transitional devices and symbolic fluency. *For the Learning of Mathematics*, *34*(2): 24–30.

# 7 Primary/secondary transition and geometrical thinking

The visual and aesthetic aspects of geometry can be appealing to students and allow an entry into consideration of mathematical relationships. There are several categorisations of geometric thinking; two notable ones that I touch on in this chapter, which have quite different purposes, are (a) the van Hiele levels and (b) 'big ideas' in geometry put forward by Sinclair *et al.* (2012).

## The van Hiele levels

There have been several versions of, and additions to, van Hiele's hierarchy of levels of geometrical thinking. The one below comes from a synthesis by Burger and Shaughnessy (1986: 31):

> *Level 0 (Visualization)*. The student reasons about basic geometric concepts, such as simple shapes, primarily by means of visual considerations of the concept as a whole without explicit regard to properties of its components.
>
> *Level 1 (Analysis)*. The student reasons about basic geometric concepts by means of an informal analysis of component parts and attributes. Necessary properties of the concept are established.
>
> *Level 2 (Abstraction)*. The student logically orders the properties of concepts, forms abstract definitions, and can distinguish between the necessity and sufficiency of a set of properties in determining a concept.
>
> *Level 3 (Deduction)*. The student reasons formally within the context of a mathematical systems, complete with undefined terms, axioms, an underlying logical system, definitions, and theorems.
>
> *Level 4 (Rigour)*. The student can compare systems based on different axioms and can study various geometries in the absence of concrete models.

The conception of geometrical thinking embodied in these levels seems strongly tied to notions of Euclidean proof. I find it helpful to consider the levels in relation to an example. Look at the simple image in Figure 7.1.

At level 0, we might see this diagram as two lines that cross and perhaps have little else to say. At level 1, we might notice that there are four angles created by the crossing of the lines. We could convince ourselves that the angles come in two equal pairs (perhaps

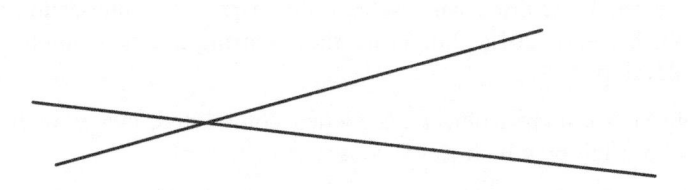

*Figure 7.1* Two lines

through animating one of the lines) no matter how the lines cross (a necessary property), and also that adjacent pairs sum to 180 degrees. At level 2, we are able to prove the equality of opposite angles, making use of the fact that angles on a line sum to 180 degrees. We might also be aware that the assumption about the sum of angles on a straight line is equivalent to an assumption about the angle sum of interior angles in a triangle, and either one is therefore sufficient to establish the opposite angles result.

At level 3 (perhaps not often attained in school?), the result about vertically opposite angles takes the form of a fully rigorous Euclidean proof, with every step of the argument justified (including steps of logic). At level 4, we recognise that the equality of opposite angles is dependent on assumptions about the lines being in a plane (as opposed to on a sphere or hyperbola). School geometry, then, tends to move through levels 0, 1, 2 and in some cases 3. The van Hiele levels do not attempt to say anything about how we can help students move from one level to the next, but there is perhaps an implicit assumption that earlier levels are present and available in higher ones and so the levels form a hierarchy that students must move through in sequence.

## 'Big ideas'

Sinclair *et al.* (2012) give an alternative perspective on the understanding of geometry. They distill 'big ideas' that are essential to gaining a flexible and deep grasp of geometry at different grade levels. They argue for the centrality of geometry, 'both as an area of study in its own right and as a means of providing insight and understanding for other areas of mathematics' (Sinclair *et al.* 2012: 7). These big ideas offer suggestions of work not only useful to do as a teacher but also useful for a teacher to give to students.

At (US) Grades 6–8 (the age range relevant to this chapter) the big ideas are as follows (along with a distillation of an example the authors use):

1   Behind every measurement formula lies a geometric result.

For example, if you consider the formula for the area of a triangle, can you find a geometric rearrangement of any triangle into an associated rectangle?

2   Geometric thinking involves developing, attending to, and learning how to work with imagery.

Whereas in the van Hiele levels, visualisation is the starting point (level zero), it is emphasised as a key way of working by Sinclair *et al.* Developing students' powers of visualisation takes place through regular use of exercises, for example: 'Imagine a square. Now make a copy of it, turn it in your mind by 45 degrees, and place one of its vertices at the centre of the first square. What is the shape of the intersection of the two squares? (Sinclair et al. 2012: 25). From these starting points geometrical awarenesses can be developed.

3   A geometric object is a mental object that, when constructed, carries with it traces of the tool or tools by which it was constructed.

If imagery is at the heart of understanding geometry (and arguably all of mathematics) then an important insight is that 'tools provide new sources of imagery as well as specific ways of thinking about geometric objects and processes' (Sinclair et al. 2012: 41). If we are working on reflection, it will make a difference if we ask students to make free-hand sketches, or offer them mirrors or get them to work within a dynamic geometry virtual environment.

4   Classifying, naming, defining, posing, conjecturing, and justifying are co-dependent activities in geometric investigations.

The authors give, as one example of a space for investigation, the possible line and rotation symmetries of quadrilaterals. Which combinations are possible? Can you make a quadrilateral with rotation symmetry order three? Along the way, the authors invite a re-naming of shapes to capture more explicitly some of their properties.

The second big idea concerns the importance of visual imagery and cultivating students' power to create and manipulate images. In Chapter 5 there was a brief description of the work of Christof Weber (2014), for whom working on visualisation is a central aspect of his teaching, much as Sinclair et al. suggest for the potential role of geometry. The fourth of these big ideas points to the importance of the activity of 'naming' properties that have been noticed. If students can be involved in the process of naming geometrical properties and concepts, Sinclair et al. suggest this will be tantamount to them being involved in conjecturing and mathematical thinking (Lakatos 1976).

In keeping with the Part Two focus on classroom activity, in the rest of this chapter I present three tasks, each one exploring a theme linked to a Big Idea. The first theme concerns the use of the strategy mentioned by Tahta (1989): 'say what you see', for the purposes of classifying, naming, defining (Big Idea 4). The second theme investigates the different geometrical activities students can engage in, given different starting points for the same task – analogous to Big Idea 3 and the way each geometrical concept carries 'traces of the tool or tools by which it was constructed'. The third theme considers Big Idea 1 (that every measurement formula hides a geometrical result) in relation to trigonometry.

**'Say what you see'**

In Chapter 4 the role of dynamic geometry software was discussed briefly and it was noted that such software offers one possible entry into considering the relationships that exist between angles within geometric figures. The task that follows makes use of a relatively simple sketch and allows for the strategy mentioned by Tahta (1989): 'say what you see'.

The sketch (Figure 7.2) allows for shifting and naming (Figure 7.3) and then a further dynamic altering of some relationships but not others (Figure 7.4).

One of the relationships made available to students, through interacting with these sketches, is that the sum of angles in a triangle is the same as the sum of the angles on

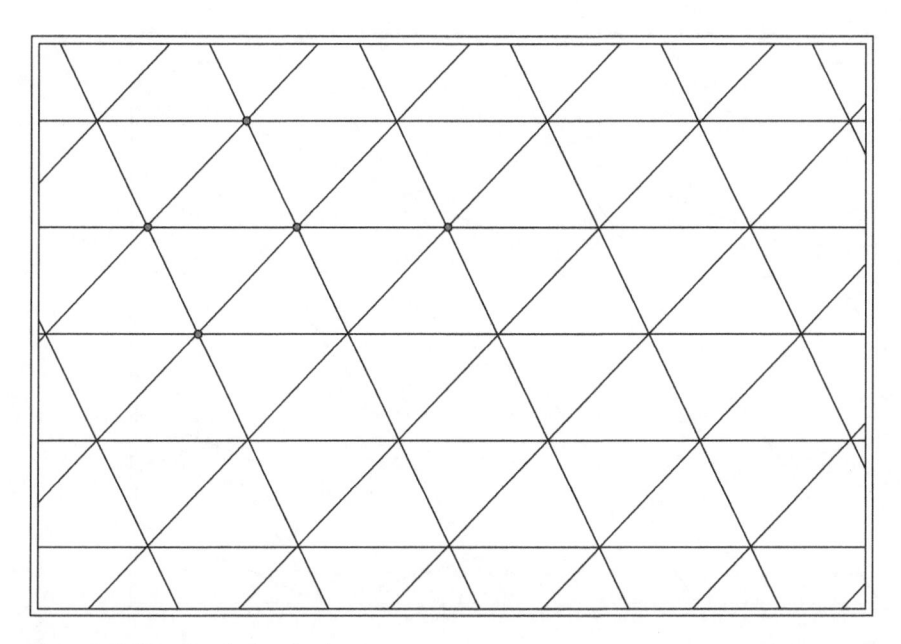

*Figure 7.2* Tessellated triangles 1

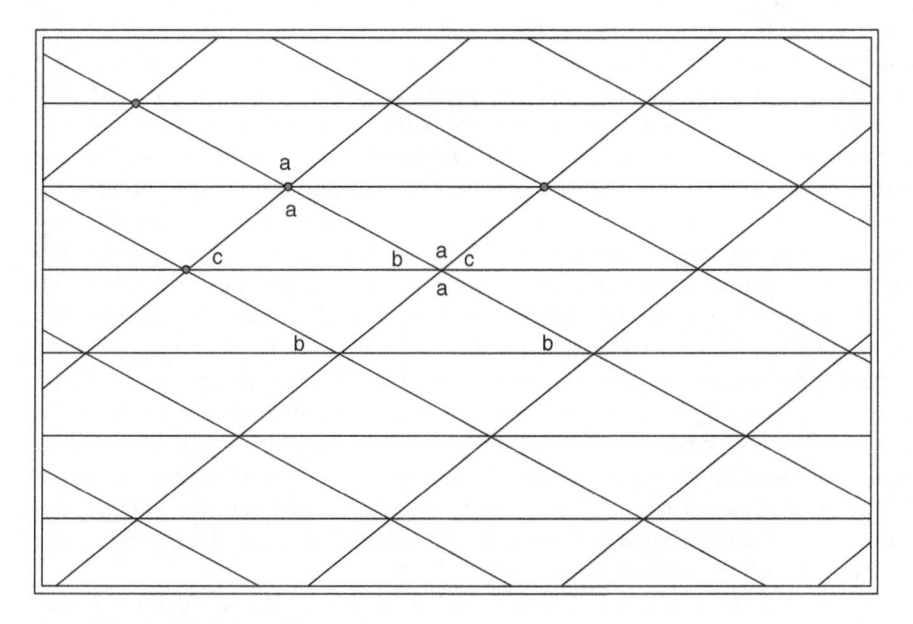

*Figure 7.3* Tessellated triangles 2

a line. Dave Hewitt (1999) writes powerfully about the distinction between what is 'arbitrary' in mathematics and what is 'necessary'. It is *arbitrary* that we label the angle sum of a triangle 180 degrees (and, in fact, mathematicians do not always use that measure: at A-level students will be encouraged to think in terms of radian measure, so that the angle sum of a triangle is $\pi$ radians). Whatever measure is chosen, however, it is *not* arbitrary

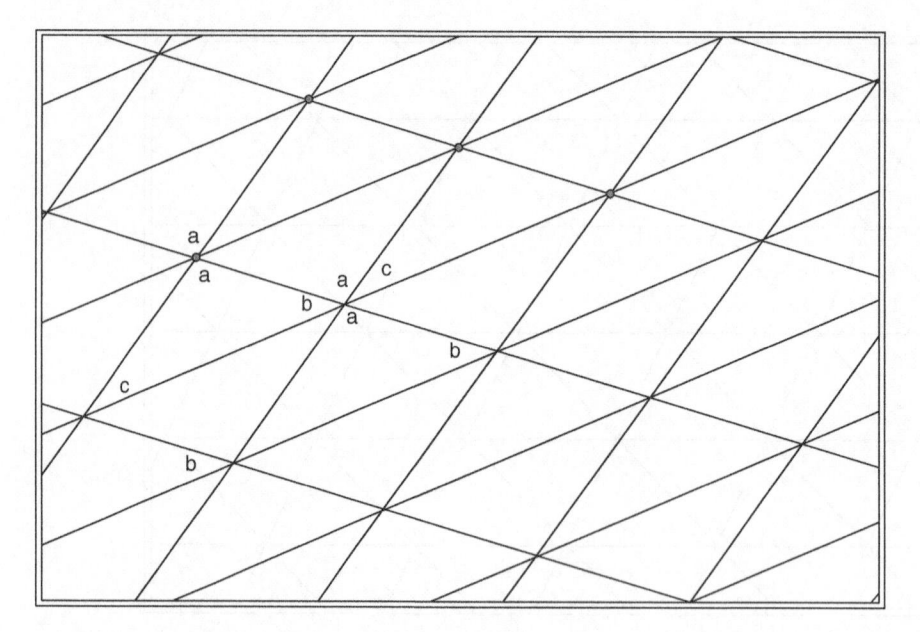

*Figure 7.4* Tessellated triangles 3

that the sum is invariant. Furthermore, if we are dealing with geometry on a plane, then it is also *necessary* that the angle sum of a triangle is the same as that of a straight line. Hewitt's point is that students need to be told the 'arbitrary' aspects of mathematics and can be left to work out the 'necessary' parts. The necessary aspects of mathematics can be accessed through students' awareness, if as teachers we can find a suitable context. This gives another way of thinking about the differences to the approach to working on the sum of the angles of a triangle discussed in Chapter 4. A sketch such as Figure 4.6 displayed an arbitrary mathematical fact (that the angle sum for one particular triangle is 180 degrees) and then the dynamicity of a software package is used to show that this arbitrary fact is true for all triangles. In contrast, an approach such as in the figures above gives the opportunity for students to become aware of a necessary relationship. In fact, many relationships are potentially available to be noticed – and the dynamicity of software can be used to work on which relationships are not particular to any one image. As students talk about the relationships they notice, there is the opportunity for the teacher to supply the (arbitrary) mathematical naming conventions (e.g. 'vertically opposite angles') and symbolism. There is something about the infinity of the tessellation that can make the awareness of relationships more obvious.

I have edited an audio recording, taken in 2007, of my year 7 class (at the time) working on an image like the ones discussed above and using the strategy 'say what you see'. Some lines of dialogue have been deleted for considerations of space, and these are indicated with three dots; however, line numbers follow the text that is included. Diagrams are included in the right-hand column to give some indication of what part of the whole of Figure 7.3 was being referred to and where letters were being placed.

| 1 | ACs | I'd like you to look at the board please (1) and (.) I'd like you (.) to tell me (.) what you see (4) What do you see? (2) S3? | |
|---|---|---|---|
| 2 | S3 | Right-angled triangles (.) Right angled. | |
| 3 | ACs | Right-angled triangles did you say? | |
| 4 | S17 | I just see triangles. | |
| 5 | ACs | Triangles? (.) S4? | |
| 6 | S4 | Um (1) lots of triangles. | |
| 7 | ACs | Lots of triangles. (1) S11? | |
| 8 | S11 | Half a quadrilateral. | |
| 9 | | . . . | |
| 10 | ACs | . . . I'm going to focus on one of these triangles and S3 started talking about angles and right-angles and whether they're just off right-angles. I'm going to call that angle in there $a$ (2)<br>[*I draw in one 'a'*]<br>I'm going to call that angle $b$ (2)<br>and I'm going to call that angle $c$ (1)<br>[*I draw 'b' and 'c' in the same triangle*]<br>and I wonder if anybody could come to the board and draw me another angle or could label another one that you know might be the same as $a$ or $b$ or $c$ could we have another one the same as either $a$ or $b$ or $c$?(7) | |
| 11 | S3 | Um (2) There (3) Would that be right or not? [*S3 draws another 'a'*] | |
| 12 | ACs | S3's saying would that be right or not? (.) So? | |
| 13 | Ss | Yeah, yeah. | |
| 14 | ACs | What I really like about what S3's done there is he's put it up and he's asking you a question (.) So can anybody try and help him on that and can we get some reasons so thinking about reasoning on the board there? (.) S23? | |

*(continued)*

*(continued)*

| | | | |
|---|---|---|---|
| 15 | S23 | It's the same because if you rotated the one that's in the middle now [it should be the same]. | |
| 16 | ACs | If you rotated the first one with all three of them it should be the same (.) Anybody want to disagree with that? | |
| 17 | S | You could put *c* up there and it would be the same but sometimes it wouldn't be cos it's on a diagonal. | |
| 18 | | [*dialogue skipped and also time for students, on their own, to fill in as many letters as they can on the diagram*] | |
| 19 | ACs | Okay let's come together then please so what have we noticed (.) What can we tell about the angles in these triangles in this kind of shape? (.) What have you seen? (.) Okay, S1. | |
| 20 | S1 | My sentence (.) Can I read out my sentence? | |
| 21 | ACs | Yeah. | |
| 22 | S1 | All I said was (.) we know that angle *a* is ninety degrees which to me is nearly half a square (.) So it is easy to tell what angle *a* is. | |
| 23 | ACs | So could somebody just come up and pick out four or five examples of *a*?(.) Of angle *a* someone who hasn't been up yet. S3 do you want to come and show us four or five *a*'s? (2) Is that alright just from seeing they're close to a right angle? (.) They're the biggest angle she was saying (.) so have a look at that because that estimating angles is really important . . . | |
| 24 | S5 | And if you look at it and keep doing it then there's a pattern in the circle sometimes it might go *b a c* or *c b a* or *a* or *a b c* or something like that around in a circle that's what it's doing on mine. | |
| 25 | S6 | Yeah I done a circle look at that. | |
| 26 | Ss | [*various voices*] | |
| 27 | ACs | Can we have some comments on what S5 has said because S5 has made two really important points there? (1) Any comments first on what S5 has said? | |

Primary/secondary transition and geometrical thinking 93

| 28 | S10 | Oh it's like where we're (1) where it goes like | |
| 29 | ACs | You could come and point if you want. | |
| 30 | S10 | It's like when all the lines go like that way every time a line meets a line it goes that way and that way (.) It goes in like a circle and then it all goes in like a little pattern every time. | |
| 31 | ACs | Is that what you're saying, S5? That every time where we've got the three lines meeting it goes in a circle and there's a pattern? | |
| 32 | S5 | Yeah um can I come and show you on the board? (3) | |
| 33 | S11 | Sir I want to show you something after (3) | |
| 34 | S5 | Cos they're opposite each other there. [pointing to angles either side of a diagonal in one parallelogram – see arrows] That one (.) That one's going to be b because (.) it's not a square or a rectangle but it still looks like a square or some'it. It's like opposite (.) and then it'll do it in each square (.) So once you've done like one triangle you can do all the rest. | |
| 35 | ACs | You can do all the rest, okay? So what I think it would be useful to draw out from this and I'd like you to write down (.) so if we can draw out (.) some simpler pictures out of this complex diagram . . . So I'd like you to draw this in your books now please because what you're discovering now here are some really key and important angle facts (.) So I just want to draw a couple of simple diagrams please (.) So could you draw two straight lines like that. [parallel lines drawn] They can be quite short (1) and one line crossing it (3) and S5 has been talking about opposite angles (.) . . . | |

The potential for discussion of Figure 7.3, in terms of both van Hiele levels and Sinclair's Big Ideas, can be glimpsed in some of the dialogue above. In line 11, a student takes up my suggested labelling of the diagram and classifies another angle (Big Idea 4) as the same as angle *a*. In line 15 another student begins to engage in reasoning (van Hiele level 1?) about why the angle *a* has been placed in a correct position. The reasoning invokes some visualisation (Big Idea 1) as we are invited to consider one part of the diagram rotated about a point. It would be possible to continue in this way and analyse each line. Big Idea 3, that each geometric object carries the trace of the tools used in its construction, can perhaps be glimpsed in line 24. Student S5 talks about a 'circle' of angles around a point. This, in my experience, is a relatively unusual way of describing angles in parallel lines and I see the emergence of the word 'circle' as linked strongly to the context, a whole page of parallel lines, in which students have been working.

At the end of the transcript, I try to force students' attention onto small sections of Figure 7.3, in order to be able to draw out some of the more standard 'angle facts'. In line 34 a student uses the word 'opposite' – although perhaps for angles that are opposite each other in a parallelogram, rather than at a point. Reading the transcript now, I wonder if, as a teacher, I jumped on the use of this 'standard' word ('opposite angles') and (perhaps too early) focused attention on one aspect of the diagram. I think now I might have wanted to check out what S5 meant by 'opposite' and perhaps asked if someone could connect this idea of opposite with what S5 had noticed about the angles around each 'circle'.

## One task, two purposes

A task that was a favourite of mine in the school where I taught (usually for year 7 students, aged 11–12) was Pick's Theorem. In this section I contrast two different ways into work on Pick's Theorem, to highlight how the use of a task is highly dependent on my purposes, as a teacher. A task is a tool and, in the same way that (Big Idea 3) the trace of the tool used to work with geometric imagery stays with my mental constructions, the way a task is used will constrain the work that students do.

Pick's Theorem concerns the relationships between the number of dots on the edge of a shape drawn on square dotty paper, the number of dots captured on the inside and the shape's area. One way into the problem, perhaps for younger age groups, is to invite students to explore shapes with the same area (as in Figure 7.5). A lesson start could be to draw two shapes with area 4 on the board, and say to the class: 'These are both 4-square shapes. Someone come and draw me another, different 4-square shape'. This approach is described in Brown and Waddingham (1982). As students come up to draw their ideas for other shapes, the meaning of the criteria can be made visible and some shapes are 'allowed' that fit the criteria and others are not (a closed start – see the design principles of Chapter 2). As can be seen in Figure 7.5, the shapes students explore often are made of squares and half-squares. It is important that students write, next to each shape, the two values from I, E and A (dots inside, dots on the edge, area) which they are varying. Without writing this information next to each shape, they will be inhibited when it comes to spotting patterns.

As can be seen in the student's work in Figure 7.5, there is scope to work with students on being systematic in their exploration and to tabulate results. A question that can arise early on in this project is whether, for example with 4 square shapes, if there are no dots inside, will there always be 10 dots on the edge? In the school where the student work in Figure 7.5 was produced, the class (age 9–10) had originally worked on paper in their exploration of shapes and areas. Many students had chosen different areas and found it hard to spot patterns. The class had their own mathematics 'learning journals' and at a later date they had space to look back over their work and reflect on it in their journals, cutting out shapes and adding comments or questions or things they had noticed. The student that produced Figure 7.5, when she transferred work to her journal, chose to

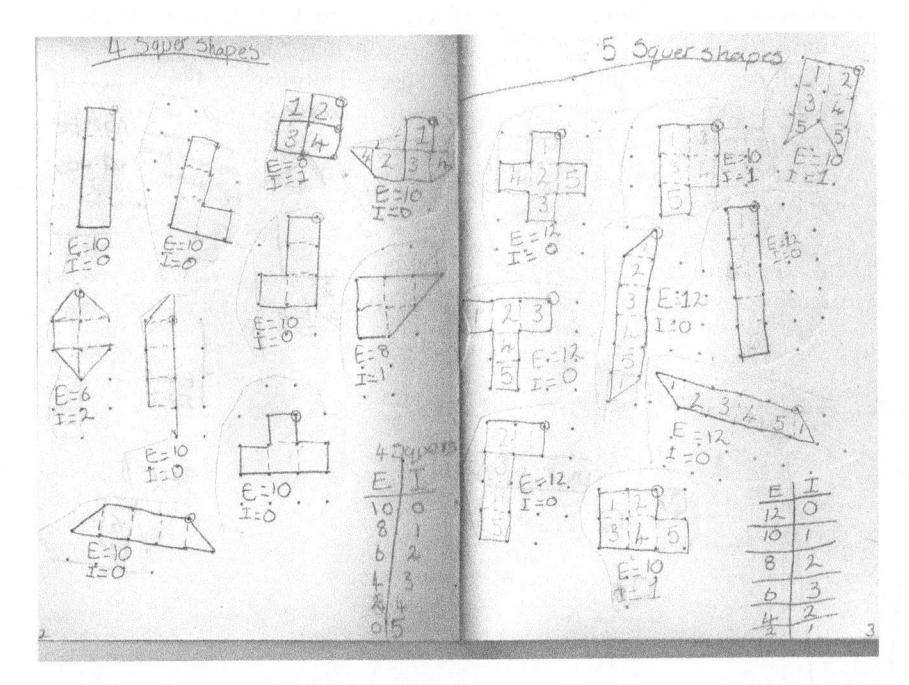

*Figure 7.5* A student's work on Pick's Theorem

organise them by area and, in doing so, was able to spot the patterns that are captured in the tables (which you may be able to see, are written directly on the page rather than cut out from previous work). The student then extended the results in the table to continue the pattern she noticed (in fact extending it into shapes that would not be possible). The importance of classifying (Big Idea 4) can be seen here – by grouping results, this student was able to engage in a level of mathematical thinking (pattern spotting and predicting) that she had not shown evidence of before.

Work on this project can extend over many lessons as students try out different areas and perhaps begin to be able to predict what the table of values will look like (again, fitting in with Chapter 2 design principles of space to spot patterns, predict and test). It can be a challenging question, to try to find a shape for each entry in a table (e.g. what is the minimum number of dots on the edge?).

Students may notice a link between the area and the number of dots on the edge when there are zero inside, if I = 0, then E = 2 × A + 2. Students may also notice that 2 × I + E comes to a constant value, when the area stays the same. They may be able to combine these two awarenesses and link all three variables, I, E, A, in one formula.

An alternative starting point, for older children perhaps, is to invite exploration of shapes with the same number of 'dots' – meaning the same number of dots if you sum those on the edge and inside. A beginning here might be to draw two '8-dot shapes' (perhaps one with 8 dots on the edge, none inside and another with 6 on the edge, 2 inside) and say: 'These are both 8-dot shapes. Someone come and draw me another, different 8-dot shape'. This is the starting point described in Banwell *et al.* (1986).

96  *Curriculum focus*

The transcript below is taken from 2008, several lessons in to work on Pick's Theorem, having begun in the way described above. The transcript has been edited for ease of reading and deleted sections are indicated by three dots. The shape being discussed is the triangle ABC in Figure 7.6: this shape had been drawn by a student (S2). The class are engaged in trying to find its area. S2 had suggested one way but others in the class disagreed with his answer. When students refer to 'dots' they are seeing a dot at every intersection of the grid lines. So triangle ABC has 8 'dots' inside it and 3 'dots' on the outside (i.e. one at each vertex and none on any edge). S2 himself had just been at the board to explain how he found the area of ABC, which he suggested was eleven square units (an incorrect value). Several students said they wanted to show how they would work out the area.

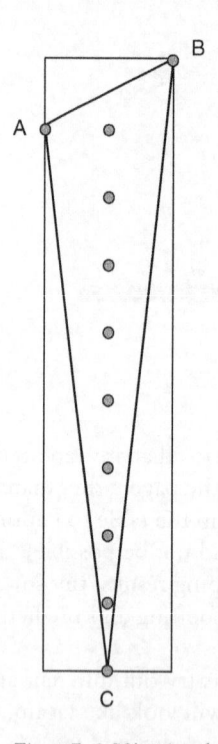

*Figure 7.6* S2's triangle

| 1 | ACs | I'll draw up some more copies of the shape and we can look at some other ways of finding out this area [*draws more copies of triangle ABC*] ... so S3 had a way ... [*S3 comes to the board*] |
|---|---|---|
| 2 | S3 | I've (.) because the outside is three (.) so I halve that ... it'll be one point five and I take away one from eight which is seven and then I add them together |
| 3 | ACs | ... show us how you do it ... |
| 4 | S3 | I'll do (.) half of the outside [*writes ½ O = 1.5*] which is one point five and then I would do (.) inside take one which equals seven [*writes I – 1 = 7*] then I would do one point five add seven which would be eight point five and that would be the area. |

*Primary/secondary transition and geometrical thinking* 97

| 5 | ACs | So (.) lovely demonstration there. Anybody want to ask a question to S3? About what she's done there (.) S2 |
|---|---|---|
| 6 | S2 | Well with the way I done it . . . so that'd be eleven to me. That (.) these are what I think |
| 7 | ACs | . . . any more comments about that? (.)<br>So we've got a difference there (.) S9? |
| 8 | S9 | I think S3's is right, because um (.) that's how you do it and it works on other ones as well. |
| 9 | ACs | It works on other ones as well that you've looked at (.) So that's S3's prediction using this rule, that the area S3 reckons is half of the outside plus the inside take away one [*writes A= ½ O + I − 1*]<br>Okay so we've still got . . .<br>Thank you S3 take a seat [*S3 returns to her seat*]<br>So we've still got the question of what is the area of this one? (.) [*pointing to ABC*]<br>S7 were you going to come and help us with that.<br>[*S7 comes to the board*] |
| 10 | S7 | I'd like do that like that . . . and draw a box round there and round the whole thing [*see Figure 7.6: the box is already shown*]<br>[and then like that like that] |
| 11 | | [*discussion continues for several minutes, focused on finding the area of triangle ABC and confirming that it does come to the answer S3 has predicted, 8.5 square units. I then ask for any further comments*] |
| 12 | S4 | I think S3's is actually right because you (.) I'm also working on ten-dot shapes as well as twenty-four-dot shapes. |
| 13 | ACs | Okay. |
| 14 | S4 | And I just writ down the way that S3 does it and then I've actually worked out one of my twenty-four-dot shapes to see if I got the same area as what I already got and I have. |
| 15 | ACs | Great . . . |
| 16 | S14 | I got a three-dot shape with twenty-four in the middle. |
| 17 | ACs | Great, okay, so you could maybe try and use S3's conjecture to see if it works. |
| 18 | S7 | The way you've done it because I've tried it like with three dot shapes on the outside and it works and then I just used a random shape and it works [ ] |
| 19 | | [*earlier in the lesson, S7 said she had found out why a rule for finding areas worked and S6 had said she wanted to work on making S3's rule into a 'theorem'*] |
| 20 | ACs | Okay (.) Brilliant. And so the question about why that S7 was working on is a really important one. So S3's got this question and S6 is wanting to know is this a theorem? To make it a theorem you've really got to say why and convince us it will work for all shapes. |

In turns 2 and 4, Student 3 suggests an algebraic rule. Student 2 is robust (turn 6) about his own, different, way of calculating the area and in line 8, Student 9 gives a reason why she believes the rule (because it has worked on other shapes she has tried). These students are engaged in classifying, justifying and predicting in relation to the geometrical figure (Big Idea 4). Similarly, Student 4 (turns 12 and 14) gives further justifications for believing S3's rule, as does Student 7 (turn 18). In turn 20, I made what I would see as a metacomment, reinforcing to the class the language of 'theorem' and the importance of asking 'why?'. It would seem as though students (at least the ones who are talking) are engaged in a communal activity, trying to make sense together, and are invested in making things make sense. In asking about 'why?' I am perhaps wanting to focus students back on a geometrical awareness. The algebraic rule of S3's appears to be a process that she has noticed. The limit of the geometrical thinking is perhaps in the checking of the rule with area calculations and the creation of the shapes (such as Figure 7.6).

The lesson start of '8-dot shapes' appears to encourage students into working with more complex shapes than the initial '4-square shapes'. Focusing on 'dot shapes' there is a need to find a way of working out areas beyond 'counting squares' – which would be an effective strategy for the shapes drawn by the student in Figure 7.2. Different starts would be appropriate with different groups of students. The focused and closed task beginnings (see design principles of Chapter 2) force students down some predictable pathways, as well as allowing space for creativity and new thinking.

## From measurement to geometric result

Big Idea 1 is: 'behind every measurement formula lies a geometric result'. The use of trigonometry in school is essentially a measurement formula. The trigonometric ratios give the measure of a length or angle, given certain conditions. Trigonometry may seem an ambitious topic to include in a chapter aimed at students in late primary, early seconday school (aged 10–13 perhaps). In the UK, students need to be able to find angles and lengths using trigonometry as well as understand something of the graphs by aged 16. It is not uncommon for them to only meet these ideas for the first time at age 15. The tasks that follow are an attempt to illustrate how it might be possible to turn a 'measurement formula' into something geometric. Rather than lesson transcripts, this section imagines possible classroom activity.

The ideas sketched below loosely follow the historical development of trigonometry. The first calculation of the 'sine' of an angle was in the context of making a connection between the angle in a circle and the length of the chord subtended by that angle. In Figure 7.7, the angle ß subtends a chord marked by the dashed line. This chord is twice the value of sin(ß), if the circle has a unit radius (see Cooke 2013 for further details). If this

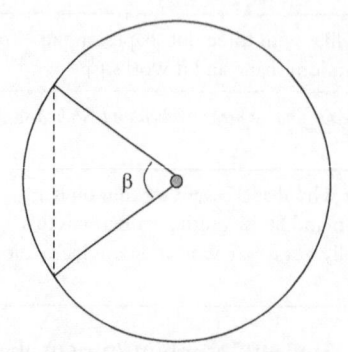

*Figure 7.7* The chord subtended by angle ß

way of thinking about trigonometry is new to you, then you may want to go through, for yourself, the steps of the activities below, which are written up addressed to a teacher, augmented with commentary for the purposes of this book.

### A first lesson

– Imagine a circle . . . and a point or dot on the circle . . . now make this point move around the circumference . . . check you can make it go faster or slower . . . move your dot clockwise . . . now move it anti-clockwise . . . now stop your dot . . . imagine your circle is standing upright on flat ground . . . move your dot to the bottom of the circle, so it is touching the ground as well . . . now start moving your dot anti-clockwise . . .
– As your dot goes around the circle, how high does it go above the ground?

As this visualisation is set up, some students may be 'seeing' it in 3D. Discussion of the height of the dot above the ground may also bring out different ways of interpreting the words used. There will be a need to agree on a way of labelling how far around the circle the dot has gone. Most useful, in terms of linking to standard trigonometric notation, would be to use angles and degrees. But if this task is being done with young children, it perhaps does not matter what convention is adopted initially. Using the clock face is a common suggestion from students.

There may be a need for some questions to provoke further thought, e.g.:

- As the dot travels around the circle, is it ever the same height in two or more places?
- When is the dot half of the full height of the circle above the ground?
- When is it ¼ (or ¾) of the height of the circle?

At some point, students may want to draw some sketches of their mind-images to help them argue – although there can be an extraordinary depth to the visualising if the class are able to hold off the desire to draw and rather keep the images in their minds. However, to help answer the last of these questions, it may be necessary to do some drawings. Students can be supported to create a graph of the changing height of the dot as it moves around the circle.

### *Where this can go*

The image in Figure 7.8 shows one way that the creation of the graph can be supported. Students draw in the vertical height at the different dots around the circumference and 'transfer' those heights to the graph. On this version, the height is measured to the ground the circle is resting on.

As the dot moves around the circle, the height above the ground can literally be copied across to build up the curve. Some labelling of the dots and a corresponding labelling on the $y$-axis is needed. In the standard version, the angle would be counted starting with zero degrees when the dot is at the '3 o'clock' position and

*(continued)*

*(continued)*

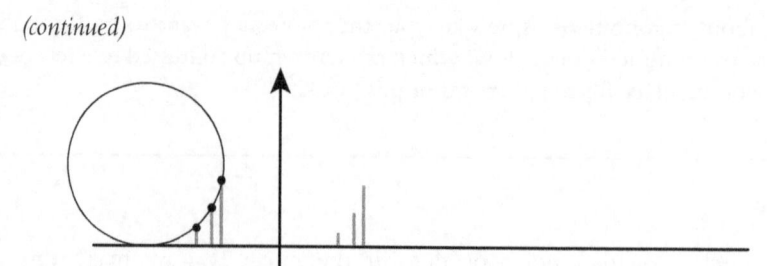

*Figure 7.8* Creating a graph of the 'sine' line

the height taken not to the 'ground' but to a horizontal line going through the centre of the circle (so the dot could be above or below). This set-up accords with the convention for the labelling used in trigonometry. The lengths of the dot above and below the line are given by the sine of the angle (assuming the radius of the circle is of unit length). A similar graph can be produced for the cosine, where instead of focusing on the vertical height, you consider the horizontal distance to a vertical line through the centre of the circle.

## Making the link to triangles

The task above of creating a graph and answering the questions about when the heights are the same seem to me worthwhile in their own right. The question about when the heights are the same can be answered from a geometrical awareness of the movement of the dot (with no measurement needed). At some point, perhaps as students near examinations, a link needs to be made to triangles, which is the context in which students are often required to demonstrate their knowledge of trigonometry. Having worked on the circle image and how the sine and cosine lengths vary students will have, in effect, been working with the image in Figure 7.9.

The hypotenuse has length 1, since we are dealing with unit circles and the 'dot' that was going around the circle has to be imagined at the top of the sin(x) line.

Many standard trigonometry questions asked in examination questions can now be dealt with as enlargements of Figure 7.9. To incorporate the tangent ratio, one addition to the image of a dot going around a circle is required, namely the

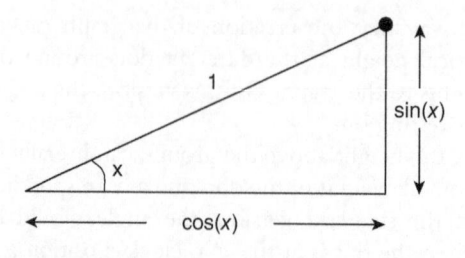

*Figure 7.9* An image of trigonometry

introduction of a vertical tangent line to the circle (see Figure 7.10). The line from the centre to the dot is then extended to meet this tangent line. The height of the tangent line that is cut off is the tangent of the angle (for a unit circle).

As with the image for sine and cosine, the circle image can be reduced to a triangle (see Figure 7.11), where the radius of the circle now runs adjacent to the angle.

And, as with Figure 7.9, the standard trigonometry questions can be dealt with as enlargements of this triangle. The measurement formulae that are trigonometry can be treated geometrically. The challenge of Big Idea 1 is that such a treatment is possible for all measurement formulae.

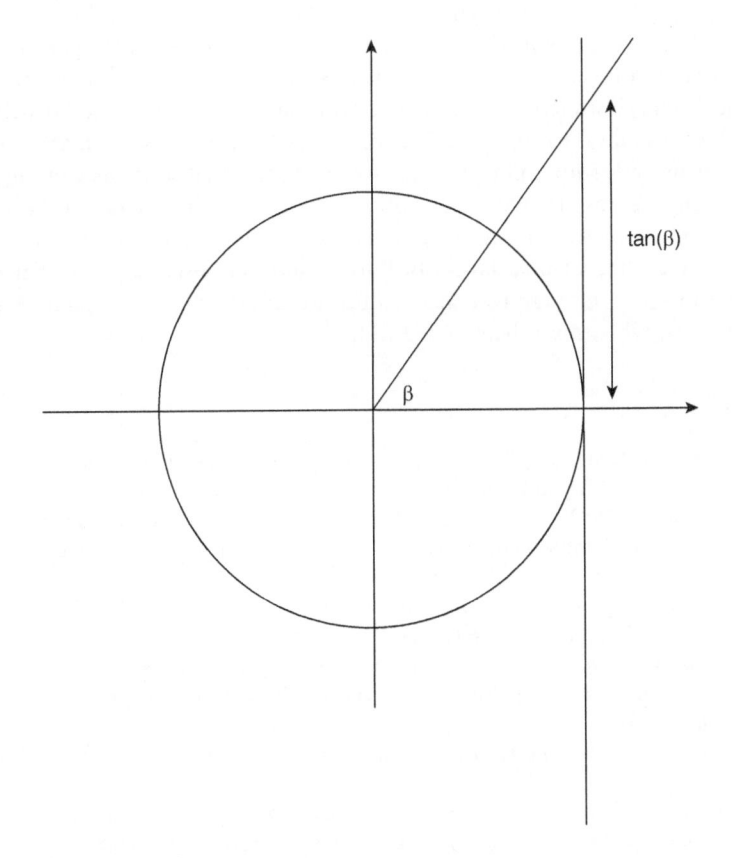

*Figure 7.10* The tangent ratio

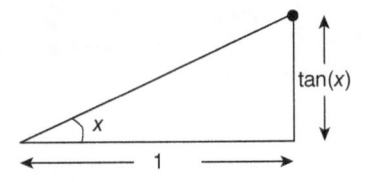

*Figure 7.11* An image of the tangent function

## Discussion

It may seem as though the diagrams for use in the trigonometry task lead to an absolute representation of sine, cosine and tangent. However, the lines represented in the diagrams (by sine, cosine and tangent) are themselves relations, or functions. In the dynamic image, as a dot moves around a circle the sine line labels the changing 'height' of the dot above or below the $x$-axis, in relation to the angle made at the centre. What is being labelled or symbolised is the connection between the angle and the length. It is as easy, with this image, to ask 'what length would be made by an angle of 45 degrees?' as it is to ask 'what angle makes the sine line ½?'. The fact these inverse processes can be considered equally easily is some evidence that a relational symbolism is being employed here.

Dick Tahta (1989: 20) reminds us that 'geometrical experience lies in imagery rather than in the words that accompany or describe such imagery'. Perhaps in all mathematics, but especially in geometry, if students are going to becoming engaged in the activity there must be (at least the possibility of) some mental work that accompanies the marks made on paper. Mental imagery is something that, in my experience, all students can engage in and can become engaged by. However, as with any skill, it needs practice to become routine. There are only so many routines I can establish as a teacher and so the question becomes one of what I value in my classroom. Do I value the visual aspects of mathematics, the mental imagery, enough to make it a feature of every lesson I teach? And a researchable question is: what might happen if I did?

## References

Banwell, C., Saunders, K. and Tahta, D. (1986). *Starting points: for teaching mathematics in middle and secondary schools.* St Albans, UK: Tarquin Publishers.

Brown L. and Waddingham, J. (1982) *An addendum to Cockroft.* Avon, RLDU. Available online at the STEM centre website www.nationalstemcentre.org.uk/elibrary/resource/6910/an-addendum-to-cockcroft.

Burger, W. F. and Shaughnessy, J. M. (1986). Characterizing the Van Hiele levels of development in geometry. *Journal for Research in Mathematics Education,* 17: 31–48.

Cooke, R. (2013). *The history of mathematics: a brief course.* New Jersey: John Wiley & Sons.

Hewitt, D. (1999). Arbitrary and necessary part 1: a way of viewing the mathematics curriculum. *For the Learning of Mathematics,* 19(3): 2–9.

Lakatos, I. (1976). *Proofs and refutations: the logic of mathematical discovery.* Cambridge: Cambridge University Press.

Sinclair, N., Pimm, D. and Skelin, M. (2012). *Developing essential understanding of geometry for teaching mathematics in Grades 6–8.* Reston, VA: National Council of Teachers of Mathematics

Tahta, D. (1989). Is there a geometric imperative? *Mathematics Teaching,* 129: 20–9.

Weber, C. (2014). Exercise in mathematical imagining: setting out a teaching instrument that evokes imaginings and utilises visualisation in secondary school mathematics. *Informal proceedings of the day conference of the British Society for Research into Learning Mathematics,* 34(1): 125–31. Available online at: www.bsrlm.org.uk/informalproceedings.html (accessed 23 November 2014).

# 8 Secondary school

Adolescence and algebraic activity

In the UK, the education of adolescents proceeds in largely the same manner as for younger students. This seems an odd situation, given what we know, developmentally, about changes taking place at that time of life. Dick Tahta (1989: 28) challenges us in strident terms to think differently:

> It is not good enough to offer adolescents merely more of the same experience they have had when they were younger. It is not good enough to use something as important and pervasive as geometry merely as a convenient medium for public examination and the selection of suitable candidates for higher education. Nor is it good enough always to algebracise geometrical experience, or to do so prematurely. What we do need to do, is to think in terms of the concerns of students themselves at this stage . . . their intellectual, emotional, social and spiritual needs. Of course, this is easier said than done. These are complex needs . . . In some ways, adults have to choose certain simplifications of them in order to survive, in order to be able to act in the world, however imperfectly. But it is the right of adolescents to explore complexity; and it is the duty of teachers to help them maintain it.

So, how might teaching be different when working with adolescents? Watson (2007) has written about the needs of an education for adolescents and suggested this can be a time when a 'scientific' understanding of concepts is developed, i.e. a time when as teachers we can try to work with students on appreciating the power of building networks of concepts. A key issue when working with adolescents is the issue of students' identity in relation to mathematics. Adolescence is a time of testing boundaries and experimenting with relationships. This is a time when the study of mathematics, if it is to engage students, needs to appear vital. Piaget wrote of adolescence as being the time when abstract thought becomes possible. The previous chapters have made clear, I hope, my conviction that abstract and algebraic thinking is possible much earlier. However, Piaget's ideas are perhaps a reminder that adolescence is a time when the abstract can become a preoccupation. In the Waldorf School tradition, there is a recognition in the teaching of art that adolescence is a time when students can become frustrated at not being able to create accurate representations of scenes but can become engaged in abstract art. Dick Tahta has wondered[1] what an equivalent recognition might be within mathematics education.

Adolescence is a time in which passions can be developed (Gattegno 1971). Our identity is linked to the communities in which we spend our time. Dick Tahta (1989) wrote about the idea of a communal mathematics in school. One challenge, then, is to find ways of creating the conditions for a communal approach to mathematics in which adolescents feel a personal engagement with abstract issues. In Chapters 5 and 7, suggestions were made for employing the power of visualisation as a teaching strategy. One way of working communally is to develop visualisation as an element of mathematics teaching, for example, along the lines suggested in those chapters.

Adolescence is also a time when students are experimenting with issues of control. Activities that have elements of self-checking can be engaging in that feedback is not always required from the teacher. The 1089 activity from Chapter 1 has this element of self-checking. This theme is taken up by Watson (2008: 24):

> [Y]ear 10 level adolescents responded well to being given authority in aspects of mathematical work: checking answers, giving explanations, asking new questions, testing hypotheses, and problem-posing. These actions appeal to the adolescent concerns of being in charge, feeling powerful, understanding the world, and being able to argue in ways which make adults listen. They offer more than belonging by doing what everyone else is doing, or being heard merely through sharing what has already been done.

The sense of 'belonging' links to the idea of adolescence being a time of exploring identities. How can we support students to feel a 'belonging' in relation to the doing of mathematics? This chapter takes up the challenges posed above in relation to the teaching and learning of algebra.

## Algebraic activity

Chapter 4 touched on the question of the nature of algebra, in relation to Gattegno's notion that mathematics is the study of relationships, and that this is inherently algebraic. It seems important to expand on the question of 'what is algebra?' before considering activities that may be appropriate for adolescents. An important characterisation of algebra was provided by Caroline Kieran (1996) in which she split algebraic thinking into three components. This was the definition of algebra adopted by a Royal Society and Joint Mathematical Council of the UK report (1997) into the teaching and learning of algebra. The three components (used in the report) were:

> *Generational activities* which involve: generating expressions and equations which are the objects of algebra, for example, equations which represent quantitative problem situations (see, for example, Bell 1995); expressions of generality from geometric patterns or numerical sequences (for example, Mason *et al.* 1985); and expressions of the rules governing numerical relationships (for example, Lee and Wheeler 1987).
>
> *Transformational rule-based activities*, for example, factorising, manipulating and simplifying algebraic expressions and solving equations. These activities are predominantly concerned with equivalence, form and the preservation of essence.
>
> *Global, meta-level activities*, for example, awareness of mathematical structure, awareness of constraints of problem situations, justifying, proving and predicting, and problem-solving. These activities are not exclusive to algebra (Royal Society and Joint Mathematical Council of the UK 1997: 4).

*Adolescence and algebraic activity* 105

The examples given in this extract point to important different aspects of working with algebra. It is perhaps a focus on the transformational aspect of algebra (which can seem pointless) that contributes to the folklore sense that algebra is unintelligible and meaningless. And, in contrast, it is perhaps the more global meta-level activities that could bring meaning to algebra (and mathematics more generally) that are less prevalent.

Generational activities might be in play if students were working on generalising number patterns arising from a growing sequence of shapes made out of matches, such as in Figure 8.1.

A typical task would be for students to count the number of matches (4, 7, 10) and then predict the number of matches in the next shape in the sequence and then generalise from the number pattern.

Taking this example, it is possible to approach the algebra in a structured manner that immediately gives the activity a more global feel. Rather than presenting students with a growing sequence of shapes, Laurinda Brown has shown the power of starting from a single example and getting students to describe how they would draw the shape. You might want to try this for yourself.

The activity might be structured with the following suggestions:

> Look at Figure 8.2 . . . draw the shape again in some kind of organised way . . . pay attention to the precise order in which you draw the lines . . . can you explain to someone else, so that they would draw the lines in exactly the same order you did?

There are usually a variety of methods within any class. Some students might draw all the matches on the top row first, then on the bottom and then fill in the middle. Others might start by drawing one square, and then add on backwards 'C' shapes of matches. Or, perhaps the first thing drawn is a single line, followed by backwards 'C' shapes. The task now is to work out the number of matches in Figure 8.2, without counting them all, and making use of the way you drew it.

Taking the three methods above in turn, would give the following expressions, for six squares:

*Figure 8.1* A growing pattern of squares

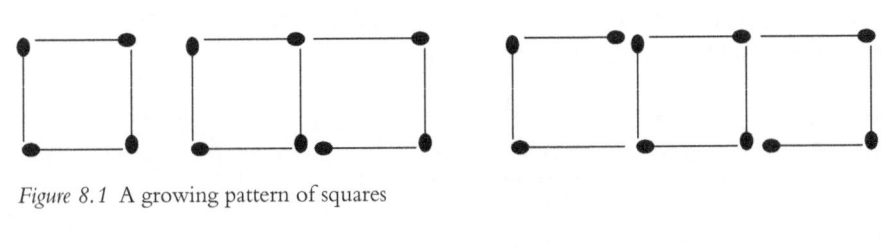

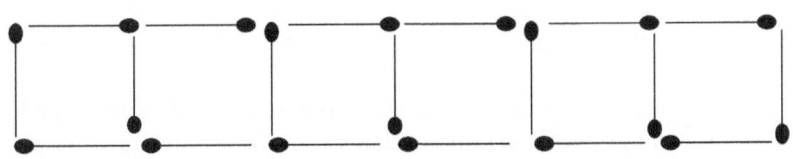

*Figure 8.2* A matchstick pattern with 6 squares

$6 \to 6 + 6 + 7$

$6 \to 4 + 5 \times 3$

$6 \to 1 + 6 \times 3$

It is possible to immediately generalise from any of these structured ways of viewing the matchstick patterns. For example, to draw 100 matches would need:

$100 \to 100 + 100 + 101$

$100 \to 4 + 99 \times 3$

$100 \to 1 + 100 \times 3$

And the pattern can be extended again to generate three different algebraic rules. Working with a focus on the global meta can provoke a need for the other forms of algebra. For example, having generated three (or more) different algebraic expressions for the same number pattern, there can be useful transformational work done in showing that the three forms are in fact equivalent.

## Algebraic thinking in the classroom

As my own teaching developed I became more and more attuned to opportunities for working on algebra no matter what the content. As a department we introduced algebra to students in year 7 (age 11) in the context of the first task we did with them at secondary school, which was '1089' (described in Chapter 1).

After perhaps six or more hours of lessons on making and testing conjectures about three, four, and five-digit numbers, students often became firmly convinced that, for example, all three-digit numbers would end up as 1,089. The question as teachers we would pose again and again was 'but why do these conjectures work?' At some point, towards the end of work on the project, we knew that we would show students an algebraic proof of the three-digit case. This would be done slowly, with a numerical example next to it. Students would be familiar with using *abc* to stand for the three digits of a number, where, for this project *a* had to be bigger than *c*. As teachers we would emphasise (often dramatically) that what we were going to do was deal with all possibilities at once. The proof would end up looking something like this:

|   | $7^6$ | $6^5$ | $^{1}2$ |   | $a^{a-1}$ | $b^{b-1+10}$ | $c^{+10}$ |
|---|---|---|---|---|---|---|---|
| − | 2 | 6 | 7 | − | c | b | a |
|   | 4 | 9 | 5 |   | a−1−c | 9 | c+10−a |
| + | 5 | 9 | 4 | + | c+10−a | 9 | a−1−c |
|   | 10 | 8 | 9 |   | 10 | 8 | 9 |

When this is done slowly, step by step with the class, working on the number example first, the first '9' to appear in the algebraic version (underneath the b) often brought out audible cries of surprise from students. Students had generally noticed that with three-digit sums there was always a '9' in the middle of the answer to the subtraction, and here it is again, but this time when starting with the algebra.

A typical teaching strategy, having gone through this proof would then be to rub it off the board and get students, in groups, to try and re-create it. Some students were then able to extend the idea to prove their own conjectures for higher or lower numbers of digits. Not all students would be able to do this, but that was never the intention. What we wanted was for students' first experience of algebra to be one where (to borrow a phrase from Laurinda Brown) the *algebra did something that could not be done without it*. There would be many more opportunities for students to develop the transformational skills needed to execute the proof, but what we hoped all students would appreciate was that algebra helped answer a meaningful question that many of them were asking: 'why is it always 1089?'

Following on from the discussion of relational symbols and representations (Chapter 5) there is a question of how algebraic symbolism can be worked on in a relational manner. It is perhaps clear from the discussion in Chapter 5 that attempts (that I have certainly made) to represent $x$ as a length or area would need to be done carefully to avoid the letters assuming a rigid absoluteness that could make the transition into fluent working with algebra (e.g., to perform transformations) problematic.

Banwell *et al.* 1986 describe a 'Function game', and there is also video footage of Bob Davis from the 1950s using the same game as a task with young children. I first saw Laurinda Brown play this game when she taught my year 8 class in my second year of teaching. I remember at the time feeling this game was so powerful it should be known by every mathematics teacher in the world! In the game (best played in silence), the teacher (with a 'rule' in mind) writes on the board (slowly, dramatically, pausing to think) two starting values, and then one for students to try, for example:

4 → 9

6 → 13

2 →

At this point, the pen can be offered to the class for someone to come up and fill in a number to the right of the arrow. The teacher will write ☹ or ☺ depending on whether the answer fits the teacher's rule or not. It can be helpful to keep incorrect answers and simply write new suggestions to the right. When a student gets it correct, they can be invited to write the next starting number. The board might look like this:

4 → 9

6 → 13

2 → 4 ☹ 5 ☺

3 →

If the silence is accepted by the class there can be a build of engagement as some students 'get' the rule. One strategy to help those who do not get it, after a while, is to invite any student who wants, to write a 'clue' on the board. The teacher can also ask students

108  Curriculum focus

to choose 'new' numbers that might help. Students might start writing large numbers. As a teacher, I might intervene and write one where students have to find the starting number:

← 21

At some point, when most or all the class have the rule, I will take the pen to ask:

N →

The algebra here is being used to describe a relation between a (by now quite long) set of pairs of numbers. Students in the UK can have a misconception that letters have specific values, so answers such as 'M' are not uncommon (☹). It is important to try to capture, algebraically all the different ways students got their answers, for example:

N → N times 2 add 1
N → N + N + 1
N → N + 1 + N
N → N × 2 + 1
N → NN + 1

Some notation will need to be explained (e.g. that NN would mean the number multiplied by itself). The equivalence, or otherwise, of these rules can be worked on as a class. A rule for going 'backwards' can also be asked for. In the department where I worked we would also spend time creating graphs of these rules (partly to test if they were all the same) and then issue the challenge of whether students could predict what the graph would look like from simply looking at the rule.

In Banwell et al. (1986) there is the suggestion that there would be a power in always adopting the same (tabular) notation whenever functional relationships are being considered. From the function game, more straightforward skills can be worked on, for example, if N + N + 1 = 31, then what was N?

It was not uncommon for year 7 students at my school to comment that there seemed to be two kinds of algebra, one where letters stood for 'all numbers' (like in the 1089 proof, or the function game rules) and one where letters had one value to be found. This awareness echoes a comment in Chapter 5 about how Bob Davis would carefully distinguish in his teaching between identities (true for all numbers) and equations (true for certain values).

How is it possible to continue working with students to develop ever-increasing algebraic skills, where there remains a sense of the power of algebra? The remainder of this chapter describes three tasks of increasing mathematical demand, where there are opportunities for communal mathematics and for global meta-level activity. These tasks are all written up as they were for the purposes of guiding teaching in the school where I was head of department, so the tone will feel different and addressed towards you, the teacher. The format is similar across the task write-ups, with some detail about a possible starting point and then suggestions of where it could go, dependent on the interest of students and teacher. I reflect on the way these tasks link to the issues raised from Part One in a discussion at the end.

## Task one: 'Both ways'

### A first lesson

Have already drawn on the board:

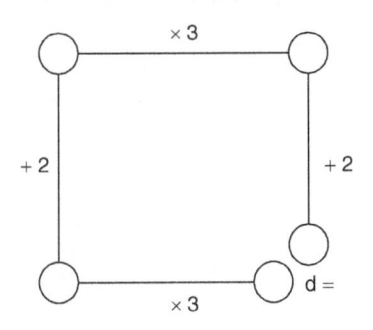

```
      × 3
   O───────O
   │       │
+2 │       │ +2
   │       │
   O───────O  d =
      × 3
```

Invite a student to suggest a number to go in the top left-hand circle. Work this through, and calculate d, the difference in answers.

*Depending on the classroom culture that exists within the group you may, at this stage, be able to ask for questions from the students; e.g. will the difference always be the same? what happens if we ×4? Otherwise work through one more example together and invite comments. At this stage it is likely someone will predict the difference will always be the same no matter what number you put in. Write this up as a conjecture.*

Invite the class to try out big numbers, negatives, fractions, decimals, staying with ×3 and +2. There is an opportunity for a common board – e.g. starting numbers where d does not equal 4.

If some students quickly become convinced d = 4 they can be invited to think about proving this, or else multiplying/adding by a different number and seeing if they can predict the difference. It is important that the operations on opposite sides of the square are always the same.

At the point where the majority of the class are convinced about d = 4 in the case above, introduce an algebraic proof (or even better get a student to show the class). Students should always write down what a proof shows them. The class are probably now ready for the challenge.

Challenge: If you × and + by any number, can you predict the difference?
Again there is an opportunity for a common board and checking, proof:

| Operation 1 | Operation 2 | d |
|---|---|---|
| ×3 | +2 | 4 |
|  |  |  |
|  |  |  |
|  |  |  |
|  |  |  |

*(continued)*

*(continued)*

## Where this can go

There is a lot of opportunity for algebraic proof in this activity. Some may even be able to generalise to × n and + m. At this point they can try operations other than multiply and add, and try to systematically work through all possible combinations.

## Mathematical aims

- Writing algebra
- Opportunities to practice algebra as generalised arithmetic
- Expanding brackets
- Collecting like terms
- Proof

## Task two: Equable shapes

### Starting point

Draw these two rectangles on the board.

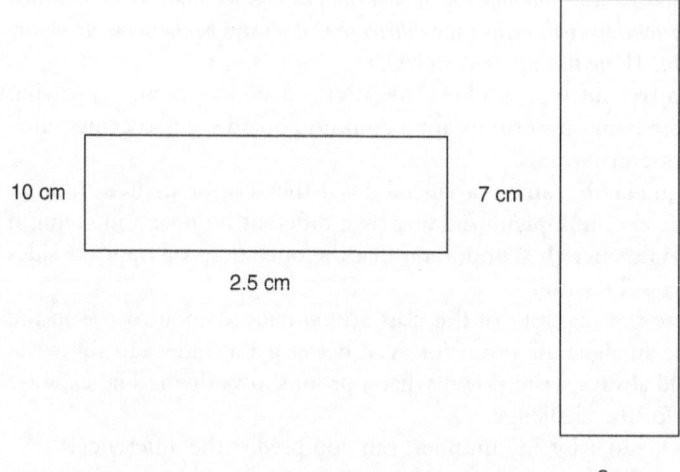

10 cm

2.5 cm

7 cm

3 cm

Question: What is the same or different about these two shapes?

*Someone will comment on the rectangles being different sizes. They may mention area and perimeter. If not, introduce these terms as ways that mathematicians determine the sizes of shapes.*

Add underneath each rectangle,
For the first rectangle, A = 25 and P = 25; for the second one A = 21, P = 20.

*Invite students to comment on what is the same or different between these values. Someone will notice that the first rectangle has the same value for Area and Perimeter and the second one does not.*

'Mathematicians call shapes which have the same value for area and perimeter, EQUABLE shapes. So our first rectangle is equable and the second one is not'.

Ask students what they could ask if they were 'thinking mathematically' about what we have just done.

Examples:

- Are there any other equable rectangles?
- Is there an equable square?
- What other equable shapes are there?

Initially the focus should be on strategies for finding other equable rectangles, rather than answers; e.g. trial and error, or students may try to use or adapt the ratio of lengths in the first rectangle – if one length is a quarter will it always be equable? If I double the lengths will it still be equable?

A useful skill for trial and error is to 'be organised' – perhaps by fixing a height and then finding the width (if one exists) that makes the rectangle equable.

A common board may be used to help with being organised:

| Height | Width | Area | Perimeter |
|--------|-------|------|-----------|
|        |       |      |           |
|        |       |      |           |
|        |       |      |           |
|        |       |      |           |

## *Where this can go*

At some point it is likely someone will suggest (or you can) using an algebra method. Using a letter for both sides leads to solving:

$$ab = 2a + 2b.$$

This is not particularly helpful. More useful is to choose a fixed length (e.g. 6) and call the other side n.

Then equating area and perimeter leads to the equation:

$12 + 2n = 6n$, which now is accessible.

It is interesting to create a table of height and widths of equable rectangles. If answers are kept as fractions there are some intriguing patterns that can be generalised and even proved.

## *Further extensions*

Looking at equable triangles/regular polygons is one way of extending the task and gets students into trigonometry and/or Pythagoras which can subsequently lead to working circles and finding approximations to pi.

*(continued)*

*(continued)*

Triangles can be approached algebraically (although this is complex!) in a similar way to rectangles – e.g. look at right angled triangles, fix the width and call the height n.

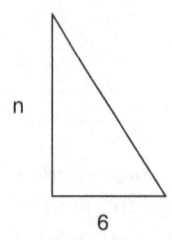

Equating area and perimeter will lead to some complex algebra – but accessible and useful practice for Higher Tier GCSE students, e.g. after going through one example with a class they could try and repeat for different fixed values.

At Foundation Tier, students can use trial and error on right-angled triangles, specifying 2 sides and using Pythagoras' Theorem to calculate the third and hence the perimeter.

To work on other polygons, stick to regular ones! Proceed by splitting up the polygon into triangles which meet at the centre. If you fix the perimeter, you then know the length and angle of a right-angled triangle. Using trigonometry you can find the height and so calculate the area and perimeter. You can use trial and error, or else call one side n (in fact 2n is easier) – see illustration of octagon below for an example.

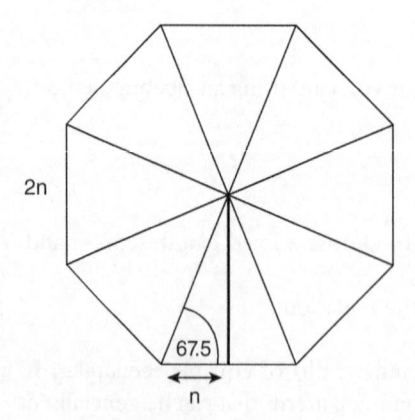

The perimeter = 2n × 8.
The area of one triangle = n × (n × Tan(67.5)).
These can be made equal and solved to find n.

A further table of results can be created to record the sizes of the equable shapes (is there only one regular one for each number of sides?). You must include the height of the triangle as a column, as there is something wonderful and slightly mysterious here!

## Task three: Graphs of rational functions

### A first lesson

*In the first lesson I try and link back to previous work on functions and graphs. The motivation to look at graphing rational functions will come simply from the mathematical extension of previous work and will be introduced by me.*

In silence, begin a linear function game, e.g.

3 → 5

5 → 9

9 →

Hopefully students will spot the rule and pattern fairly quickly, and I or they will introduce algebra to express this, $x \to$

Again, much more quickly than in previous years, sketch these points on a grid (no need for students to copy it) and highlight the gradient and *y*-intercept and how these link to the rule.

*My attention here is not on whether everyone remembers this, or can now use $y = mx + c$. There will be opportunity to revisit this idea within the more complex space of rational functions. This beginning is more about reminding students how to generate co-ordinates from rules.*

– Up to this point in maths most of the graphs you have ever looked at are of this form; some number multiplied by *x* and then another number added or subtracted. One way that mathematics advances is that someone one day decides to see what happens if you apply an idea from one context to a different context. This is what we are going to do today. You have all met the idea of division since you were in primary school. What probably none of you have done is apply this idea to graphs. In this project we are going to be exploring what kinds of graph we get if instead of just looking at $y = ax + b$, we look at graphs of the form $y = \dfrac{ax+b}{cx+d}$ or even $y = \dfrac{ax^2 + bx + c}{dx + e}$.

[*Decision here about whether to introduce the second type at this point – I personally always like to get in as soon as possible the extent of the complexity of the task.*]

So, could someone give me an example of a graph of the first type? Make up any numbers you like for a, b, c and d.

a is 1, b is 2, c is 3 and d is 4.

– Okay, so we are going to plot, $y = \dfrac{x+2}{3x+4}$, we will work together until everyone can do this and then you will have a go at doing your own ones, with the challenge of being able to predict what they will look like before working out any points. Anyone got any ideas on this one before we begin? [*You may not get any response to this, but still worth asking!*]

– All we need, in fact, with these graphs, is to get an accurate sketch. We don't need to plot loads and loads of points, we just need to capture the key features. So, any suggestions about how to begin?

*(continued)*

114 *Curriculum focus*

*(continued)*

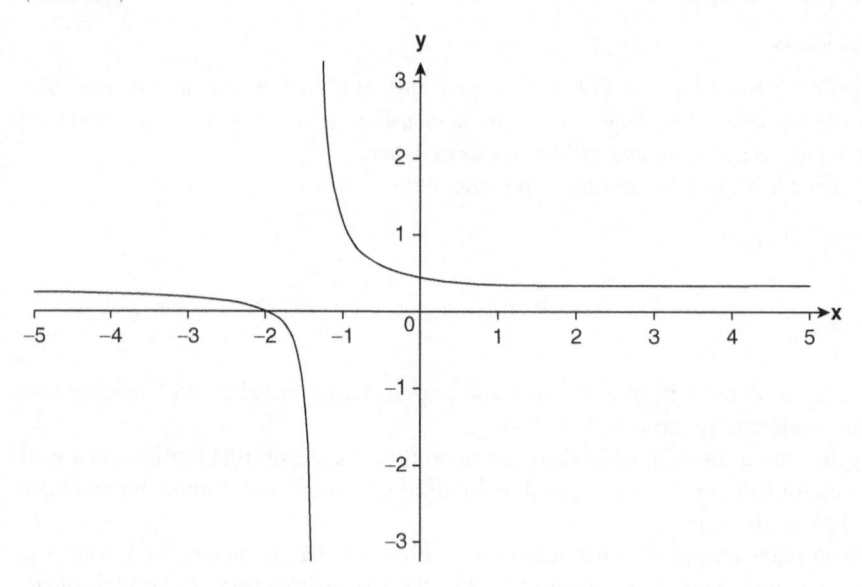

*Figure 8.3* Graph of a rational function

Some key points need to come out of this discussion, for sketching these graphs, which need to be written clearly somewhere for students to refer to when doing their own ones:

1. Find what happens when $x = 0$
2. Find what happens when $y = 0$
3. Find when the denominator $= 0$ (introduce the words 'vertical asymptote' to describe this)
4. Find what happens for large +ve and −ve values of $x$ (to give the horizontal asymptote – you can also deal with this by dividing top and bottom by $x$ and then considering what will happen as $x$ tends to + or − infinity)
5. (Depending on how the discussion goes) Find what happens either side of the vertical asymptote

It will probably take most of a lesson to establish these points and go through them for the one example. It is important students do end up with a sketch in the first lesson, with asymptotes labelled and also points where the graph crosses the axes.

### Where this can go

The basic task is for students to try their own rules and try to predict what the graph will look like. Do not be surprised if these take a long time for some students to do! Graphs should be done on paper and pinned up on a wall, with the equation written large. Workings can be done in students' exercise books.

Students may get conjectures around:

- predicting the horizontal asymptote (e.g., $y = \frac{a}{b}$);
- generalising the equation of the vertical asymptote;

- predicting overall shape (i.e., 'which way around' it is);
- generalising where the intercepts are.

## Possibilities

Students can go onto the second type of graph. In general there will no longer be a horizontal asymptote, but an oblique one, which can be a little tricky to find – one method is to rearrange the top so it factorises with the bottom, e.g., for $y = \dfrac{x^2 + 5x + 7}{x + 2}$ :

$$y = \dfrac{x^2 + 5x + 7}{x + 2} \Rightarrow y = \dfrac{x^2 + 2x + (3x + 7)}{x + 2} \Rightarrow y = \dfrac{x^2 + 2x}{x + 2} + \dfrac{3x + 7}{x + 2}$$

$$\Rightarrow y = x + \dfrac{3x + 7}{x + 2}$$

As $x \to \infty$

$$\Rightarrow y \to x + 3$$

So the graph tends towards $y = x + 3$.

## Typical mathematical content

- Reading algebra
- Substituting into formulae, including very large numbers
- Plotting co-ordinates
- Arithmetic with negatives
- Gradients and intercepts of straight line graphs
- Generalising with algebra
- Transforming equations
- Solving linear equations

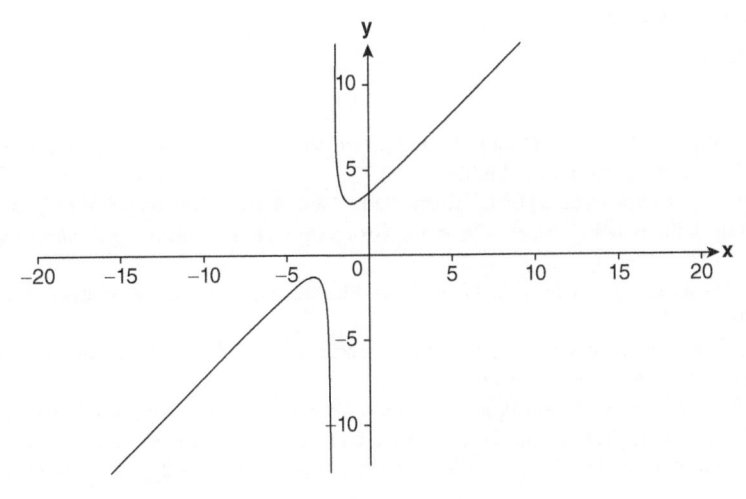

*Figure 8.4* Graph of a rational function with quadratic numerator

## Discussion

A similarity of the three tasks detailed above is the complexity of what is on offer and the algebra serving a purpose. With the 'Both Ways' task, students first notice a pattern in the differences; the algebra can help them express or discover the structure of the problem that leads to this pattern. Algebra is used for justification (hence global meta-level). Transformational moves that I have seen confuse students, particularly around the use of brackets, can become obvious with this task. For example, when generalising the starting problem suggested above, if you start with $n$, going down you get $(n + 2)$ which must be multiplied by 3. If students have tried out several numbers in the Both Ways puzzle, it is possible to gain an intuitive sense that the starting number and the '+2' bit are multiplied by 3. In other words, it can become intuitive that 3 lots of $(n + 2)$ must be $3n + 6$. The algebra can express the relationships in the simple puzzle, in other words '$n$' can become a relational symbol (see Chapter 4).

In the 'Equable Shapes' task, solving equations for rectangles such as $12 + 2n = 6n$ can function in a similar way to the Both Ways expansion of brackets. Because the algebra arises from a context and symbolises the action of equating area and perimeter it is possible for students, again, to gain an intuitive sense of solving these kinds of equation.

The three tasks are good exemplars of the design principles from Chapter 2, for example, starting with closed tasks and things for students to contrast that naturally lead to questions. 'Graphs of Rational Functions' forces students to engage in relating algebraic symbols to each other within a complex but meaningful activity, in that there is always a linking back from what is done (transformationally) with the functions and what this means for the graph. In the UK, students would only need to be able to sketch such functions in the context of an exam at age 17 or 18. When we used this task in the school where I worked, it was with 14- and 15-year-olds. By working on these more complex ideas, what students seemed to actually sort out were skills such as substituting into equations, solving equations with fractions and graphing $y = mx + c$, in other words, all the skills that were on the syllabus for their age.

## Note

1 Informal personal communication.

## References

Banwell, C., Saunders, K., and Tahta, D. (1986). *Starting points: for teaching mathematics in middle and secondary schools*. St Albans, UK: Tarquin Publishers.

Bell, A. (1995). Purpose in school algebra. In C. Kieran (ed.) New perspectives on school algebra: papers and discussions of the ICME-7 Algebra Working Group (special issue). *Journal of Mathematical Behaviour 14*: 41–73.

Gattegno, C. (1971). *The adolescent and his will*. New York: Educational Solutions Worldwide Inc., republished in 2010.

Kieran, C. (1996). The changing face of school algebra. Invited lecture presented at the *Eighth International Congress on Mathematics Education*, Seville, Spain.

Lee, L. and Wheeler, D. (1987). *Algebraic thinking in high school students: their conceptions of generalisation and justification* (research report). Montreal, Canada: Concordia University, Mathematics Department.

Mason, J., Graham, A., Pimm, D. and Gower, N. (1985). *Routes to roots of algebra*. Milton Keynes: Open University Press.

Royal Society and Joint Mathematical Council (RS/JMC) (1997). *Teaching and Learning Algebra pre-19.* Report of a RS/JMC Working Group. London: Royal Society, Carlton House Terrace.

Tahta, D. (1989). Is there a geometric imperative? *Mathematics Teaching, 129*: 20–9.

Watson, A. (2007). Adolescence and secondary mathematics. In D. Kuchemann (ed.), *Proceedings of the British Society for Research into Learning Mathematics, 27*(3): 108–14.

Watson, A. (2008) Adolescent learning and secondary mathematics. *Proceedings of the 2008 Annual Meeting of the Canadian Mathematics Education Study Group*, pp. 21–32. Available online at www://cmesg.ca/ (accessed 17 September 2010).

# 9  Post-16 and infinity

With post-16 mathematics in the UK, there is a need for a different way of working (again) compared to approaches for earlier years. Typically, textbooks play a significant role in students' learning and the question arises: how such study can be made engaging?

There is a strong sense that notions of infinity can be engaging with students of any age. At the post-16 level, considerations of infinity can become more rigorous and the 'taming' of infinity can shed light on the power of a mathematical endeavour. Taming is perhaps the wrong word here, but there is certainly a sense that infinity can be considered as an object or a process about which things can be said. At this age, students may become committed to further study of mathematics at university.

## Shot through with infinity

Gattegno (1984: 20) wrote that 'all mathematics is shot through with infinity' and although this is a phrase used already in the book, it warrants further unpacking. To take the phrase literally may require a rethinking of what 'mathematics' means. I can see 'infinity' in some of the tasks already described in this book.

- The '1089' task (Chapters 1 and 8):
    - being able to choose 'any' three–digit (with first digit bigger than last);
    - extending to work on four, five-digit calculations (and the possibility of working on any number of digits);
- The 'Frogs' task (Chapter 3):
    - being able to choose any number of students on each side;
    - finding a rule to predict the number of moves for any number of students;
- 'Arithmogons' (Chapter 5):
    - being able to place any numbers in the boxes;
    - finding a rule to solve the triangle arithmogons in every case;
    - extending to arithmogons with any number of sides.

In these tasks, the infinity arises out of the awareness of structure or awareness of relationships. It is at the moment that, as a learner, I recognise a conjecture about three-digit numbers (with the '1089' task) that questions arise about all other numbers of digits. In other words, the infinite potential of the tasks arise at the moment I become aware of features of their structure (e.g. that there are a limited number of 'answers' with the 1089 task, or that in 'Frogs' there is a pattern in the minimum number of moves). Appendix 2 to this book gives a task at post-16 level (linked to introducing complex numbers) that shares this sense of an exploration of an infinite structure.

However, the focus of this chapter is on a different aspect of infinity, or on how to symbolise infinite processes. Perhaps one of the most intuitive ways to access ideas of infinity in a manner that requires some symbolism is through consideration of recursive processes. A simple but surprising illustration of recursion can be achieved through hooking up a video camera to a display and then pointing the camera at that display. You may want to think for a moment what you would see (Figure 9.1 offers a sketch of the result). How would you represent what is happening here and why?

A similar sense of recursion is achieved in paintings or prints where somewhere in the picture is a depiction of the picture itself.

Another way of approaching recursion is through computer routines that call up themselves. Students may have experience of the openware MSW Logo, or the related programme Scratch, also produced by the Massachusetts Institute of Technology. In this environment, you control a 'Sprite' that can leave a trail as it moves. It is possible to define 'blocks' of commands and then, within a block, call up the block itself. The simple programme in Figure 9.2 creates the spiral on the right, in an unending routine.

The block 'Spiral' is defined with a variable 'number1'. This 'Spiral' moves the Sprite on the screen 10 units (which is a fairly short distance) and then rotates the Sprite

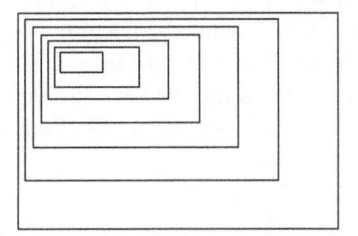

*Figure 9.1* An image of recursion

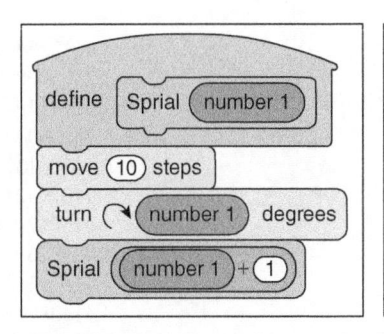

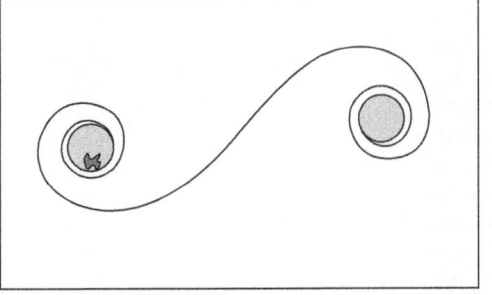

*Figure 9.2* A simple recursive programme in Scratch

'number1' degrees, before calling up the block again, with the angle of turn one degree more. Altering the '+1' value can change the number of 'nodes' of the spiral (trying to predict the shape is an interesting task!).

Recursion can be used to solve equations. When faced with a quadratic equation, an alternative to the formula, or completing the square, is to make $x^2$ the subject, divide through by $x$ and treat the equation as a recurrence relation. For example, to solve:

$x^2 - 6x + 7 = 0$, you can rearrange it to get $x^2 = 6x - 7$, and from there to: $x = (6x - 7)/x$ and now all that is needed is a starting value for $x$. A spreadsheet allows for quick calculations. Starting with $x = 1$, the recurrence relation converges to a value around $x = 4.414$ (see Table 9.1).

Some experience with recursion can perhaps give students the sense that infinite processes can be used and represented. It may be that working with activities involving recursion pre-16 can prepare students for the more formal treatment of infinite processes that comes later on.

## Limits and limiting processes

A lot has been written, academically, about students' difficulties with the concept of limit, a limit being an infinite process. The example below illustrates the dangers of arguments from limiting processes.

Imagine a square of unit length. If you can only move in the directions of the sides, what is the minimum length required to get from one corner to the opposite corner? The diagrams in Figure 9.3 show three different routes. What is their length?

It is not hard to verify that in all three cases the length of the route is 2 units. The number of steps can be increased and the length remains at 2. It would be possible to have so many steps that the route covered was indistinguishable from a straight line across the square. Hence it may appear intuitive to conclude that 'in the limit' we have shown that the length of the diagonal of a square is 2 units. However, a consideration of Pythagoras'

Table 9.1 Recurrence calculation for $x = (6x - 7)/x$

| $x$ | $(6x - 7)/x$ |
|---|---|
| 1 | −1 |
| −1 | 13 |
| 13 | 5.461538462 |
| 5.461538462 | 4.718309859 |
| 4.718309859 | 4.51641791 |
| 4.51641791 | 4.450099141 |
| 4.450099141 | 4.427001337 |
| 4.427001337 | 4.418794243 |
| 4.418794243 | 4.415857445 |
| 4.415857445 | 4.4148039 |
| 4.4148039 | 4.41442561 |
| 4.41442561 | 4.414289736 |

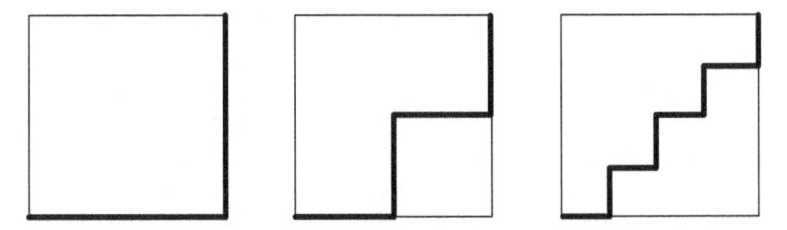

*Figure 9.3* Routes across a square

Theorem tells us that the diagonal of a unit square has length $\sqrt{2}$ units, roughly 1.4. Our 'limiting' argument has gone wrong. We must be wary, perhaps, when we are not arguing about processes that tend to zero in a straight line!

David Tall (1992: 5) wrote about students' difficulties with limits in the context of work in the calculus and, in summary, he lists some of the issues as:

- restricted mental images of functions;
- the Leibniz notation – a 'useful fiction' or a genuine meaning;
- difficulties in translating real-world problems into calculus formulation;
- difficulties in selecting and using appropriate representations;
- algebraic manipulation – or lack of it;
- difficulties in absorbing complex new ideas in a limited time;
- difficulties in handling quantifiers in multiply-quantified definitions;
- consequent student preference for procedural methods rather than conceptual understanding.

To circumvent some of these problems, one of Tall's suggestions is to follow the approach taken at Harvard in their work on the calculus, which is to recognise (Tall 1992: 9):

> the need for versatile movement between representations. Graphics give *qualitative global insight* where numerics give *quantitative results* and symbolics give *powerful manipulative ability*.

This is not so much to suggest that all three approaches (graphical, numerical and symbolic) need to be considered at the same time, but rather that what is important is to support students in being able to make movements ('versatile movements') between them. For Tall, the mark of the mathematician is to be able to select the 'most useful' representation in any given context and to be able to move between representations as required.

In the text that follows I have tried to suggest opportunities for all three of Tall's modes of representation and also highlight opportunities for students to consider when limiting arguments are or are not valid, so that they can begin to feel some control over the infinite processes they are using. In keeping with the conclusions of Chapter 4, I have also been mindful to present activities that allow students to start using new notation as

122  *Curriculum focus*

quickly as possible. There are two tasks and both are taken from Core Mathematics; as for Chapter 7, the tasks have been augmented with some commentary for the purposes of this book.

---

**Task one: fundamentals of calculus**

Notions of infinity and infinite limits are at the heart of the theory of the calculus. The approach below aims to use work on a proof of the fundamental theorem of calculus to support an understanding of these limits and of how integration and differentiation are connected. The inverse connection between finding areas and finding gradients is surely the highlight of the calculus at secondary school mathematics. I know in my own teaching I wanted students to appreciate a sense of the wonder of this connection.

*Differentiation*

How do you introduce the idea of differentiation? An investigative approach might involve the measurement of gradients of a graph and the spotting of a pattern in order to guess at the derived function. It is hard to make these measurements accurately enough for a satisfying sense of pattern to emerge. A more analytic process can involve numerical approximation and students having to move been the graphical and symbolic from the start. From this numerical process, a definition of the differential of a function, from first principles, can perhaps be appreciated.

The gradient of the graph $y = x^2$ at $x = 1$ can be approximated by the gradient of a chord (see Figure 9.4):

The approximation suggested by Figure 9.4 is

$$\text{Gradient at } 1 \approx \frac{1.01^2 - 1^2}{1.01 - 1}$$

More and more accurate approximations can be taken and the process generalised:

$$\text{Gradient} \approx \frac{(1 + \delta x)^2 - 1^2}{1 + \delta x - 1}$$

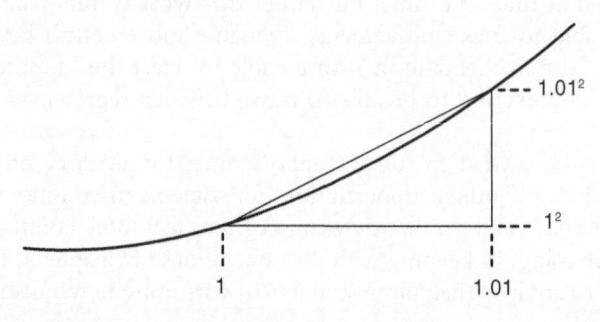

*Figure 9.4* A numerical approach to finding the gradient of $y = x^2$ when $x = 1$

Expanding brackets gives

$$\text{Gradient} \approx \frac{1 + 2\delta x + \delta x^2 - 1}{\delta x}.$$

Hence

$$\text{Gradient} \approx 2 + \delta x.$$

As we let $\delta x$ tend to zero, this tells us the gradient is 2, when $x = 1$. What happens for different values of $x$, including negatives?
After a while, the process itself can be generalised for any starting value, $x$:

$$\text{Gradient} \approx \frac{(x + \delta x)^2 - x^2}{\delta x}$$

Expanding brackets gives us

$$\text{Gradient} \approx \frac{x^2 + 2x\delta x + \delta x^2 - x^2}{\delta x}.$$

After simplifying, the numerator can be divided through by the denominator, and hence:

$$\text{Gradient} \approx 2x + \delta x.$$

At this point, the algebra should match the numerical work, i.e. the gradient tends to twice the value of $x$. A student who has followed this process has access to a sense of how the gradient will get closer and closer to $2x$ and the algebra indicates that as $\delta x$ goes to zero, the gradient becomes $2x$.

Having seen their numerical process generalised to an algebraic rule for $y = x^2$ what about, for example, $y = x^3$ and higher powers, or $y = x^2 + x$ and other variations? After a relatively closed starting point of finding the gradient of one function in a particular manner (see design principles from Chapter 2), students can explore a range of functions, making use of arguments involving limiting processes.

If students are given the space to explore, it is perhaps not a big leap again to generalise to any function, and arrive at the definition, from first principles, of the differential of a function:

$$f(x) = \lim_{\delta x \to 0} \left( \frac{f(x + \delta x) - f(x)}{\delta x} \right)$$

Given the suggestion that it might be useful for students to consider the limits of limiting arguments, there would be an opportunity to consider if there are functions where the argument used to derive this equation break down. What would a

*(continued)*

*(continued)*

function have to look like for the argument to break down, that the limit of a chord gives the gradient of the tangent? A proto-definition might be possible of what it means for a function to be differentiable.

### *Integration*

In a remarkable book (*Calculus by and for young people (ages 7, yes 7 and up)*) Don Cohen (1988) describes a route into working on the integral function that he has used successfully with young children.

Cohen begins by getting students to work out the area (perhaps by counting squares) underneath the curve $y = x^2$, at different values of $x$. See Figure 9.5.

A crucial step in allowing for generalisation is to see the area under the curve as a fraction of a rectangle, where the size of the rectangle is given by $x \times y$. Remembering that $y = x^2$, the area under the curve is going to be a fraction of $x \times x^2$, or $x^3$. In other words, in the left-hand image of Figure 9.5, the task is to find

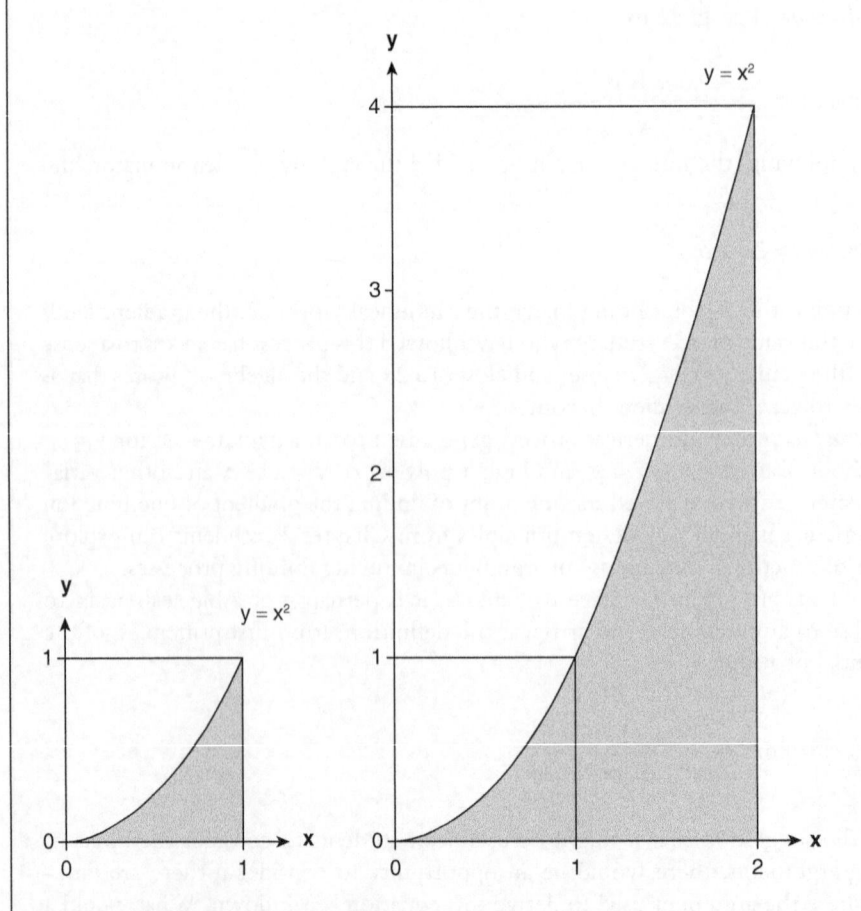

*Figure 9.5* Finding the area under a curve

Reproduced with kind permission from D. Cohen from www.mathman.biz/html/map.html

the number of the shaded area as a fraction of a rectangle of size 1 × 1². In the right hand image, the shaded area will be a fraction of a rectangle of size 2 × 2². A typical answer to the area (if drawn on graph paper) up to $x = 1$, is 34 squares out of 100. Cohen asks his students to think of what simple fraction is close to the results they get, and encourages the notation below (also from Don Cohen's website) to be read as 'the area under the curve $y = x^2$ from $x = 0$ to $x = 1$':

$$A_{0,1}x^2 = \frac{1}{3} \times 1 \times 1^2 = \frac{1}{3} \times 1^3.$$

If students collect results in this manner, they may become convinced after a while that:

$$A_{0,x}x^2 = \frac{1}{3} \times x^3.$$

Working in a similar manner with other functions (for example, Cohen suggests $y = x$ next), students can convince themselves of the general integration formula for polynomials.

## The fundamental theorem of calculus

Having seen the process of deriving the two key processes of differentiation and integration, the link can be made between them. Gattegno suggested that, as teachers, whenever we teach a process we should teach its inverse.

It is worth considering what might motivate the search for the connection between differentiation and integration. If students are used to considering inverse processes, it may be natural for them to work on how to reverse the process of differentiation. In other words, the question may be natural for them to consider: if my derived function is $f(x)$ then what function did I start with? This might allow students to get to an algebraic rule that fits what they found out for integration, but will not *explain* the link between the inverse of differentiation and the areas under the graph. In other words it is possible, symbolically, to appreciate that the formulae for integration and differentiation are the inverse of each other, but what might allow 'qualitative global insight'?

One alternative way in to working on the question of finding the area under a graph (in a typical mathematician's move) is to begin by assuming we already know the 'area' function that gives the area underneath a curve between 0 and $x$. This calling into being of what is as yet unknown is a central insight of algebra, i.e. that the unknown can be named and worked with (there is also a link here to Big Idea 4 of geometrical thinking discussed in Chapter 7). The area function of $f(x)$ (Figure 9.6), would give the value of the area marked by dashed lines from zero to $x$. So, $A(x)$ would be the value of the dashed area, and $A(x + \delta x) - A(x)$ would be the value of the shaded area (Figure 9.6).

The area of the shaded region is a value that lies between the area of two rectangles. The shaded area must be larger than $\delta x \times x^2$ and smaller than $\delta x \times (x + \delta x)^2$ (see Figure 9.6). We can be more precise.

*(continued)*

*(continued)*

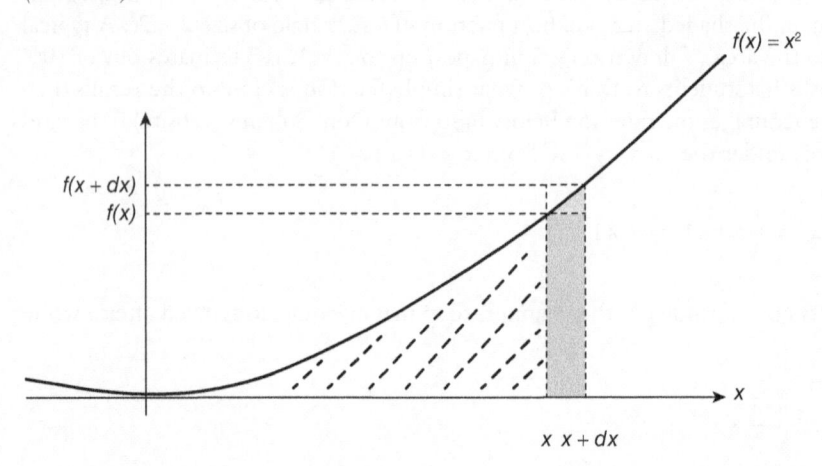

*Figure 9.6* The area under the graph $y = x^2$

Applying the rule for differentiation from first principles to the imagined area function, we get:

$$A'(x) = \lim_{\delta x \to 0} \frac{A(x + \delta x) - A(x)}{\delta x}.$$

Remembering that $A(x + \delta x) - A(x)$ is the area of the shaded region, and (from above) that this lies between the area of two rectangles, we can say:

$$\lim_{\delta x \to 0} \left\{ \frac{\delta x \times x^2}{\delta x} \right\} < A'(x) < \lim_{\delta x \to 0} \left\{ \frac{\delta x \times (x^2 + \delta x)^2}{\delta x} \right\}.$$

Simplifying the brackets, we get the result:

$$\lim_{\delta x \to 0} \{x^2\} < A'(x) < \lim_{\delta x \to 0} \{x^2 + 2x\delta x + (\delta x)^2\}.$$

So we have 'captured' the value of $A'(x)$ in between $x^2$ and $x^2$ plus some terms that tend to zero. This result may need some time to 'unpack'. What we have found is that, by differentiating the area function of $y = x^2$ we get back to the function itself. Students might be able to work on what this means and whether they could now guess at an area function. Students must, in effect, find a function that differentiates to $x^2$.

The argument can be applied in other specific cases or else generalised to any function.

Again, the link between differentiation and integration can be appreciated by applying the fundamental theorem of calculus to the imagined area function of the general function in Figure 9.7:

$$A'(x) = \lim_{\delta x \to 0} \frac{A(x + \delta x) - A(x)}{\delta x}$$

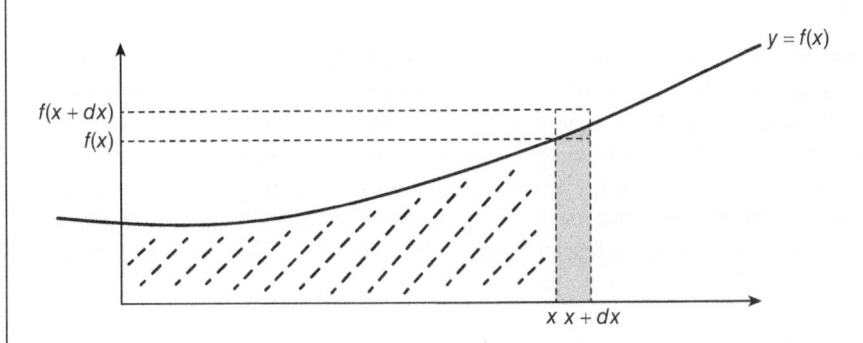

*Figure 9.7* The 'area' under the function *f(x)*

As before, the numerator of the fraction inside the limit is the grey shaded area in Figure 9.7. The shaded area has a value somewhere in between the areas of two rectangles of width $\delta x$, one with height f(x), and the other with height f(x+ $\delta x$). Therefore, when the shaded area is divided by $\delta x$, the result is a value in between the heights of the two rectangles, i.e. a value between f(x) and f(x+ $\delta x$), so that:

$$\lim_{\delta x \to 0} \{f(x)\} < A'(x) < \lim_{\delta x \to 0} \{f(x + \delta x)\}$$

As $\delta x$ tends to zero, these values will converge, for certain kinds of function at least. There is the possibility for investigation here; could students devise some functions or draw some graphs where, at particular points, the argument above does *not* hold? In other words, graphs where f(x + $\delta x$) and f(x) do not converge?

I suspect that what matters in a line of argument such as above is not so much the absolute rigour, but the extent to which it gives the 'global insight' Tall writes about. Lines of proof offer the promise of insight, but work is needed by the reader. The convention of mathematical proof is for lines of direct implication (A implies B, B implies C, and so on). It is not clear that such a format is helpful to students, in terms of appreciating the insights behind the proof. Given some of the work above what further work would be needed in order for students to feel confident that, given certain conditions:

$$A'(x) = f(x) ?$$

Alternatively, I wonder how students might respond to the question 'say what you see', given the equation above? Perhaps with 'Differentiating the "area function" of a function gets you back to the original function again' or 'If you have a function, *f*, to find its area function, you need to find the function that would be differentiated to *f*' or even 'You need to do the inverse of differentiating *f* in order to integrate it (and find its area function)'. As in so many places in this book, what seems to matter is not so much the way this is described, but having some way of describing it (and hopefully, over time, several ways).

*(continued)*

*(continued)*

In earlier parts of this book there were tasks that focused initially on students becoming fluent with the use of symbols (and not worrying initially about what they 'understood' outside of a symbol's relationship to other symbols). The task looking into the connection between integration and differentiation may be more powerful once students have got some sense of what these processes are and how they work. It may be that students will appreciate more of the beauty and surprise of the connection between integration and differentiation if they have already got some appreciation of the separate processes.

**Task two: the chain rule and product rule**

Having established meanings for symbols such as $\frac{dy}{dx}$, the UK syllabus quickly moves on to more complex processes involving the use of deltas. There is an unhelpful ambiguity between the sense that $\frac{dy}{dx}$ is a single entity that cannot be split, and the 'cross-multiplication' that seems to occur in the derivation of the chain rule and integration by parts. Some of this ambiguity is referred to by Tall (1992: 9) when he wrote: 'the Leibniz notation – a "useful fiction?" or a genuine meaning'. It is worth remembering that each $dx$ or $dy$ is itself the result of an infinite limiting process. A choice we all face as teachers is the extent to which it is important to us to demonstrate some consistency in working with infinite limits and how much we want to emphasise shifts between graphical, numerical and symbolic representations. In the next section I present some non-standard graphical representations in the spirit of exploring connections.

### *Chain rule*

The chain rule is about how rates of change combine. If we know how $y$ varies with respect to $t$, and how $t$ varies with respect to $x$, how does $y$ vary with respect to $x$?

The answer contained in the chain rule is that, if $x$, $y$ and $t$ are related variables, then:

$$\frac{dy}{dx} = \frac{dy}{dt} \times \frac{dt}{dx}.$$

An intuition about what is going on here can perhaps be gained by thinking about linear functions. The limiting arguments around the calculus might convince students this is a reasonable starting point.

So imagine $y = \frac{1}{2}t$ and $t = 3x$.

Rather than draw these relations on typical Cartesian axes, what would happen if we separate out three number lines? The relationship between $y$ and $t$, and, $t$ and $x$ could be visualised as in Figure 9.8.

The gradient of a function, within this representation, can be seen in how quickly the arrows 'spread out' in relation to each other.

Figure 9.8 shows one image of how $y$ varies with respect to $t$, and how $t$ varies with respect to $x$, from which you can *observe* how $y$ varies with respect to $x$. Figure 9.8 might suggest, empirically, that for these two linear functions, to find how $y$ varies with respect to $x$, we simply multiply the rates of change, i.e., $\frac{dy}{dx} = \frac{3}{2}$

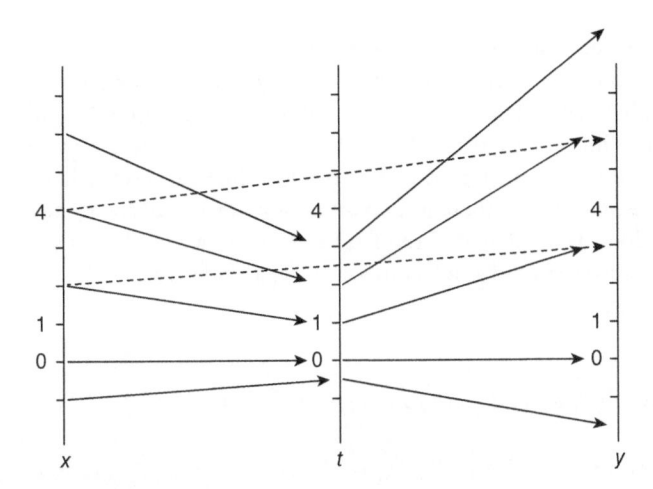

Figure 9.8 Visualising the chain rule for linear functions

An alternative representation, where the gradient of linear function can be read in the spacing of the number lines, not the arrows, is to insist that arrows from one number line to another have to be parallel to each other, meaning that the target number line is scaled (Figure 9.9).

The $t$ line is scaled ×3 from $x$. The $y$ line is scaled $\times \frac{1}{2}$ from $t$. And reading across it can be seen that the $y$ line is scaled $\times \frac{3}{2}$ from $x$. In other words, for the case of these two functions:

$$\frac{dy}{dx} = \frac{dy}{dt} \times \frac{dt}{dx}.$$

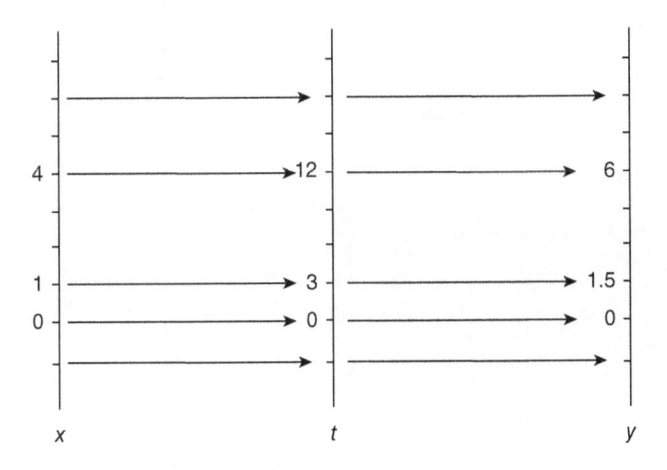

Figure 9.9 An alternative chain rule representation

*(continued)*

### (continued)

The tasks above do not generalise to non-linear functions and so do not attempt to give a rigorous justification of the chain rule, but more to give a 'qualitative insight' or perhaps a structure within which it is possible to make sense of the symbols, without having to think about 'splitting' any of the limits. Perhaps the alternative representations do not help – but they are given in the spirit of suggesting that, as teachers, it is necessary to have *some* story for why these important limiting processes are as they are. Is it stretching the Big Idea from Chapter 7 too far, to suggest that the chain is a measurement formula and hence there is some geometrical result underlying it?

### Product rule

The product rule states that, if $f$ and $g$ are functions of $x$, then:

$$(f(x) \cdot g(x))' = f'(x) \cdot g(x) + f(x) \cdot g'(x).$$

In order to make sense of this, I am helped again by a non-standard representation. In Figure 9.10, the values of $f(x)$ and $g(x)$ are represented by the lengths of two perpendicular vectors, hence the value of $f(x).g(x)$ is represented by the area of the resulting rectangle. In the snapshot that is Figure 9.10, $f(x) = 2.5$ and $g(x) = 4.4$, for some imagined value of $x$.

Differentiating $f(x).g(x)$ means considering how the area of the rectangle changes, given a small increase in $x$. A small increase in $x$, in Figure 9.10, adds the areas of the three rectangles around the outside (labelled A1, A2 and A3). Finding the differential, in this context, therefore means finding the limit of: the change in area divided by $\delta x$ as $\delta x$ tends to zero. This is the limit of (A1 + A2 + A3)/ $\delta x$, as $\delta x$ tends to zero.

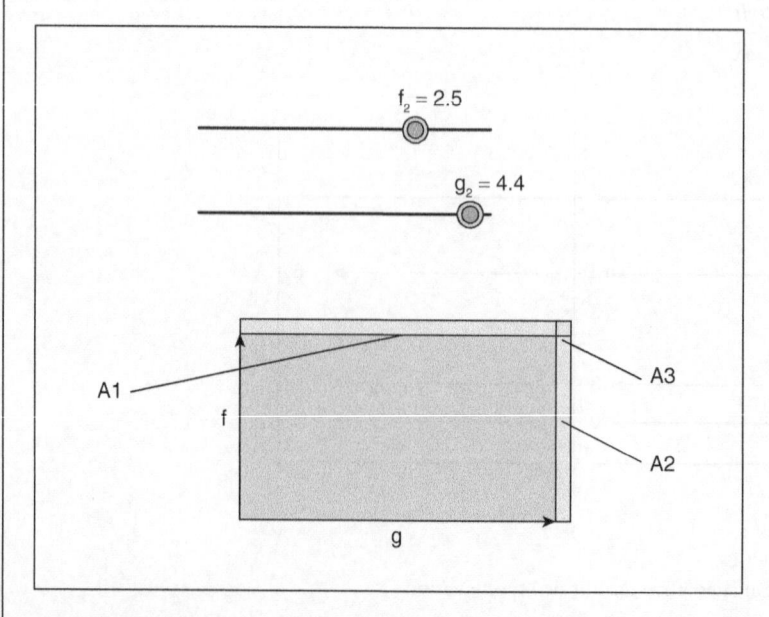

*Figure 9.10* A representation of the product of two functions

But: $A1 = g(x)\left[f(x+\delta x) - f(x)\right]$,

and: $A2 = f(x)\left[g(x+\delta x) - g(x)\right]$,

and A3 can be safely ignored, as its area is an order of magnitude smaller than A1 and A2. Applying the definition of differentiation to *f(x).g(x)*, we therefore get:

$$\left(f(x)\cdot g(x)\right)' = \lim_{\delta x \to 0} \frac{A1 + A2}{\delta x},$$

and applying what we know about A1 and A2, it is a nice task to verify from here that:

$$\left(f(x)\cdot g(x)\right)' = f'(x)\cdot g(x) + f(x)\cdot g'(x).$$

As with the activities on differentiation and integration, the idea here is not to provide a rigorous justification but to give a context in which it is possible to 'see' how the product rule works. Apparently[1], David Wheeler (a close collaborator of Gattegno's) used to say that he would have two bones to pick with God about the design of the universe; the first was that the tempered musical scale is not perfect, and the second was that the derivative of a product is not the product of the derivatives. I have to say I am not so sure this second one is a flaw!

## Discussion

In looking back over the tasks described in this chapter, I am reminded of the quotation from Anne Watson (2008: 23) in Chapter 2:

> But mathematics is not *only* an empirical subject at school level; indeed it is not *essentially* empirical. Its strength and power are in its abstractions, its reasoning, and its hypotheses about objects which only exist in the mathematical imagination. Enquiry alone cannot fully justify results and relationships, nor can decisions be validated by enquiry alone. Many secondary school concepts are beyond observable manifestations, and beyond everyday intuition. Indeed, those which cause most difficulty for learners and teachers are those which require rejection of intuitive sense and reconstruction of new ways of acting mathematically.

The use of numerical examples, particularly in the first task, could be seen as advocating empirical enquiry. And this is where David Tall's sense of the need to be able to shift flexibly between numerical and other modes of representation is important. The numerical cannot validate results that require proof, but can give insight into the graphical and symbolic. Prospective teachers on the PGCE course on which I teach are often so sophisticated algebraically that they resist any number work where possible (when working on a task for themselves) – and yet number examples can give a sense of structure that is obscured by too quick a move into algebra, perhaps in the same way that Dick Tahta warned against too quick a shift out of geometrical thinking into algebraic symbolism. However, to link to the discussion in Chapter 4 of different modes of representation, if the symbolic can capture a relationship or action then it may be possible for the learning of mathematics to be both intuitive and yet relate to objects (relationships/actions) that exist only in the mathematical imagination. It may be that mathematical concepts such as the product rule are beyond 'everyday' intuition (to borrow Watson's phrase), but we can educate our intuitions, and surely there is an intuitive insight behind every mathematical connection or result.

## Note

1 Thank you to David Pimm for this anecdote (conversation with author, 2 February 2015).

## References

Cohen, D. (1988). *Calculus by and for young people (ages 7, yes 7 and up)*. Champaign, IL: Don Cohen The Mathman.

Gattegno, C. (1984). Infinity. *Mathematics Teaching*, 107: 18–22.

Tall, D. (1992). Students' difficulties in calculus. *Plenary presentation in Working Group 3, ICME, Quebec.* Available at: www://homepages.warwick.ac.uk/staff/David.Tall/pdfs/dot1993k-calculus-wg3-icme.pdf (accessed 28 November 2014).

Watson, A. (2008) Adolescent learning and secondary mathematics. *Proceedings of the 2008 Annual Meeting of the Canadian Mathematics Education Study Group*, pp.21–32. Available online at www://cmesg.ca/ (accessed 17 September 2010).

# Part III
# Reflections

# 10 Engaging in engaging learners

The first two sections of the book have focused on different images of what it might mean to engage students in learning mathematics. In this chapter, the focus shifts to teachers. What is it that motivates any teacher to engage in the process of developing their teaching to be able to engage students in the learning of mathematics? How is it possible to work with other teachers in a way that provokes change and growth?

## Personal change

This first thing to say about working to develop your own teaching is that it is hard to do on your own. If I look back over my own journey in teaching, I have relied heavily on others, most notably Laurinda Brown with whom I have been fortunate to collaborate. An important element, for me, along the way to developing conviction about my teaching was also doing a Master's degree and later a PhD study.

The first task of the initial unit I undertook on the Master's course at the University of Bristol was to find an issue in my teaching that I wanted to work on. The core text for that first module was *Teachers investigate their work: an introduction to the method of action research* (Altrichter et al. 1993) and pages 31–32 invited me to do one of the following tasks to help refine what my interest was:

- Select one of next week's lessons. Write a memo about the course of events in your diary. Include all thoughts that come to your mind during reflecting and writing.
- Tape one of next week's lessons. Select five minutes of the tape for transcription . . . Leave a margin for comments beside your transcription. Then note in the margin all associations that come to your mind when reading specific sections of the transcript . . .
- Prepare a 'cluster' of all associations that come to your mind when you think of the phrase 'Being a teacher' . . .
- Every day next week cut out from a newspaper some words, phrases or pictures which you intuitively like or which you spontaneously feel concern your profession. At the end of the week prepare a collage from the cuttings. Feel free to complement the collage by handwritten words and your own drawings.
- Imagine an extraterrestrial visitor entering you classroom (or your personal workroom) from the top left corner without being noticed by anybody in the room. Describe in a short piece of writing what he or she would see and think.

I wrote out a cluster of associations around 'being a teacher' and became interested in my interactions with students. I noticed how sometimes, after a student asked me for help and I went over to see them, I would leave them and they would still not know what to do next. I had observed other teachers help students and when they left the students would be energised and refocused. What was different? What was I doing that was getting in the way? I began audio recording my interactions with students and playing them back, to listen again after the lesson, was a painful procedure. I realised how little I was actually hearing the students, how many mathematical ideas I was missing and how often I was simply imposing my own ideas and explanations – it was no wonder that I was not supporting students to become engaged by mathematics in my lessons.

The discipline of Master's study encouraged me to continue researching my own teaching, alongside further readings and working with others. The physical act of walking into a university building I always felt helped me to think differently about my own practice – perhaps seeing it from a helpful distance in order to be able to conceptualise possibilities for how it could be different.

Part of the initial action research process I went through in that first Master's module involved having something in mind to try out and evaluate in my teaching – having a 'purpose' for a lesson, beyond the content.

## Purposes

The sense of having an idea in mind to guide development, as a teacher, is something Laurinda Brown has labelled having a 'purpose', an idea she developed over a series of papers and book chapters (Brown and Dobson 1996; Brown (with Coles), 1997; Brown and Coles, 2000; Brown, 2005). When I began collaborating with Laurinda and during my Master's studies, I remember working on a number of different purposes. To help get a sense of what a purpose is, it may be useful to spend a little time explaining a selection.

### *Using silence*

This was the first 'purpose' I worked with consciously and has been alluded to in Chapter 5. The label came out of a conversation between Laurinda and me about my first year of teaching and a recognition that the times I valued most in terms of the learning of my students were linked to my own (deliberate) silence during an activity. Laurinda and I began to plan deliberately for lesson starts that would begin with silence.

### *Don't comment, metacomment*

Linked to my first Master's module described above, I became interested in how I responded to student contributions. The idea of this purpose was, in responding to student questions, to only make a comment *about* what they asked, rather than respond directly to the content of their question. I worked on myself quite deliberately to do this in some lessons.

### *It's not the answer that's wrong*

This purpose was again about ways of interacting with students and managing class discussions. Whenever a student gave an answer that was 'wrong', the inspiration for this purpose was the idea that they have made a sensible response (unless there has simply been a calculation error) and so there must be some assumption about the context that is not shared or that has been interpreted differently. So, from Chapter 1 and the 1089 task, you can get answers of 198, under certain assumptions and for some starting numbers. Instead of rejecting this interpretation of the task, I would use the opportunity to discuss how mathematicians need to choose rules and be consistent about applying them. Students could likewise choose their rules, a 'wrong' answer helps illustrate an important aspect of mathematical thinking. Another strategy linked to this purpose is to simply collect all student responses to a question and then discuss them, including how different answers were arrived at.

## *How do I know what they know?*

I recognise this purpose as much now from working with prospective teachers as from my own practice. A teacher may come out of a lesson I have observed and initially feel exasperated at how things went. Focusing in on the detail of events and discomforts, it might emerge that a particularly uncomfortable moment was when a task was given to students and soon afterwards, six hands went up of students who were stuck and, shortly after this, behaviour deteriorated. Probing further, the discomfort was linked to not knowing that these students might be stuck – hence the label. Having identified a label for the issue, it is possible to consider a range of strategies so that I *can* know what students know before giving them a task.

A significant element of each of these purposes is that the labels are easily stated. They are not about specific teaching strategies, or specific lessons. Equally, they are not abstract aims or ambitions. They are in a middle position between the abstract and the detail of behaviour. Purposes are ideas that can accrue links to a range of teaching strategies. Using 'purposes' is a central principle behind the organisation of sessions with groups of prospective mathematics teachers on the PGCE course on which I work (see Brown and Coles, 2012). The easy articulation of a purpose is important in allowing the possibility of keeping these ideas in mind, in planning and/or during a lesson itself.

In working with others, it seems essential that there is a move between the detail of experience/description and the raising of issues at a more general level – to then think through or discuss a range of strategies to support that more general idea. This is a complex suggestion and one on which I elaborate further below.

## A whole department approach to engaging in engaging learners

In the description of the 1089 activity in Chapter 1, I mentioned in several places that in the school where I taught there was a whole department focus on 'thinking mathematically'. There is a power in a group of teachers deciding on a common focus for the development of teaching. My experience, as a head of department, was that there was a 'critical mass' needed of teachers with the time and energy to engage in reflecting on their practice for conversations to build over a school year and for a sense of progress against an issue. This critical mass, or perhaps it was a critical proportion, only happened for a few of the seven years I spent as head of department.

It is perhaps easy for departmental meetings to be taken up with administrative decision-making and procedures. I always found it a useful discipline to limit the length of any administrative discussions to allow the majority of meetings to be dedicated to work that was focused on developing teaching. If a decision needed to be made, I would aim to speak individually to each member of the team and gauge their reaction. If there was divided opinion, then I would not waste time in meetings rehearsing positions and instead work on finding an alternative that everyone could get behind. If there was general agreement about a decision then I would be confident this could be raised and dealt with quickly at a meeting.

One of the most powerful developmental activities that I would undertake as a head of department was using meeting time to watch short video clips of each other teaching. Making use of video is the focus on the next section.

## Finding purposes through video[1]

In the conclusion of an edited book on the use of video with teachers, Brophy (2007: 298) states an essential practice is 'establishing norms to ensure discussion is reflective and constructively critical', something echoed by many others (e.g. van Es and Sherin 2002). However, establishing such norms can be problematic; for example, van Es and Sherin (2002: 264) report on the workings of a 'video club'[2] in which some teachers

> would often evaluate or call into question the teachers' pedagogical approaches as viewed in the clip, offering advice on what the teachers should have done differently. This approach to video analysis is different from the interpretive stance that was promoted in the meetings. Similarly, rather than look closely at the specific events in the video, these teachers drew more from their own classroom experiences as a foundation for their comments.

For the two teachers in question it was not until a tenth and last meeting of the video club that there was an observable shift in the way they discussed the clips. The description by van Es and Sherin of the evaluative comments of some teachers to video is mirrored in Nemirovsky et al. (2005). Drawing on an empirical study of teacher talk Nemirovsky et al. (2005: 365) distinguish 'grounded narrative whose aim is to articulate descriptions of classroom events' from 'evaluative discourse' which 'centers on the values, virtues and commitments in play'. They conclude (Nemirovsky et al. 2005: 388): 'Evaluative discourse is in our experience, by far, the most prevalent mode used in conversation about videotaped teaching episodes'.

Strikingly similar findings were reported many years earlier in Jaworski (1990), drawing on her work at the Open University (OU). Jaworski (1990: 63) cites the following statements as common reactions to watching video, and ones that constitute barriers to valuable discussion (and which I read as 'evaluative discourse'):

> 'He was railroading them – they didn't have a chance to think for themselves'.
>
> 'I couldn't do that with my pupils, they can't work quietly enough'.
>
> 'They're not intelligent enough'.
>
> 'They don't wear uniform'.
>
> 'We can't arrange the classroom like that'.
>
> 'I could never do that – I just don't have the right sort of personality'.

As Jaworski (1990: 63) goes on to analyse:

> The problem with comments such as these is that they invest all of their energy in interpretation and judgement of the acts and intentions of the particular teacher of the video. Such comments, particularly if from the first speaker to open the discussion, can condition what follows and result in little of value for the teachers concerned.

A very particular practice was developed at the OU to overcome the difficulty of such evaluative talk; this practice was rooted in Mason's (e.g., 2002) distinction between 'accounts of' and 'accounts for' data. Accounts *of* phenomena aim to report on them as directly as possible, avoiding interpretations, judgements or evaluations. Accounts *for* phenomena aim to explain what is perceived or interpret it, for example by classifying. I interpret the 'grounded narrative' of Nemirovsky *et al.* as essentially accounts *of*, and their 'evaluative discourse' as one type of account *for*. Jaworski (1990) reports on the practice of using video with teachers in a two-part process, in order to avoid judgemental and unhelpful comments from teachers, particularly at the start of discussion. The OU practice has been such an influence on me that it is worth quoting in full.

> [T]he first step, on switching off the machine is to invite everyone to spend a minute or more silently replaying what they have seen, trying to reconstruct for themselves the most significant parts of it. Participants are then asked to join together in pairs, and try to *agree* on what they have seen, if possible without overtly entering into interpretation at this stage. This might be described *as giving an account of* what was seen. It is often surprising to the members of a group that what they notice in a video excerpt varies very considerably from one to another – how what is significant for one might go unnoticed by another – and this draws attention to what emphasis they put on what they see . . . If there has been disagreement about what was seen, then it may be appropriate to replay the excerpt . . . Discussion can then move into interpretation, and it is now more possible to back up any interpretation which is made by reference to what happened in the video excerpt. This stage might be called *accounting for* what was seen – trying out possible meanings and explanations. People are less likely now to jump in with unjustified interpretations, and at this stage it is likely that personal feelings about the teacher viewed have been deflected. Experience shows that extremely profitable discussion can result, that issues are raised which are important to the participants, and that the constructive atmosphere can lead to genuine consideration of classroom consequences (Jaworski 1990: 63–4).

In the first part, then, the facilitator begins by asking for accounts *of* what was observed in attempt to reconstruct the precise words or actions and their chronology, before moving to accounting *for* what was seen. Although the OU videotapes generally had a focus (e.g. 'practical work'), Jaworski (1990: 62) is explicit that discussion of the tapes was not limited to this focus:

> rarely would any particular issue of concern be the *only* possible focus of any excerpt on video-tape.

and in the creation of the tapes themselves she goes on to write of her 'desire to constrain the viewer as little as possible'. In other words, although the videos had been created with some ideas in mind, there was an open agenda in terms of where teachers took their discussions and what they noticed. Jaworski also recommends using short sections of lessons for observation.

## Facilitating discussion

I have, on occasion, made the decision not to follow the discipline of starting discussion of video with an 'account *of*' the events. In all cases, I have regretted the decision! However, it is not straightforward to facilitate discussion in the manner suggested by Jaworski. In a study linked to the use of technology in teacher learning Goldman (2001: 37) acknowledges the complexity involved in facilitating productive discussion (online or face-to-face):

> For facilitators, it is no easy task to decide what to say when, and how much information to provide . . . Knowing when to insert a question, reframe the issue, redirect the conversation toward more productive conjectures, or offer the 'accepted' disciplinary view requires that facilitators have sensitivity, patience, faith in the group-learning process, and deep content knowledge. Furthermore, facilitators can model the inquiry process by sharing their own puzzlements and points of confusion with the group. This helps establish a collaborative learning community by softening the often held 'infallible expert' view of facilitators and other professional development staff.

There are precious few articulations of such complexities involved in running a course for teachers. As Goldman (2001: 36) also notes:

> The avenues by which facilitators can acquire this knowledge are by no means clear. This is a serious issue of capacity building . . . there are scant opportunities to develop content and pedagogical content knowledge for purposes of mentoring adults.

Through interrogating audio recordings of teacher meetings at my school, when we worked on video, I identified some decision points that seemed always to be around for the facilitator.

### 1 Starting with reconstruction and moving to interpretation

In line with the practice described in Jaworski (1990), having had a period of time with 'accounts of' what was watched it is possible to move to 'accounts for' and avoid judgemental comments. In setting up this second phase of working on video, I use a similar form of words each time to signal the move. In the second phase, I saw the aim of discussion as the identification of one or more 'purposes' that could then be taken up by teachers and used to inform future actions.

### 2 Setting up discussion norms

It was evident from the transcripts that there were some rules or norms in play that were more or less explicit. In particular, during a period of 'reconstruction' one of the roles of the facilitator is to stop any evaluative or judgemental comment. This requires noticing when something being said is not a comment about the detail of events. As a facilitator, particularly with a group of teachers new to working with video in this way, I would often have to intervene or cut off a teacher in order to make explicit what it means to 'stay with the detail' and not slip into judgement. Another norm was that during the interpretation phase, the teacher whose lesson we were watching would not talk – this was so that discussion would not veer into asking the teacher to explain or justify decisions made.

## 3 Re-watching the video

In running a session looking at video, I am aware of crucial decisions about when, and how often, to replay any clips. In discussing the same issue in relation to working on silent mathematical animations with post-16 students, Love (quoted in Pimm 1995: 47) commented, 'If I keep showing them the film, they'll think it is about remembering. I ask them to reconstruct the film communally'. I also want a communal reconstruction that is not about memory, and see a strong connection to my practice, despite the different purposes at play here, in that Love is wanting his students, in their minds, to begin visualising moving images from the film whereas for me reconstruction is aimed at avoiding the problems of evaluative talk identified by Jaworski. There is a subtle mixture of intentions here; like Love, I do not want the task to be just about remembering. Equally, I do not want to get bogged down in the detail of every moment of the three minutes (perhaps for Love it is more important that students can reconstruct all of, or entire sections of, his animations). I am aware of being alert to any disagreements about the reconstruction. I know I am looking for an excuse to slow down the reconstruction and disagreements about what is said can provide that, often prolonging discussion, the issue finally to be resolved by re-watching(s). The purpose of the slowing down is to let the complexity of what is happening come to the surface, and to allow a focus on the fine detail of a small section of the clip. I find, in a teacher meeting, it is not possible, or even desirable, to do this for every section of the clip, due to the time it takes.

## 4 Metacommenting

Laurinda Brown and I have reported on the practice of 'metacommenting' in lessons and teacher meetings (e.g. Brown 2004). Identifying a purpose that is being talked about, and naming it (e.g., 'it seems that the issue everyone is talking about here is . . .'), is an example of a metacomment – a comment *about* the discussion. I see the making of these metacomments as a vital aspect of my role in facilitating discussion of video. Identifying a purpose potentially supports other teachers in responding in new or different ways in their own classrooms.

## 5 Selecting a video clip

There is one further aspect to this way of working, a choice made prior to the transcript recordings begin – the selection of what to watch. Teachers in the department who had lessons recorded were always volunteers. The member of staff would select a class and a time. Before the lesson I would set up the camera on a tripod at the back of the room, set it to record and then leave, returning at the end of the lesson to retrieve the equipment. Students were told in advance of these recordings, and given the option to sit out of shot, or have any other concerns discussed. Having taken the video recording, I would transfer it to DVD and watch it, looking for any sections that might be suitable for discussion with other staff. I was looking for small sections of the recording where something 'interesting' (as I thought about it at the time) was occurring. The department had agreed on a shared focus for development around the running of class discussions and 'managing pupil talk'. It was therefore only the times of whole-class discussion that I was selecting from. Indeed the nature of the recordings, and the way the camera was set up, meant that little else from the lesson could be discerned than these periods. By an 'interesting' section of video, I mean a time when, for example, students were responding to each other in a whole-class discussion (i.e. the dialogue fell out of a pattern of teacher-student-teacher), or when there was some ambiguity that was discussed as a class (e.g. two or more students expressing conflicting ideas), or if there was a section where several different students were contributing ideas to discussion. I set myself a rule to choose one continuous section from the lesson that did not last more than five minutes, and in general I aimed to make the clip around three minutes long.

### Identifying levels of communication

One of the subtleties of the ideas above, of reconstruction and of purposes, is to become sensitive to what *kind* of a communication you are hearing (alongside the content of that communication). To impose a discussion norm of starting from the detail of events, I must notice and act on the difference between a comment such as 'the students seemed distracted at the start' (a judgement and so not allowed) compared to 'the student at the back of the class had her head on the desk at the start' (a comment about the detail of events). If I am to support a group or individual in finding a 'purpose' to guide their future planning and actions in a classroom, I need to notice the difference between discussion of the detail of events and the raising of a more general issue, or when there is the potential for the raising of a more general issue. There is clear link between noticing these differences and the discussion of forms of listening, as discussed in in Chapter 5.

Eleanor Rosch (in Varela *et al.* 1991) researched the different categories we use to speak and communicate and identified three distinct layers. The extremes are a detail/behaviour layer (we sometimes talk about specific items or events, or discuss the detail of our experience) and a superordinate layer (we sometimes talk in abstract terms about broad categories or philosophical ideas).

But, most often, we pitch our discourse at a layer in between these two, which Rosch labelled 'basic-level'. The categories in this layer (basic-level categories) are the most abstract labels that are linked to similar kinds of actions. We often use words like table, chair, knife, fork, tree, or pen. These are (for most of us) basic-level because we perform similar actions with all members of those categories. We much less often talk about specific tables or chairs, and equally do not often use the more abstract words like furniture, cutlery, or stationery. These more abstract (superordinate) words are not linked to similar actions – I do different things with a sofa compared to a chest of drawers, yet both are furniture. Although, of course, if I were to become a furniture remover, I would begin performing similar actions with these items (i.e. pack and unpack them) and the word 'furniture' would then become basic-level. Rosch's categories are not fixed.

Rosch's categories give one possible explanation for what can go wrong when watching video and for what makes the OU method so powerful. If we generally speak using basic-level categories, then when a group of teachers watch a video clip it is likely they will reflect on what they have seen with words at this layer, in other words, using words that are linked to actions they already perform in the classroom. Students might be described as 'disruptive' or 'engaged', for example. Both these ways of describing and therefore experiencing the video are likely, for an experienced teacher, to be strongly linked to typical actions (particularly the former word!). And this is the point, if I begin discussing or reflecting at this basic-level, then the opportunities for being surprised, for seeing something different, or raising the possibility of a different way of acting in my own classroom, are severely limited.

The OU method for working with video forces discussion (at the start) into the detail/behaviour layer. I am therefore immediately tripped out of my habitual ways of experiencing and seeing. From this detail layer, with skilful facilitation, there is the possibility of arriving at a new synthesis of my experience. I may be able to get to a new basic-level category that then has the possibility of becoming linked to new actions in the classroom. And part of the skilful facilitation that will make this possible is being able to recognise when someone is talking at the basic-level and when they are in the detail. One clue to this is that the basic-level can carry judgement. An insight that Laurinda Brown has articulated (2005) is that 'purposes' are always at this middle, or basic-level.

## Relational symbols

In Chapter 4, I distinguished, within mathematics, between absolute and relational symbols. Absolute symbols denote an object in a direct manner whereas relational symbols symbolise an action on an object or a relation between objects. There is an intriguing parallel to this distinction in thinking about what purposes are. When people start to teach and reflect on lessons, or on what they need to do to develop, it is not unusual to hear comments such as: 'I need to be more confident', or 'the kids were disruptive'. This first kind of comment is all about self, the second kind of comment is all about the 'other'. Neither comment is useful in terms of something to aid growth and change – the first kind of comment offers nothing that can actually be done, and the second kind of comment suggests a permanent and unchangeable state. In contrast, purposes, it seems to me, are always labels (symbols) for *relationships*. 'How do I know what they know?' is a purpose about how I interact with students in order to assess what they can do. 'Don't comment, metacomment' is a purpose about my interactions with students, as is: 'it's not the answer that's wrong'.

When I began teaching I thought about wanting students to be 'autonomous'. As well as being a statement, that is too abstract for Rosch's middle, basic layer and so a statement that cannot be linked directly to action, I am also struck now by how the statement is all about the students – it is not relational. Thinking about 'autonomy' did not help me develop in the way that working with purposes did. What I needed to find were the statements that linked me to students ('how do I know what they know?') that helped me develop strategies I could employ in the complex decision-making of teaching (Brown and Coles 2000).

## High diligence

Wodehouse (1924: 217), writing about the development of education within any system (at school, regional or national level) wrote:

> There is no automatic safeguard. No subject and no curriculum can dispense with the teacher's periodic effort of heart and mind, or with his (sic) sensitiveness to growing possibilities and changing needs. The central problem of organisation is to safeguard and promote such high diligence and such awareness, and to help them to their full effort.

Whatever curriculum is in place, whatever assessment regime is being adopted, there is surely great wisdom here: what makes a difference is, as teachers, our periodic effort of heart and mind. What a teacher-leader can do is so organise the structure around the classroom to make such 'high diligence' possible.

## Notes

1 I have written elsewhere about the use of video to promote teacher learning (Coles 2013a, 2014) and I will attempt to summarise the key ideas. This section draws on writing from my own PhD study (which was the basis for Coles (2013b)).
2 Seven teachers joined this 'video club'; they met for ten meetings in 2001–2. At each meeting they watched and discussed video clips, taken by the researchers on the project, of each other teaching.

## References

Altrichter, H., Posch, P. and Somekh, B. (1993). *Teachers investigate their work: an introduction to the methods of action research*. London and New York: Routledge.
Brophy, J. (2007). Discussion. In J. Brophy (ed.), *Using video in teacher education*, pp. 287–304. Bingley, UK: JAI Press.
Brown, L. (2004). It's about learning: from purposes to basic-level categories to metacommenting. In A. Noyes (ed.) *Proceedings of the British Society for Research into Learning Mathematics, 24*(3): 1–6.
Brown, L. (2005). Purposes, metacommenting and basic-level categories: parallels between teaching mathematics and learning to teach mathematics. *Paper presented at the 15th ICMI Study Conference*. Available online at stwww.weizmann.ac.il/G-math/ICMI/log_in.html (accessed 21 July 2006).
Brown, L. and Coles, A. (1997). Being true to ourselves. In V. Zack, J. Mousley and C. Breen (eds), *Teacher as researcher: researcher as teacher*, pp. 103–111. Victoria, Australia: Deakin University.
Brown, L. and Coles, A. (2000). Complex decision making in the classroom: the teacher as an intuitive practitioner. In T. Atkinson & G. Claxton (eds), *The intuitive practitioner: on the value of not always knowing what one is doing*, pp. 165–81. Buckingham, UK: Open University Press.
Brown, L. and Coles, A. (2012). Developing 'deliberate analysis' for learning mathematics and for mathematics teacher education: how the enactive approach to cognition frames reflection. *Educational Studies in Mathematics, 80*(1-2): 217–31.
Brown, L. and Dobson, A. (1996). Using dissonance – finding the grit in the oyster. In G. Claxton, T. Atkinson, M. Osborn and M. Wallace (eds), *Liberating the learner: lessons for professional development in education*, pp. 212–27. London: Routledge.
Coles, A. (2013a). Using video for professional development: the role of the discussion facilitator. *Journal of Mathematics Teacher Education, 16*(3): 165–84.
Coles, A. (2013b). *Being alongside: for the teaching and learning of mathematics*. Rotterdam: Sense Publishers.
Coles, A. (2014). Mathematics teachers learning with video: the role, for the didactician, of a heightened listening. *ZDM, 46*(2): 267–78.

Goldman, S. (2001). Professional development in a digital age: issues and challenges for standards-based reforms. *Interactive Educational Multimedia, 2*: 19–46.

Jaworski, B. (1990). Video as a tool for teachers' professional development. *Professional Development in Education, 16*(1): 60–65.

Mason, J. (2002). *Researching your own practice: the discipline of noticing.* London: RoutledgeFalmer.

Nemirovsky, R., Dimattia, C., Ribeiro, B. and Lara-Meloy, T. (2005). Talking about teaching episodes. *Journal of Mathematics Teacher Education, 8*(5): 363–92.

Pimm, D. (1995). *Symbols and meanings in school mathematics.* London: Routledge.

van Es, E. and Sherin, M. (2002). Learning to notice: scaffolding new teachers' interpretations of classroom interactions. *Journal of Technology and Teacher Education, 10*(4): 571–96.

Varela, F., Thompson, E. and Rosch, E. (1991). *The embodied mind: cognitive science and human experience.* Cambridge, MA: The MIT Press.

Wodehouse, H. (1924). *A survey of the history of education.* London: Edward Arnold & Co.

# 11 Learning across the lifespan

In this book I have attempted to present images of engagement in learning, with the hope of provoking new possibilities for action and inquiry. I have identified some themes that emerge when looking at what is the same about the stories of learning from the early primary school years, through to post-16 teaching and to the professional development of adults. These themes are:

- vulnerability to change;
- sharing ways of seeing;
- making new distinctions;
- symbolising experiences;
- putting symbols to use.

These themes are overlapping. I am not suggesting they are necessary for learning, but perhaps that learning can be fast and engaging when these elements are around. I will take each theme in turn.

## Vulnerability to change

Chapter 5 dealt with issues of making the mathematics classroom a safe place to be for learners. In order to allow the process of engaging in learning to actually happen, learners and teachers must make themselves vulnerable to the new – and this can only take place in certain kinds of environments. Ways of working and routines that focus on the mathematics have to become established. Gattegno referred to the idea that, in a classroom, the students learn the mathematics and the teacher learns the students. Vulnerability to change is no less important for either endeavour. Am I able to allow for the possibility that my students might be different today from how they were yesterday? What does it take to resist the pressure to categorise students as 'bright' or 'less able' and instead to find a way to allow each individual to demonstrate their intelligence, or brilliance, even?

The sense of making ourselves vulnerable inevitably touches on personal issues. It is simply not easy to do – or at least not easy to do always, or perhaps even impossible to do always. It is also possible to so control the communication in a classroom that nothing surprising can take place. Students can still learn in such environments. But we have the evidence from the teaching of Gattegno, Davis, Tahta, Brown and others of how great the possibilities and potentials are for leaning when the new and the creative are allowed to have space, alongside a structure that provides safety.

## Sharing ways of seeing

The idea of visualising mathematics has cropped up in several chapters. One way of engaging learners is to find a starting point that will generate different responses, so that there is something for them to share. Many of the tasks described in this book begin with contrasting examples (see the design principles of Chapter 2) or something for students to look at or do and then share.

With teachers, starting with 'accounts of' (Chapter 10) the events on a video is a parallel to the classroom, in terms of an activity that is likely to generate different responses. In facilitating discussion of video, I recognise looking out for points of disagreement among what people have seen. These points of difference can engage participants in, for example, wanting to re-watch a clip.

On your own, of course, sharing ways of seeing is difficult to do – how do you see something differently to how you already see it? This is one of the paradoxes of learning: how do we come to recognise that which we do not recognise? One mechanism for reflecting on learning in a way that allows the possibility of throwing up new awarenesses is to keep a diary of events. Looking back over written descriptions may allow a different view. Of course, it is much easier to work with others – and the suggestion has come up more than once (drawing on Dick Tahta) that mathematics in classrooms could become a *communal* activity.

## Making new distinctions

The purpose of sharing ways of seeing is to allow for the possibility of new distinctions to arise from the awarenesses of the group. In a classroom one of the roles of the teacher can be that of providing a name for distinctions noticed by the students.

Of course, to be able to provide a name for a distinction that is made by a student presupposes that I notice and hear what is said – something that comes back to the extent to which we can make ourselves vulnerable to the new and the unexpected. A teacher's metacomments on the processes of mathematical enquiry that are taking place can be one aspect of naming distinctions to support new patterns of activity.

In working with teachers, the discipline of focusing on the detail of events inevitably leads to 'seeing more' than was first apparent. De-briefing with a prospective teacher on a lessons of theirs I have observed, there is often a need to slow down discussion and focus in on the first comment they make (before dealing with the second), to allow new distinctions to arise.

## Symbolising experiences

Closely related to the naming of a new distinction is the possibility of the new distinction now being symbolised. In a classroom, the idea of setting up contexts where mathematical symbols can stand for relationships or actions on objects has been alluded to in several chapters. In Chapter 7, when students are discussing the infinite tessellation of triangles, in lines 34 and 35, a student makes a connection between two angles and I, as teacher, add the precise term 'vertically opposite angles' to name the distinction being discussed (this naming occurs after the transcript ends).

Working with teachers in the context of professional development, finding purposes which also symbolise relationships, becomes a possibility if a mechanism (such as the OU video technique) can be found to shift discussion initially out of the basic-level, down into the detail, so that there is the possibility later for the creation of new categories and distinctions that can lead to new ways of acting (and being) in the classroom.

## Putting symbols to use

For Tall (see Chapter 9) one of the purposes of symbolising is to provide 'powerful manipulative ability'. If I can symbolise a distinction, I may be able to begin to consider that symbol in relation to other symbols. In a classroom, the making of new distinctions and the labelling of symbols is not enough to mean students learn. For students to become fluent in their use of symbols, they must engage in the process of relating symbols to each other, they need to have a sense of the structure within which the symbols operate. And, as Tall (1992) notes, they must be supported in flexibly shifting representations.

With teachers, equally, the identification of a 'purpose' is only the beginning. If the process of identifying purposes is to be useful, these new labels, or new symbols, need to inform planning and action in the classroom.

## Symbolising symbols

I have paid a lot of attention to symbols over the course of this book and only briefly touched on what a symbol is – how might we symbolise the role of a symbol?

Picking up on a theme from Chapter 5, there is an important sense of needing, at times, to suppress the meanings of symbols in order to use them fluently. For example, in solving a problem that requires some algebra, I might form an equation that relates to the problem (the symbols at this stage have a metaphorical meaning – standing for particular relations). I then 'crunch' the symbols to arrive at a solution (and at this stage only consider the symbols metonymically, in relation to each other), before perhaps re-interpreting my solution back into the context of the original problem (metaphorically). However, such binary distinctions do not capture well the sense that symbols (and the concepts they are used to denote) exist within a complex web of associations. As a mathematician, if I am presented with an expression such as $2x^2 + 7x - 9$ a whole host of associations arise – pending (as Laurinda Brown would say) what I may be asked, or decide, to do next. I may recognise the statement as an expression that can be factorised, I may picture the graph, or the quadratic formula may come to mind. The point is that the concepts involved in the expression gain their use and meaning from their relation to other concepts. Furthermore concepts are never fixed, as each use adds a different complexion to the web of connections that surrounds it.

If concepts have been introduced as relations, then a symbol's link to physical objects or images takes its places as just one among a myriad of connections. Concepts, as relations, are at once material (arising from a consideration of objects) and abstract (the relation of, say, 'double' does not exist 'in' either one of two objects being compared but only in their comparison by an observer).

Translating this sense of the role of symbols in the classroom to my learning as a teacher, I may work with a particular purpose for a period of time until new behaviours become established, before working on a new purpose. As with mathematical symbols, a purpose, in my experience, is never lost once worked on but adds to the myriad complexity of my teaching practice. Behaviours quickly become automatic but, if necessary (particularly if a behaviour ceases to be effective), it is possible (to use a phrase of Francisco Varela's) to reconstruct the 'intelligent awareness' that gave rise to that action (Varela 1999: 31). If a habitual action stops 'working', I need to trace back the awareness that led to the action and bring that awareness into question, to allow for the possibility of acting differently in the future.

## Conclusion

Dick Tahta, along with David Wheeler, was Gattegno's closest colleague in the UK. In a review of Gattegno's *Science of Education* (1987), Dick had the following to say about mathematics teaching (Tahta 1988: 12–13), which is worth quoting at length:

> Either we continue to enquire what children can do as individuals and then create 'learning environments' (microworlds?) in which they can create 'their own mathematics', and so on. Or – and this may not be palatable for some readers – we try to find out what it is that all children have done and can do, and then teach them – in groups – in a more directed and sustained way. A related challenge, in the specific field of mathematics teaching, has also been put very forcibly by Charles Desforges and Anne Cockburn in their devastating account (*Understanding the mathematics teacher*, Falmer Press, 1987) of the gap between the practice of first-school teachers and the aspirations held up to them by teacher-trainers. In an absorbing book, which is rich in classroom observations of teachers and children, these authors claim that the teachers' job is more constrained, and more complex, than sometimes seems to be assumed by those who advise them how to teach mathematics.
>
> The teachers in our study seemed very conscious of the amount of material they had to cover ... When the authors of the Cockcroft Report exhort teachers to follow issue x or question y as these are spontaneously raised, they perhaps do not quite know what they are asking for (Desforges and Cockburn 1987: 131).
>
> My own interpretation is that the whole mathematics curriculum, as well as proposed methods of teaching it, has been over-elaborated. I assume that no sensible teacher takes any notice in practice of the absurd lists of Stages or Levels that the commercial schemes tell us that learners have to go through. But these do leave a sense of guilty failure in many who would be far better served by a ruthlessly *economic* set of principles and minimal list of required *awarenesses*. I assume that no sensible teacher would modify practice on the basis of the vague exhortations of a government commissioned report. But I note that these exhortations continue to be repeated, over and over again – to the point where they have already become ritual clichés that tend to distract people from any serious inquiry of their own.

This is an extraordinary piece of writing to look back on some thirty years after it was written. I wonder what Dick would have made of the ubiquitous use of levels in the teaching and assessing of mathematics in successive National Curricula in the UK over the last twenty years. His comment, several years before the introduction of the first national curriculum, about the 'absurd lists of Stages or Levels' is perhaps a useful reminder that things do not have to be the way they are. The curriculum for 2014, in the UK, did away with these levels and it remains to be seen what difference this might make to how we think about teaching and learning.

Dick mentions two choices for mathematics teaching: a focus on individual students creating their own mathematics and a more directed, group approach, based on what 'all children have done and can do'. It is this second approach that I have tried to articulate in this book, while also believing there is space for creativity. The challenge remains of finding an 'economic' set of principles for teaching and the minimal list of required 'awarenesses' for succeeding at school mathematics. I suspect these are challenges to be worked on in the practice of every teacher and teacher educator – in other words, the importance of the challenges is in the process of working on them rather than in getting to any definitive lists. The principles and awarenesses that appear in this book are ones that have seemed important in my practice and, as I have said before, where they are put forward it is not to recommend them to others, but in the spirit of raising awareness of the power of having *some* principles and awarenesses with which to work.

I end with a story and reflection.

> My father has worked as an educational therapist for fifteen or so years, generally seeing students who have been excluded from school or who are having significant difficulties, on a one-to-one basis over a period of time. He usually invites students to draw a picture or create a plasticine model in the first session. On several occasions he has seen a student through to some kind of resolution or even transformation. In all these cases there was a traumatic event in the child's life and once the child had been able to speak about it, somehow a way through their difficulties became possible. My father has noticed that when he looks back at these children's first piece of art work, the traumatic event is there, represented. At the time, as the therapist, he cannot know which part of that first work is the most significant, but looking back it is clear.

I relate this story because it seems linked to the role of symbols. In the first session, the child represents a traumatic event (among other things) but this is not healing. What seems necessary is for the child to be able, not just to represent the event, but to symbolise it, to notice that it is represented perhaps, to speak about it. It is the way we symbolise our experience that can make all the difference.

## References

Gattegno, C. (1987). *The science of education. Part 1: theoretical considerations.* New York: Educational Solutions Worldwide Inc.

Tahta, D. (1988). The science of education. *Mathematics Teaching* 118: 10–13.

Tall, D. (1992). Students' difficulties in calculus. *Plenary presentation in Working Group 3, ICME, Quebec.* Available at: www://homepages.warwick.ac.uk/staff/David.Tall/pdfs/dot1993k-calculus-wg3-icme.pdf (accessed 28 November 2014).

Varela, F. (1999). *Ethical know-how: action, wisdom and cognition.* Stanford, CA: Stanford University Press.

# Appendix 1

The material below is taken from notes provided to teachers in the context of the primary school research project described in Chapter 6. The notes are addressed to those teachers, who were working with students aged 5 to 10.

---

### Intervention materials

*Some general principles*

There is evidence that we use different aspects of our brains when we consider number relations (e.g. linking number symbols one to another) compared to when we make judgements about sizes of collections of objects or when we link numerals to collections of objects. There is evidence that these ways of working develop independently. It also seems that it is what we do when working with numerals in themselves that is most closely correlated with what we do when we use more complex arithmetic. Hence, if a student is struggling with mathematics, repeated work focusing on linking numbers to objects may not help them access higher levels of the subject.

The basis of this intervention is to test the proposal that all students (and particularly those who are under-achieving) will be helped by a regular focus on the relational and structural use of number. The activities in this booklet are designed to support students gain awareness of the structure of the number system (in itself) and relations between number symbols (in themselves).

To gain fluency with symbols, it is vital that students are given space to 'play' with numbers and are offered some open tasks (as suggested in this booklet) and share their findings both orally and in writing.

We imagine each week following a similar pattern. The pattern is not intended as a straightjacket and we imagine you will sometimes do more than one day's work in a session and equally that you will may need to re-cap previous work before moving on. The kinds of thing you can do are:

- work with the whole class as they respond in unison (chanting);
- move from chanting, to *you* modelling how to write down the chant (e.g. simply a sequence of numbers, or including operation signs);

*(continued)*

*(continued)*

- move from you writing down a sequence, to students doing the writing (e.g. one student at the front, or everyone on mini white boards/books);
- space for students to do some exploration (e.g. trying their own sequences or journeys);
- space for students to talk to the whole class about what they have done and found out (and what they want to do next).

### First activities with the tens chart

#### Naming numbers

AIM

When introducing the Gattegno chart to a group for the first time, students need to see how numbers are named on the chart. Rather than concern about the meaning or place value of numbers, the focus of this activity is on how to say and write numbers and to gain awareness of how they are ordered.

A STARTING POINT

Tap on a number in the units row and get the class to chant back in unison the number name. Continue for other numbers of the units row and extend to numbers in the tens row.

Tap on '4' (class chant FOUR) and then '40' (class chant FOUR-TY); tap on '6' and then '60'; tap on '8' and then '80'. Focus attention on how the number name changes. All we do is add '-ty' to the end of the digit number. Practise this (you may want to allow students to say 'five-ty' and 'three-ty' for 50 and 30).

Having established these names, tap on '40' followed by '2' – students need to chant back 'FOUR-TY-TWO'.

Keep tapping out two-digit numbers. When students seem confident in calling back these number names, invite a student to the board to write 'forty-two' – or, if this is new to students, show them how to write it and invite someone to write 43, 44, etc.

Students could count up in 1s from different starting points, focusing on how the digit names keep repeating in sequence.

A TASK

Students, in pairs or small groups, could be challenged to create their own '100 square', i.e. order the numbers 1–100 (or as an extension, 100–200). The Gattegno chart can be kept in view as support.

#### Multiples

AIM

Support students in exploring patterns in number, leading to awareness of multiplication table facts.

A STARTING POINT

With no introduction, say to the class: 'One hundred'. Invite a response – someone will usually say 'Two hundred', you can then reply 'Three hundred' and get the class to continue chanting multiples of 100. As they do this, begin tapping out the numbers on the Gattegno chart. When you have gone slightly higher than feels comfortable, invite the class to give you another starting number, or choose one for the class (e.g. 10 or 5 or 2).

Work on multiples of the new starting number, get the class to chant in unison – again, tapping out the numbers they say on the chart. Someone can write down the numbers as well. Invite the class to talk about any patterns they notice.

A TASK

Students pick their own starting number and write out multiples, going as high as they can. Students can be invited to pay attention to any patterns they notice. At some point you might want to gather the class on the carpet and invite individuals to describe the patterns they have seen. Other students can be asked if they can continue these patterns.

*Addition and subtraction journeys*

AIM

Students to develop an awareness of what happens at the 'transition' between tens and/or hundreds.

A STARTING POINT

Tap on a number and get students to chant back the number *one* higher. Choose different numbers, particularly those ending in a '9'.

A TASK

Students choose a starting number and add one. They then keep on adding one, looking for patterns in their answers, writing, for example:

$17 + 1 = 18$

$18 + 1 = 19$

$19 + 1 = 20$

$20 + 1 = 21$

When they have gone as far as they want, they choose a new starting number.

The same process could be gone through with subtracting one, or going up/down in numbers other than one.

*(continued)*

*(continued)*

## More complex activities with the tens chart

*Multiplication and division by powers of 10*

AIM

Students to gain an awareness of how to multiply and divide by powers of ten and awareness of the relations between these operations.

A STARTING POINT

Tap on a number, get the class to chant back the number that is 10 times bigger. Initially choose single-digit numbers, then progress to others, returning to single-digit if the class lose confidence. At some point, invite someone to say how, on the chart, they get their answer. Focus attention on how you can get the answer simply by moving down one row on the chart. Try to steer the class away from mention of changing numbers of zeros as such methods do not extend to decimals. Return to chanting with the awareness of movement. Then point on a number and invite the class to chant back that number divided by 10. Repeat for multiplication and division by 100 (and possibly 1000).

A TASK

Students have to choose a number off the chart, then go on a 'journey' multiplying or dividing by 10, 100, etc. Their challenge is to return to the number they started with. Do one 'journey' with the class and then let try out their own.

You may want to show some of the decimal rows of the chart in order to help students extend their journeys. Be prepared for some big numbers!

After some time, gather students to discuss what they have done. They might have questions they want to explore further. This activity has continued with energy over four hours and more with some groups. Questions might emerge about how long they can make their journeys, or whether they can go on a journey and get back in one go, or whether they can get journeys that shift between columns (see *Fraction Journey* activity).

*Fraction journeys*

AIM

Let students develop an awareness of fractions as operations.

A STARTING POINT

This activity is best done following on from 'Multiplication and division by powers of 10'. In that activity, students may have noticed that their 'journeys' only move vertically (up or down). It may be that a student asks how they could do different journeys. This activity is best set up if this question has arisen in such a way.

The key to the starting point is to establish, through chanting on the chart, that to get from the first (1s) column to, say, the fifth (5s) column, we multiply by 5. To go in the reverse direction, we multiply by one fifth. To go from the 1s column to the 7s column, we multiply by 7. To go in the reverse direction we multiply by one seventh.

A TASK

Students have to pick *two* numbers from the chart: a starting number and a finishing number. Their task is to find a journey from one to the other. For example:

From 200 to 70

$200 \times \frac{1}{2} = 100$

$100 \div 10 = 10$

$10 \times 7 = 70$

You may need to do a few such journeys all together. We have seen year 3 classes confidently working with fractions in this way, having spent time beforehand working on multiplication and division by 10 on the Gattegno chart.

*Percentages*

AIM

Develop a method for finding a percentage of any number.

A STARTING POINT

Tap on a number, get the class to chant back 10% of that number. Repeat many times. As with multiplication and division by powers of ten, at some point focus attention on what you are doing visually (going up one row). Then repeat with finding 1% of a number (going up two rows).

A TASK

Students can set challenges for each other of finding percentages of a number. They should find their percentages initially by splitting it up into 10s and 1s. For example:

31% of 60

10% of 60 = 6

10% of 60 = 6

10% of 60 = 6

1% of 60 = 0.6

31% of 60 = 18.6

*(continued)*

*(continued)*

They may notice ways to get 20% or 5% based on 10% and this can speed up their calculations.

A harder challenge is to choose two numbers from the chart and find, as close as possible, one as a percentage of the other. For example:

Choose numbers 16 and 60. What percentage of 60 gives us an answer as close as possible to 16?

   10% of 60 = 6

   10% of 60 = 6

   5% of 60 = 3

So, 25% of 60 is 15
   Can you get closer?

## An approach to fractions

Having worked on the pilot materials it seems as though enthusiasm has been generated by students working with big numbers and also taking on the role of 'teacher' when they come up and do the pointing. We have found it useful to think about possibilities for whole-class work with the chart as pairs of activities, e.g. 'I point, you say' or 'I point, you write'. Several of you have worked with: 'You (singular) point, you (plural) say'.

If you think about the activities of: Point, Say, Write – done by 'I', 'you' (singular/plural) or 'we' – then there are many many possible combinations! E.g., 'You write, I say'; or 'You point, we say', etc.

The materials that follow suggest a development for work on fractions. These are not split by year group or by time but suggest a sequence of activities. Different year groups may need to spend more or less time on different sections. And not all sections will be appropriate for all years.

It can be useful to think about three aspects of fractions:

- fractions as parts of a whole (eg shading shapes);
- fractions as numbers (eg on a number line);
- fractions as operators (eg finding a fraction of a number).

All of these are important. Our approach would be to leave the first aspect until last – the sense of fractions as parts of a whole is so common, that aspect will not be discussed here.

### *Fractions as numbers*

*Naming fractions*

Aim: students to be able to 'read' the decimals on the chart as fractions
   Some activities:

Tapping on different numbers, simply get students to say back what the number is, e.g. 40, 500, 7, 2000, 340 . . . and at some point move to 0.4.

Students are likely to reply 'zero point four'. Without explanation, simply ask them to say this number as 'four tenths'. Tap and get responses to: 0.5, 0.7, 0.1, etc.

You might then want to combine tenths with units, e.g. tap on '4' and '0.2' and students should respond 'four and two tenths'.

In some years, this may be as far as you want to go with naming numbers on the chart.

If you want, you can move to the hundredths row and get students saying those as fractions, e.g. 0.07 → 'seven-hundredths'.

If you want to combine tenths and hundredths, you may need to use an alternative name for the tenths row. Tapping on 0.3, students need to respond 'thirty hundredths'. You may want to write out some equivalences here, e.g. $\frac{3}{10} = \frac{30}{100}$.
Having established this, you can then tap on, say, 0.4 and 0.05 and students respond 'forty-five hundredths'.

Students could play the role of 'teacher' as they name numbers. You could also get students writing (as fractions) the numbers to which you (or they) point.

*Addition and subtraction with fractions*

Aim: students to develop awareness of the processes of addition and subtraction using fractions.

Some activities:

'Starting at 1, I want you to count up in steps of 3'. The class respond: 'one, four, seven, ten, thirteen, sixteen, . . .'. As they speak, you tap on the chart to keep up with their responses.

You might want to do this starting at 1 and going up in different steps. You could then start at 100 and go in steps of 300: 'one *hundred*, four *hundred*, seven *hundred* . . .' the pattern of movement is the same and also some of the words.

At some point, when they seem confident with counting up in different steps: 'I now want you to start at one-tenth and count in steps of three-tenths'. The class may need some support to respond: 'one-tenth, four-tenths, seven-tenths, one, one and three-tenths, etc.'.

It is probably important to do some writing down of sequences:

$$\frac{1}{10}, \frac{4}{10}, \frac{7}{10}, 1, 1\frac{3}{10}, 1\frac{6}{10}, \text{etc.}$$

You could then start at one-tenth and go up in other steps. Perhaps students could choose what steps they want to go up in (direct the less confident students to go up in steps of one-tenth).

Once students have seen and described some patterns, perhaps they could start at another fraction, like one-sixth and go up in steps of, say, two-sixths:

$$\frac{1}{6}, \frac{3}{6}, \frac{5}{6}, 1\frac{1}{6}, 1\frac{3}{6}, \text{etc.}$$

*(continued)*

*(continued)*

Again, they could extend this work into their own choice of fraction and step.

In some sense you are focusing on the language aspect of fractions: ONE-sixth, add TWO-sixths is THREE-sixths.

Having got confident with writing sequences of fractions, you might want to focus students on alternative ways of writing out what they are doing. So, starting at one-tenth and going up in steps of three-tenths could be written as:

$$\frac{1}{10} + \frac{3}{10} = \frac{4}{10},$$
$$\frac{4}{10} + \frac{3}{10} = \frac{7}{10}, \text{etc.}$$

Again, students could go 'up' or 'down' in different steps and look at what patterns they notice.

### Fractions as operators

*Multiplication by fractions*

Aim: get students comfortable with movement around the chart (to and from the 1 column) in terms of multiplications.

This activity probably needs students to have worked on Multiplication Journeys from the earlier materials.

'I am going to tap on two numbers. What do I need to multiply by to get from the first to the second?'

Tap on (1, 10), students respond '10' or 'multiply by 10'.

Tap on (5, 50), 'multiply by 10'.

Tap on (30, 300), 'multiply by 10'. Explore others that are 'multiply by 10'. Perhaps do some 'multiply by 100' as well.

Tap on (1, 2), 'multiply by 2'. Tap on (100, 200), 'multiply by 2', explore other 'multiply by 2's (all going from the 1 column).

When multiplying by 2, 3, 4, ..., 9 on the chart, I think it is important to always do these from the 1 column (1, 10, 100, etc.). While you could multiply by 2 in moving from, say 3 to 6, there is a danger students may generalise from here in unhelpful ways!

After working on ×10, ×100, ×2, ×3, ×9 etc., return to movements from 1. For example (1, 10); (1, 2); (1, 100) ... hopefully forcing an awareness that the number you land on (starting at 1) is the number you multiply by. Then tap: (1, 0.1). You want students to say 'multiply by one-tenth' (this may need support). Then (2, 0.2), (6, 0.6), etc., and then moving further around the chart, e.g., (30, 3), (600, 60) – all 'multiply by one-tenth'. If there is confusion in moving away from the unit row, perhaps go back to some where you multiply by 10 and show (without telling!) students how they know this works anywhere on the chart – then return to multiplication by a tenth.

If you can get students confident with these ways of describing movements on the chart, then you can get them writing down what they are doing, e.g.

$300 \times \frac{1}{10} = 30$, $30 \times \frac{1}{3} = 10$, and maybe try to do and say some the other way around: $\frac{1}{5} \times 50 = 10$.

Students could attempt some 'journeys' (that they should be familiar with) but only using multiplication. For example:

400 to 30

$400 \times \frac{1}{4} = 100$,

$100 \times \frac{1}{10} = 10$,

$10 \times 3 = 30$

One challenge would be to do this in one go, combining $\frac{1}{4}, \frac{1}{10}$, and 3.

*Fractions of amounts*

Aim: continue to develop awareness of fractions as operators.

Some activities:

Using the Gattegno chart, reinforce the way fractions work as operators between columns. Point to a number in the '4' column and get students to chant back one-quarter of your number, e.g. $\frac{1}{4} \times 40 = 10$.

Get students to chant back one-eighth of your number and tap on something in the '8' column, e.g. $\frac{1}{8} \times 800 = 100$. Continue for other columns, writing out the resulting sums.

Then ask students how you could do a third of a number NOT in the '3' column, e.g. $\frac{1}{3} \times 6$.

Students may recognise 6 as 3 × 2 and they know that $\frac{1}{3} \times 3 = 1$. What you want to get to is for students to write out sequences of fraction operations:

$\frac{1}{3} \times 3 = 1$; $\frac{1}{3} \times 6 = 2$; $\frac{1}{3} \times 9 = 3$; $\frac{1}{3} \times 12 = 4$, etc.

and, eventually, being able to get straight to, e.g. $\frac{1}{3} \times 18 = \frac{1}{3} \times 3 \times 6 = 6$. But the initial focus can be simply on writing out the sequences of fraction sums, going up in multiples.

Students can choose their own fractions statement to start with, e.g.:

$\frac{1}{4} \times 40 = 10$, and write out multiplies as far as they want to go:

*(continued)*

*(continued)*

$$\frac{1}{4} \times 80 = 20$$

$$\frac{1}{4} \times 120 = 30$$

$$\frac{1}{4} \times 160 = 40, \text{ etc.},$$ with students writing down what they notice.

As students share the work they have done and the lists they have produced, you could focus them on saying how you could go straight to a number in the sequence without having to work out all the others in between.

As an extension, for anyone feeling very confident, it is also possible to work on fraction sequences in this way:

$$\frac{1}{4} \times 40 = 10; \quad \frac{2}{4} \times 40 = 20; \quad \frac{3}{4} \times 40 = 30; \quad \frac{4}{4} \times 40 = 40; \quad \frac{5}{4} \times 40 = 50, \text{ etc.}$$

The challenge here could be to them combine the two kinds of sequences (i.e. this one and the ones from above), to be able to get straight to the answer to questions like $\frac{3}{4} \times 160$.

You could start creating posters for different fractions:

$$\frac{1}{3} \times 3 = 1; \quad \frac{2}{3} \times 3 = 2; \quad \frac{3}{3} \times 3 = 3;$$

$$\frac{1}{3} \times 6 = 2; \quad \frac{2}{3} \times 6 = 4; \quad \frac{3}{3} \times 6 = 6; \quad \frac{1}{3} \times 3 = 8;$$

$$\frac{1}{3} \times 9 = 3; \ldots \text{ etc.}$$

# Appendix 2

**Further mathematics – complex numbers**

How do you introduce complex numbers? A challenge I always give myself in teaching is to consider if there is a starting activity that can provide students an appreciation of the entire range of techniques and issues to be tackled within any topic. The task that follows is one exemplar of what I mean.

Much as the number ½ can be seen as an operator (finding a half) or as a place on a number line, complex numbers can be seen as operators, or as points on a set of axes (the Argand diagram, where the imaginary part is the *y*-axis and the real part is the *x*-axis). The lesson ideas that follow presuppose familiarity with the notion *i* to stand for the square root of negative one, and also how to represent complex numbers on the Argand diagram.

A complex number, as a function, transforms shapes. Because complex numbers need two dimensions to represent them, to get a sense of how they might transform a shape, we need two sets of (2D) axes.

Starting with the a unit circle drawn on the Argand diagram, centre (0,0), students can be invited to conjecture what the shape would be transformed to, if both real and imaginary parts were doubled. This is represented by the operation, $z \to 2z$ and the result is a circle of radius 2 units. If any student is unhappy with the result, they can be invited to test out particular points. For example, *i*, at (0,1) on the original circle, will be mapped to 2*i*, at (0,2) on the image circle. Consideration of this case may lead students quite quickly to conjecture what transformation would be associated with $z \to k.z$, for any real number, *k*.

Students can become independent in testing out other complex transformations and generating their own pairs of images. Good starting points to test out include the following, but students may come up with their own ideas.

$z \to z + 2$

$z \to z - i$

$z \to 2z + 3i$

$z \to iz$

$z \to z^2$

In each case, students can be invited to predict and test what transformation will be described by the functions above. The last one may need some support, since it is unlike any transformation students are likely to have seen before. It is here that the infinite appears, for me, but perhaps more in the sense of 'shot through with infinity' than the grappling with infinite processes. Students can consider *any* complex function and find the corresponding transformation.

One thing that appeals to me about this task is that students are learning how to add complex numbers, how to multiply them, practising how to represent them on an Argand diagram and making constant shifts between graphical and symbolic representations. Students can try out (numerically and graphically) with particular points, how a function transforms the Argand diagram. From these tests it may be possible to generalise. One awareness, that may help synthesise a number of results, is that multiplication by a complex number, $z$, transforms a given point, rotating it by the argument of $z$ and enlarging it by the modulus of $z$. Furthermore, if $z$ is on the unit circle (with modulus 1), and hence can be expressed in the form

$$Cos(\theta) + iSin(\theta),$$

it may also be possible to give sense to deMoivre's theorem, by considering $z$ as a transformation applied $n$ times, i.e.:

$$\left(Cos(\theta) + iSin(\theta)\right)^n = Cos(n\theta) + iSin(n\theta).$$

One potential mathematical appreciation on offer in this activity is also around the mapping of one entire system (transformation geometry, e.g. translations, rotations, reflections, enlargement) into another system (complex numbers). It is also possible to work on the connection between the transformation entailed in a 2 by 2 matrix and the equivalent complex number.

# Index

adolescence 103–17
algebra 17, 21, 25, 35, 65–6, 97–8, 103–17, 123, 125, 131, 148
arithmogons 65–6, 118
Association of Teachers of Mathematics xii
awareness xii, 13, 16–20, 33, 40, 57–8, 80, 100, 104, 150

Barwell, R 24
Bateson, G 4
Brown, L 3, 10, 15, 63, 65, 94, 107, 135–7

calculus 122–31
cardinality 39–41
categories 142–3
classroom environment 12
climate change 25–6
concepts 33–5
conjecture 8–23, 64, 69, 75, 106–7, 118, 140
creativity 75, 85, 150

Davis, R 43–6, 107–8
division 76–80
distinctions 21–2, 27, 53, 146–7
dynamic geometry 56–7

flow 67
fluency 35–8, 43, 49, 51–3, 59, 80, 84–5
fractions 37, 49–50, 62, 109, 124–5
Freud, S 3
Freudentahl, H 5

Gattegno, C 17–18, 22, 38–9, 46–50, 63, 103; chart 76–80, 84; infinity 118
geometry 28, 51–3, 56–7, 86–103
graphing 53–6

Hewitt, D 89–90
Hiele, P, van 86–7, 93

inner task 16
intuition 23, 37, 68, 131–2

limits 120–1
listening 64–5, 67, 142

manipulatives 35
Mason, J 15, 16, 38
mathematical concepts 33–6; modelling 23; thinking 17, 75
Maturana, H 3
meaning making 32, 36, 85
metacomment 10, 17, 64, 67, 98, 138, 141–4, 147
multiplication 76–80

neuroscience 39–41, 84

ordinality 39–41, 75, 84

Piaget, J 39–40, 103
Pick's Theorem 94–8
Pimm, D xi, 36
planning 14–28, 63
powers of the mind 17
Post Graduate Certificate of Education 61
psychology 69–70
purposes 136–8, 140–3, 147–8

real world 23
recursion 119–20
relational symbols 50–2, 107, 143

Scratch 119
silence 65
Sinclair, N 57, 86–8, 93
story 15
sustainability 24–7

Tahta, D xi, 16, 35, 38, 43, 88, 102–3
task design 21
technology 52–9
trigonometry 98–101, 112

Varela, F 3
video 138–43
visualising 68–9, 88, 99–101

Walkerdine, V 4, 37
Watson, A 15, 23, 35, 103–4, 131
Weil, S xi
Wodehouse, H xii, 12, 27, 58, 60, 88, 144

Zwicky, J 13, 37